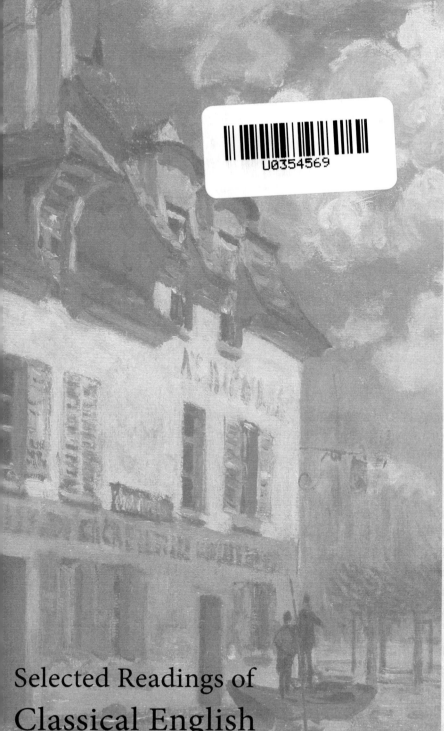

新编英国文学
经典作品选读

程朝翔 · 总主编
欧光安 · 主编

Selected Readings of
Classical English
Literary Works

北京大学出版社
PEKING UNIVERSITY PRESS

图书在版编目（CIP）数据

新编英国文学经典作品选读：英文 / 程朝翔总主编；欧光安主编. —北京：北京大学出版社，2023.8

ISBN 978-7-301-34174-2

Ⅰ.①新… Ⅱ.①程… ②欧… Ⅲ.①英语–阅读教学–高等学校–教材②英国文学–文学欣赏 Ⅳ.① H319.4：Ⅰ

中国国家版本馆 CIP 数据核字(2023) 第 125123 号

书　　　名	新编英国文学经典作品选读
	XINBIAN YINGGUO WENXUE JINGDIAN ZUOPIN XUANDU
著作责任者	程朝翔　总主编
	欧光安　主编
责任编辑	李　娜
标准书号	ISBN 978-7-301-34174-2
出版发行	北京大学出版社
地　　　址	北京市海淀区成府路 205 号　100871
网　　　址	http://www.pup.cn　新浪微博：@北京大学出版社
编辑部邮箱	pupwaiwen@pup.cn
总编室邮箱	zpup@pup.cn
电　　　话	邮购部 010-62752015　发行部 010-62750672　编辑部 010-62759634
印　刷　者	北京溢漾印刷有限公司
经　销　者	新华书店
	720 毫米 ×1020 毫米　16 开本　18 印张　420 千字
	2023 年 8 月第 1 版　2023 年 8 月第 1 次印刷
定　　　价	68.00 元

未经许可，不得以任何方式复制或抄袭本书之部分或全部内容。
版权所有，侵权必究
举报电话：010-62752024　电子信箱：fd@pup.pku.edu.cn
图书如有印装质量问题，请与出版部联系，电话：010-62756370

前　言

　　《新编英国文学经典作品选读》和《新编美国文学经典作品选读》是北京大学与石河子大学的又一次缘分。

　　2002年年初，中东部重点高校对口支援西部高校的序幕拉开，教育部指定北京大学对口支援石河子大学。是年3月，北京大学外国语学院的程朝翔教授作为第一批支援者，不远千里来到石河子大学为英语专业大三的学生讲授英国文学。程师的拿手好戏是莎翁作品研究，当时教室里并无多媒体设备，他便用粉笔在黑板上满屏书写，生怕落下一个知识点。莎翁之外，程师还重点讲解了乔伊斯的著名短篇《阿拉比》（"Araby"）。继程师而来者为王继辉教授，王师所讲为其专长之乔叟与中古文学。王师或西装革履，或着白衬衫一丝不苟，上课时仅手持几张小卡片而知识源源而至，倾倒一片。之后便是何卫老师来讲授语言学，何师风格与王师迥然相异。何师常着T恤衫与牛仔裤，授课如邻家大哥亲切自然。2004—2005年间，北大外院胡壮麟教授来校举办功能语言学讲座，姜望琪教授为专业学生讲授语用学等课程。2006年，早已年过花甲的刘意青教授来石大做讲座，刘师融自身经历于学理讲授，而常怀忧国忧民之襟抱，为学生所崇仰。刘师风格极为亲和，被学生和年轻老师戏称为"刘姥姥"，但她毫不介怀。2008年，年近古稀的刘师欣然挂职石河子大学外国语学院的援疆院长。她不仅亲自为学生授课，还组织年轻教师做读书会，为他们讲解文学难点。她得知当时学院缺乏合适的文学选读教材，便组织骨干教师自主编纂选读材料。刘师亲自选定篇目和选段，之后由参与者作篇内注释。内容确定之后，交由复印店打印成册，作为教学的自主编纂教材。这便是读者面前这两部经典作品选读的前身。自2009年起，该自主编纂教材便在石大外院英语专业本科课程及部分大学英语选修课程中使用，屈指算来，已有14年之久。

　　2008年年底，刘师听说部分年轻教师在职称评定时经常铩羽而归，原因是缺乏有分量的著作和教材，她便主动提出在选读中选出若干短篇小说，以专题的形式分为若干章节，每章依术语阐释、正文、注释、赏析的体例编排，并附上若干短篇作为附录。书稿编成之后，刘师即联系北京大学出版社，得到出版社张冰主任的热情支持，并委任素养超强的李娜老师作为责任编辑。该教材很快于2010年8月出版，题名《英语短篇小说选读》，署名方岩主编，刘意青审定，叶春莉、欧光安等参编。实际上，刘师不仅校对了全部的文字，不少篇章的赏析文字亦出自其手。2015年，在一次学术会议上，编者与刘师和张冰主任等同席讨论，得隙向张冰主任提议对《英语短篇小说选读》进行修订，张冰主任欣然同意，而刘师亦当即同意继续承担审定工作。2018年6月，该书第二版成功推出。2021年，该书荣获石河子大学首届优秀教材奖一等奖。[①] 而同在2010年，在一个寒风凛冽的冬日，刘师在由办公室回住处的路上摔倒在薄冰覆盖的路面，骨裂而伤，无奈只好由石返京，而她对石大外院的关注却从未停止过。

除2002年集中为石大学生授课外，自2002年迄今，程朝翔老师不时来石大外院，或讲学，或交流，其中最重要的活动之一是在2012年组织北京大学、淡江大学和石河子大学联合举办外国文学研讨会，一时影响甚广。2018年，程朝翔老师更是来石大外院任援疆院长[②]，从各方面提携年轻教师，其中一项便是为了推动外院翻译专业建设，组织臧红宝等老师翻译《韦氏英汉双解扩词手册》，该词典同样由北京大学出版社出版（2021年10月初版）。2021年，编者提议将英美文学经典作品选读进一步调整体例出版，程师当即表示赞同并立即联系北京大学出版社，同样得到张冰主任的大力支持，此次则由李娜老师和吴宇森老师担任责任编辑，这可说是刘意青先生、程朝翔院长对石大外院倾力支持的前后赓续。

钱锺书先生曾考证近代第一首译为汉语的英诗乃朗费罗之《人生颂》（"A Psalm of Life"），其汉译时间约为19世纪60年代。与诗歌相比，小说的读者接受群应该更广，在我国近代英文小说被译介为汉语的时间也应该不会太晚，林纾在19世纪末、20世纪初"翻译"的那些西文小说更是影响深远。不过在中国学生中使用英文原文教材的情况，可能在20世纪10年代之后才较为常见。钱锺

---

① 一等奖为最高，只有两部教材获此殊荣，另一部教材为石大传统强势学科农学类教材。
② 继刘意青先生担任石大外院援疆领导的还有北大外院凌建侯教授（常务副院长，2011—2012年度），他曾在北大连招三名石大外院教师为博士。

书先生的老师吴宓，20世纪10年代就读清华学校时，就读过不少原文小说①。留学归来后，吴宓一度将萨克雷的名著《钮康氏家传》(*The Newcomes*)和《名利场》(*Vanity Fair*)的前几章以文言译出，刊登于《学衡》杂志，成为中国现代文学史上的独特风景。20世纪30年代，吴宓回到母校清华任教，同样提倡阅读文学作品的原文，并曾为清华外籍教师吴可读（A. L. Pollard-Urquhart）编著的英文著作 Great European Novels and Novelists 题写书名《西洋小说发达史略》，该著作即吴可读教授学生时所用教材②。吴宓常被视为文化保守主义者，其人主张"昌明国粹，融化新知"，实际上并非反对引入和译介西洋文学，而是希望有一种比较的视野和方法。百年后回顾之，其观念仍自有价值。因此，我们在编排中一方面注重原文阅读和注释，同时在提问等环节以比较的视野来实践文明互鉴的宗旨，也是试图在同类的文学选读著作中"走一点不一样的路"。钱锺书在清华就读时，曾因年轻气盛和好玩调皮，常与同学一道嘲笑有时过于迂腐的老师吴宓，而一生坚持随事随记的吴宓将这些记入日记中。近半个世纪后，曾经的学生钱锺书在读到老师的日记时，为自己曾经的鲁莽"愧生颜变，无地自容"，并为老师的宽容而更感愧疚，希望自己这个"头白门生倘得免乎削籍而标于头墙之外"③。我们也希望自己所做的这两本小册子，能够抵得上北大外院诸位教师教诲之一毫，而不被逐出门墙之外。

本套经典文学作品选读分英国卷和美国卷，由程朝翔教授任总主编，英国卷由欧光安任主编，编者为张娟、刘小姣、阿依努尔；美国卷由叶春莉任主编，编者为邹晓惠、卞赛赛、马艺文。目前任教于石大的外籍教师 Ralph Leong 校对了全部英文，在此表示感谢。

编者
2023年6月

---

① 无独有偶，吴宓在清华读书时喜爱朗费罗的长诗 Evangeline，并将前几节改译为《沧桑艳传奇》。小说方面，他喜读华盛顿·欧文的《见闻杂记》(*The Sketch Book*)，而"最爱其中'The Wife'一篇"（吴宓：《吴宓自编年谱》，吴学昭整理，北京：生活·读书·新知三联书店，1995年，第122页）。

② 据吴心海考证，吴可读在中国期间至少出过五部编著，其中除《西洋小说发达史略》之外，还被用作教材的尚有《英国散文选》(*Selections of English Prose: From Chaucer to Thomas Hardy*，商务印书馆1931年11月初版)。见吴心海：《吴宓珍视的一本书及其作者》，载2013年8月18日《东方早报》。

③ 钱锺书：《吴宓日记序》，载吴宓：《吴宓日记》（第一册），吴学昭整理注释，北京：生活·读书·新知三联书店，1998年，序言第2页。

目 录

Part One Old and Middle English Period

1. **Beowulf** 1
   Beowulf 2
2. **Sir Gawain and the Green Knight** 7
   Sir Gawain and the Green Knight 8
3. **Geoffrey Chaucer** 13
   The Canterbury Tales 15
4. **Popular Ballads** 22
   Get up and Bar the Door 23
   The Three Ravens 26
   Sir Patrick Spens 27

Part Two The English Renaissance

5. **Edmund Spenser** 32
   Sonnet 75 33
6. **Christopher Marlowe** 36
   The Passionate Shepherd to His Love 37
7. **William Shakespeare** 40
   Sonnet 18 40
   Hamlet 42
8. **Francis Bacon** 46
   Of Studies 47

Part Three The Seventeenth Century

9. John Donne ··· **52**
    Death, Be Not Proud ··· 53
10. John Milton ··· **56**
    To Mr. Cyriack Skinner Upon His Blindness ································ 57
    Areopagitica ··· 59
11. John Bunyan ··· **62**
    The Pilgrim's Progress ·· 63

Part Four The Eighteenth Century

12. Daniel Defoe ··· **68**
    Robinson Crusoe ·· 69
13. Jonathan Swift ·· **76**
    A Modest Proposal ·· 78
14. Samuel Johnson ·· **89**
    Samuel Johnson's Letter to Lord Chesterfield ······························ 91
15. Thomas Gray ·· **95**
    The Epitaph ··· 96
16. William Blake ··· **99**
    Laughing Song ··· 100
    The Chimney Sweeper ··· 101
    The Chimney Sweeper ··· 102
17. Robert Burns ·· **105**
    A Man's a Man for A' That ·· 106
    Scots Wha Hae ··· 109
    A Red, Red Rose ·· 111

Part Five The Romantic Period

18. William Wordsworth ·· **114**
    I Wandered Lonely as a Cloud ·· 115

  Michael: A Pastoral Poem ············· 117

19. George Gordon Byron ············· **125**
  Sonnet on Chillon ············· 127
  She Walks in Beauty ············· 128

20. Percy Bysshe Shelley ············· **130**
  Ode to the West Wind ············· 131

21. John Keats ············· **135**
  On the Grasshopper and Cricket ············· 136
  To Autumn ············· 138

22. Jane Austen ············· **142**
  Pride and Prejudice ············· 143

Part Six The Victorian Literature

23. Charles Dickens ············· **148**
  David Copperfield ············· 149

24. William Makepeace Thackeray ············· **158**
  Vanity Fair ············· 159

25. Matthew Arnold ············· **170**
  Dover Beach ············· 171

26. Charlotte Brontë ············· **176**
  Jane Eyre ············· 177

27. Emily Brontë ············· **184**
  Wuthering Heights ············· 185

28. Alfred Tennyson ············· **195**
  Break, Break, Break ············· 196
  Crossing the Bar ············· 197

29. Robert Browning ············· **200**
  My Last Duchess ············· 201

30. Oscar Wilde ············· **204**
  The Happy Prince ············· 205

31. Thomas Hardy ... **216**
    Afterwards ... 217
    Jude the Obscure ... 219

Part Seven   The Twentieth Century

32. William Butler Yeats ... **229**
    The Lake Isle of Innisfree ... 230
    When You are Old ... 232
    The Second Coming ... 233

33. John Galsworthy ... **236**
    Told by the Schoolmaster ... 237

34. D. H. Lawrence ... **246**
    The Rocking Horse Winner ... 248

35. James Joyce ... **265**
    Ulysses ... 267

36. William S. Maugham ... **270**
    Home ... 271

Part One

Old and Middle English Period

1. Beowulf

    Beowulf, an epic of 3,182 lines, is the most representative work of Anglo-Saxon (Old English) literature. The first part of the epic tells of the Geatish hero Beowulf fighting and killing the monster Grendel, who has been attacking the Danish king Hrothgar's brilliant palace Heorot, and Grendel's mother, who comes to avenge her son the next day. In the second part, the elderly Geatish king Beowulf fights with a fire dragon that is attacking the sovereign's subjects, one of which has been stealing some treasure from the cave where the dragon has been a guard, and both are fatally wounded in the end. Generally, *Beowulf* is considered a pagan epic that is intertwined with Christian elements that run through the whole poem. Its consistency in the structure highlights the entire narration.

    Beowulf is also a treasure house for artistic features of Anglo-Saxon literature. For instance, alliteration ("head rhyme", the repetition of the same sound or sounds at the beginning of two or more words in a line), the most prominent rhetoric device in Anglo-Saxon literature, is used in almost every stanza. In each line, there is a caesura (a pause or break) to separate the whole line that normally consists of two metrical feet in the first part and two more in the second part, with an accented syllable and a varying number of unaccented syllables in each part. Another special figure of speech–kenning–is often employed to add splendor to the poem, in which two common words are used to refer to a special object. For example, "brain biter" refers to sword, "ring giver" refers to king and "swan road" actually means sea.

Beowulf

(Modern Translation, Excerpt)

Down off the moorlands' misting fells[1] came
Grendel stalking[2]; God's brand[3] was on him.
The spoiler[4] meant to snatch away
From the high hall some of human race[5].
He came on under the clouds, clearly saw at last
The gold-hall of men, the mead[6]-drinking place
Nailed with gold plates. That was not the first visit
He had paid to the hall of Hrothgar the Dane:
He never before and never after
Harder luck nor hall-guards found.[7]

Walking to the hall came this warlike creature
Condemned to agony. The door gave way[8],
Toughened with iron, at the touch of those hands.
Rage-inflamed[9], wreckage-bent[10], he ripped open
The jaws of the hall[11]. Hastening on,
The foe then stepped onto the unstained floor[12],
Angrily advanced: out of his eyes stood

An unlovely light like that of fire.
He saw then in the hall, a host of young soldiers,
A company of kinsmen caught away in sleep,
A whole warrior-band. In his heart he laughed then,
Horrible monster, his hopes swelling[13]
To a gluttonous[14] meal. He meant to wrench[15]
The life from each body that lay in the place
Before night was done. It was not to be;
He was no longer to feast on the flesh of mankind

After that night[16].
     Narrowly the powerful
Kinsman of Hygelac kept watch how the ravager
Set to work with his sudden catches;
Nor did the monster mean to hang back.
As a first step he set his hands on
A sleeping soldier, savagely tore at him,
Gnashed[17] at his bone-joints, bolted[18] huge gobbets[19],
Sucked at his veins, and had soon eaten
All of the dead man, even down to his
Hands and feet.
     Forward he stepped,
Stretched out his hands to seize the warrior
Calmly at rest there, reached out for him with his
Unfriendly fingers[20]: but the faster man
Forestalling[21], sat up, sent back his arm.
The upholder of evils at once knew
He had not met, on middle earth's
Extremest acres[22], with any man
Of harder hand-grip: his heart panicked.
He was quit of the place no more quickly for that[23].

Eager to be away, he ailed for[24] his darkness
And the company of devils; the dealings he had there
Were like nothing he had come across in his lifetime.
Then Hygelac's brave kinsman called to mind
That evening's utterance[25], upright he stood,
Fastened his hold till fingers were bursting.
The monster strained away: the man stepped closer.
The monster's desire was for darkness between them,
Direction regardless, to get out and run
For his fen-bordered lair[26]; he felt his grip's strength

Crushed by his enemy. It was an ill journey

The rough marauder[27] had made to Heorot.

The crash in the banqueting-hall came to the Danes,

The men of the guard that remained in the building,

With the taste of death. The deepening rage

Of the claimants[28] to Heorot caused it to resound.

It was indeed wonderful that the wine-supper-hall

Withstood the wrestling pair, that the world's palace

Fell not to the ground. But it was girt[29] firmly,

Both inside and out, by iron braces

Of skilled manufacture. Many a[30] figured[31]

Gold-worked[32] wine-bench, as we heard it,

Started[33] from the floor at the struggles of that pair.

The men of the Danes had not imagined that

Any of mankind by what method soever

Might undo[34] that intricate, antlered hall[35],

Sunder[36] it by strength–unless it were swallowed up in

The embraces of fire.

Notes

1. fell: *n.* a hill or an area of hills

2. stalk: *v.* to move slowly and quietly towards a person or an animal

3. God's brand: This is an allusion to the biblical story that Adam and Eve's first son Cain kills his younger brother Abel and is punished by having a mark or brand on his forehead, being a symbol of sin and a mark that is specially put on God. The use of the allusion is to hint that Grendel is a monster or an evil offspring of Cain.

4. The spoiler: *n.* a person or thing that intends to sabotage or mess up things; here it refers to Grendel.

5. In this line, the words "high", "hall" and "human" form an alliteration, which also happens in the next line with "came", "clouds" and "clearly".

6. mead: *n.* an alcoholic drink made from honey and water

7. The normal sentence order should be "He never found harder luck nor hall-guards before (in the past) and after (in the future)". Here please notice that "found" is used to go along with both "luck", an abstract noun, and "guards", a concrete noun, which are irrelevant. This kind of rhetoric device is called syllepsis.

8. give way: step back; here it means that the door is open.

9. rage-inflamed: full of anger or fury

10. wreckage-bent: intending to make a mess

11. the jaws of the hall: the door; here it is a typical example of kenning.

12. unstained floor: the floor that is not stained (with blood).

13. swelling: growing or developing

14. gluttonous: *adj.* tending to eat too much food or drink; "glutton" is one of the seven sins according to Catholic tradition.

15. wrench: *v.* to pull or twist violently

16. Notice here the interpolation is happening, which indicates the singer or the person who writes down the lines is making a short break between lines.

17. gnash: *v.* to bite one's teeth because one is extremely angry

18. bolt: *v.* to eat or devour very quickly

19. gobbet: *n.* the small amount of something (especially food)

20. Here notice the use of rhetoric device "understatement"; Grendel is not only unfriendly, actually he is with malicious intentions.

21. forestall: *v.* to act first before the enemy makes a move or attacks

22. on middle earth's extremest acres: the farthermost places on the world; no matter which place in the world

23. was quit of: was clear of; the whole line means "although Grendel wants eagerly to get away from the hall, he could not."

24. ail for: feel bad at the moment and long for

25. utterance: *n.* vow or oath (Beowulf made the oath to fight and kill Grendel that night.)

26. fen: *n.* moor, low flat wet land; lair: *n.* a place where a wild animal sleeps or hides; fen-bordered lair: the place or home (of Grendel) that is near the moorland

27. marauder: *n.* a person or thing that goes around to steal or attack

28. claimant: *n.* a person who claims that he/she owns something; here it refers to

both Beowulf and Grendel who think that they are the guardians or owners of the hall.

29. girt: the past participle of "gird" (to surround or enclose)

30. many a: many

31. figured: carved with figures, shapes or lines

32. gold-worked: made from gold or gilded with gold

33. start: *v.* to spring up or bound up

34. undo: *v.* to break down or destroy

35. antler: horn of the male deer; antlered hall: a hall that is decorated or adorned with antlers, which is a way of showing the bravery of warriors

36. sunder: *v.* to break apart or split with force

Questions for Discussion

(1) How is Beowulf's bravery described in the selection?

(2) How do you understand the pagan spirit in the selection and the intertwining of Christian elements in the selection?

(3) How many more cases of figures of speech as alliteration and kenning can you find in the selection besides what have been picked out in the notes?

(4) What can we learn from the comparison between Beowulf and Homeric epics such as *Iliad* and *Odyssey*?

(5) Alliteration is one of typical artistic features of Old English literature, whereas the earliest Chinese literature such as the *Book of Songs* uses rhyming at the end of the lines. Make a reflection on that.

Suggested Reading

(1) *Beowulf: A Verse Translation.* Translated by Michael Alexander, London: Penguin Books Ltd., 1973.

(2) *Beowulf: A Translation and Commentary, Together with Sellic Spell.* Translated by J. R. R. Tolkien, New York: Harper Collins, 2014.

(3) *Beowulf: A New Verse Translation* (Bilingual Edition). Translated by Seamus Heaney, New York: W. W. Norton & Company, Inc., 2002.

(4) Bruce Mitchell, Fred C. Robinson. *A Guide to Old English.* Beijing: Peking

University Press, 2005.

(5)《贝奥武甫：古英语史诗》，冯象译，北京：生活·读书·新知三联书店，1992年。

(6)《贝奥武甫》，陈才宇译，南京：译林出版社，2018年。

(7) 李赋宁编著：《英语史》，北京：商务印书馆，2005年。

(8) 陈才宇：《古英语与中古英语文学通论》，北京：商务印书馆，2007年。

2. Sir Gawain and the Green Knight

Sir Gawain and the Green Knight is one of the most famous poems that is categorized as a "romance", originally meaning a vernacular language and later evolving into a tale in poetic form. It usually narrates the life and adventures of knights who embody such chivalry qualities as loyalty, faithfulness, bravery and tenderness. As far as subject matters are concerned, "romance" includes the matter of France (mostly related to Charlemagne the Great and Roland), the matter of Rome (such as the siege of Troy) and most importantly the matter of Britain (mainly on King Arthur and knights of Round Table).

Sir Gawain and the Green Knight deals with the adventures of Sir Gawain who takes the challenge of a green knight at King Arthur's New Year banquet by cutting the head of the green knight and letting the latter behead him a year later. Soon after the banquet, Sir Gawain sets off and undergoes a multitude of odd twists and turns on the way until he comes to a Green Chapel on Christmas Eve. Agreeing to exchange what they get on the day between him and the host, Gawain fulfills the first two agreements and conceals the girdle given to him by the tempting hostess in the third one, thus being dishonest. Finally, the truth comes out that the host is the green knight himself and Sir Gawain is punished with two cuts. Gawain dodges the first one being scared, but being ashamed of his own cowardice and covetousness before, he courageously takes the second one.

Artistically, *Sir Gawain and the Green Knight* is a mixture of Anglo-Saxon poetry with French poetry, an influence from the Norman Conquest. It features the blending of alliteration with metrical technique (fixed number of accented and unaccented syllables). It inherits the unified structure from Old English literature while adding climaxes and ups and towns in the plot. Furthermore, symbolic meaning and psychological analysis achieved in the narration became an inspiration for later literature. Lastly, another unique feature is the way each stanza ends with a line of two syllables (called specially as "the bob") with four accented lines (called specially as "the wheel").

Sir Gawain and the Green Knight

(Excerpt)

Now he rides in his array[1] through the realm of Logres[2],
Sir Gawain, God knows, though it gave him small joy!
All alone must he lodge through many a long night
Where the food that he fancied was far from his plate;
He had no mate but his mount[3], over mountain and plain,
Nor man to say his mind to but almighty God,
Till he had wandered well-nigh[4] into North Wales.
All the islands of Anglesey[5] he holds on his left,
And follows, as he fares[6], the fords[7] by the coast,
Comes over at Holy Head[8], and enters next
The Wilderness of Wirral[9]—few were within
That had great good will toward God[10] or man.
And earnestly he asked of each mortal[11] he met
If he had ever heard aught[12] of a knight all green,
Or of a Green Chapel[13], on ground thereabouts[14],
And all said the same, and solemnly swore
They saw no such knight all solely green

     In hue[15].
   Over country wild and strange

> The knight sets off anew;
> Often his course must change
> Ere[16] the chapel comes in view[17].

Many a cliff must he climb in country wild;
Far off from all his friends, forlorn[18] must he ride;
At each strand[19] or stream where the stalwart[20] passed
'Twere[21] a marvel if he met not some monstrous foe[22],
And that so fierce and forbidding[23] that fight he must.
So many were the wonders he wandered among
That to tell but the tenth part would tax[24] my wits.
Now with serpents he wars, now with savage wolves,
Now with wild men of the woods, that watched from the rocks,
Both with bulls and with bears, and with boars besides,
And giants that came gibbering[25] from the jagged steeps[26].
Had he not borne himself bravely, and been on God's side,
He had met with many mishaps[27] and mortal harms.
And if the wars were unwelcome, the winter was worse,
When the cold clear rains rushed from the clouds
And froze before they could fall to the frosty earth.
Near slain by the sleet[28] he sleeps in his irons
More nights than enough, among naked rocks,
Where clattering from the crest the cold stream ran
And hung in hard icicles high overhead.
Thus in peril and pain and predicaments dire[29]
He rides across country till Christmas Eve,
> our knight.
> And at that holy tide[30]
> He prays with all his might
> That Mary may be his guide
> Till a dwelling comes in sight.

By a mountain next morning he makes his way

Into a forest fastness[31], fearsome and wild;

High hills on either hand, with hoar[32] woods below,

Oaks old and huge by the hundred together.

The hazel and the hawthorn were all intertwined

With rough raveled[33] moss, that raggedly hung,

With many birds unblithe[34] upon bare twigs

That peeped most piteously for pain of the cold.

The good knight on Cringolet[35] glides thereunder

Through many a marsh and mire, a man all alone;

He feared for his default[36], should he fail to see

The service of the Sire[37] that on that same night

Was born of a bright maid, to bring us his peace.

And therefore sighing he said, "I beseech of Thee[38], Lord,

And Mary, thou[39] mildest mother so dear,

Some harborage[40] where haply[41] I might hear mass[42]

And Thy[43] matins[44] tomorrow–meekly I ask it,

And thereto proffer[45] and pray my pater[46] and ave[47]

    And creed."

  He said his prayer with sighs.

  Lamenting his misdeed,

  He crosses himself, and cries

  On Christ in his great need[48].

Notes

1. array: *n.* (literary) a particular dress or armor

2. Logres: There are quite a few names for Arthur's kingdom and this is one of them.

3. mount: *n.* horse; notice that "amount" is "get on a horse" and "dismount" is "get off a horse".

4. nigh: (literary or archaic) near

5. Anglesey: the name of an island that is located off the coast of North Wales

6. fare: *v.* (literary or poetic) travel or move forward

7. ford: *n.* a shallow place in a river where it is possible to walk or ride through

8. Holy Head: a coast place in North Wales

9. Wirral: a place of Cheshire in Northwest England

10. Notice that in this line "great", "good" and "God" form alliteration. The selection is in modern English and if we read the original Middle English version there are much more examples of alliteration.

11. mortal: *n.* a human or an ordinary person

12. aught: *pron.* (old use) anything

13. chapel: *n.* a small church or a separate room or hall in a church or cathedral

14. thereabouts: *adv.* (usually used after "or") near the place around

15. hue: *n.* (literary or technique use) a color or a particular shade in a color

16. ere: (literary or old use) before

17. Notice that in these four lines, the words at the end of each line are forming ending rhyme ("strange" with "change", "anew" with "view"), which is a development of poetic technique from Old English literature that features in alliteration.

18. forlorn: *adv.* lonely

19. strand: *n.* (literary) the edge of a river, lake or sea

20. stalwart: *n./adj.* a loyal or faithful supporter or being loyal or supportive; here means Sir Gawain.

21. 'Twere: It were. In Middle English, there are such usages as "'t" (it), "'er" (over) and so on.

22. foe: *n.* enemy

23. forbidding: threatening

24. tax: *v.* to require a great deal of or even too much of

25. gibber: *v.* to speak quickly but could not be understood

26. jagged steeps: rough and sharp cliffs

27. mishaps: *n.* misfortunes or bad accidents

28. sleet: *n.* a mixture or rain and snow

29. predicaments dire: dire predicaments, that is, awful and unpleasant situations; notice that in poetry sometimes the normal order of words in a line is changed or reversed to achieve effect on rhyming or metrical arrangement.

30. holy tide: holy time (Christmas Eve)

31. fastness: *n.* a place that is difficult to attack; a fortress or a stronghold

32. hoar: *adj.* (old use) white and gray as if covered with frost

33. raveled: mixed or complicated

34. unblithe: unhappy or anxious

35. Cringolet: the name of Sir Gawain's horse

36. default: *n.* failure to fulfill one's duty or to pay one's debt

37. the Sire: Jesus Christ

38. beseech of: (formal) to seek help from or to plead dearly; Thee: you (in the objective case)

39. thou: you (in subjective case)

40. harborage: a shelter or a safe place

41. haply: (old use) perhaps, accidentally or occasionally

42. mass: (often in the form of "Mass") It refers to a church service, especially in Roman Catholic tradition, it means a ceremony held in memory of Jesus's last supper with his disciples.

43. thy: your

44. matins: prayers in the morning

45. proffer: (old use) offer

46. pater: father (Here it refers to God.)

47. ave: short for "Ave Maria or Ave Mary" (starter for a prayer that praises Mary, the mother of Jesus)

48. need: Here means "great difficulty or misfortune".

Questions for Discussion

(1) Unlike *Beowulf*, *Sir Gawain and the Green Knight* uses both ending rhyme and alliteration. What is the relationship here between the development of language and the evolution of literature?

(2) As a human, Sir Gawain has his share of mistakes, but he also dares to admit his mistakes, show his chivalry. How are the images of Sir Gawain and Beowulf characterized in story narration?

(3) The legend of King Arthur and the Knights of the Round Table (of which Sir Gawain is one of its prominent knights) is of Celtic origin. However, the Anglo-Saxon people, who were enemies of the Celts, picked many of these legends up and forged them into an important part of English literature. What are the reasons for that? How were concepts such as "nation", "language", and "identity" formed?

(4) Read the entirety of *Sir Gawain and the Green Knight* and other romances (including matters of France, Rome and Britain). How were the concepts and principles of knighthood or chivalry spirit at that time formed? What is its influence on later Western literature, and in particular British literature?

(5) What are the most pertinent elements of romance in the context of European literature? The very term "romance" is often rendered as 传奇 in Chinese. Compare Chinese works of 传奇 and romance works in English literature.

Suggested Reading

(1) Marie Borroff, Laura L. Howes. *Sir Gawain and the Green Knight*. New York: W. W. Norton & Company, 2010.

(2) Alfred David, James Simpson. *The Norton Anthology of English Literature: The Middle Ages* (Volume A) (The Eighth Edition). New York: W. W. Norton & Company, 2006.

(3) 布莱恩·斯通：《高文爵士与绿衣骑士》，陈才宇译，杭州：浙江工商大学出版社，2019年。

(4) 冯象：《玻璃岛：亚瑟与我三千年》(第二版)，北京：生活·读书·新知三联书店，2013年。

(5) 刘建军：《欧洲中世纪文学论稿——从公元5世纪到13世纪末》，北京：中华书局，2010年。

3. Geoffrey Chaucer

Geoffrey Chaucer (ca.1340–1400), "the father of English literature", was born into a rising vintner family that later came to enjoy contact with royal family members. Chaucer joined the English army in the Hundred Years' war (Edward III's invasion of France) but was captured and put in prison in France. After being ransomed, he served in diplomatic missions on the European continent for ten years. Returning to London, he undertook various positions that are more or less related to court and was even elected as a Member of Parliament from Kent where he was the knight of the shire. Under the patronage of John of Gaunt, Chaucer carried out his tasks with enormous energy, while still leaving some energy and time to his literary pursuits. His career is generally divided into three periods–literature under French influence (*Book of the Duchess*), literature under Italian influence (*Troilus and Criseyde*, *The Parliament of Fowls*, *The House of Fame*) and literature of his own creation (*The Canterbury Tales*). Chaucer lived between the end of the Middle Ages and the dawn of the Renaissance. His works are not only closely related to his own personal experience but are also a brilliant reflection of his time. He was buried in the Poets' Corner in Westminster Abbey that heralds a tradition of resting renowned men of letters in this magnificent church.

The Canterbury Tales, Chaucer's magnum opus, describes 31 pilgrims' traveling to Canterbury from a London inn and their agreement that each will tell four tales to and fro the holy place. However, only 24 tales were finished including the author's two tales and the characters in these tales represent almost all walks of life, forming a panoramic view of contemporary times. The particular poetic technique employed by Chaucer is termed as "heroic couplet", a pair of end-rhymed lines with iambic pentameter (unstressed + stressed in meter in each foot and with five feet in each line), and the special structure of the book is "frame within frame" (see Boccaccio's *Decameron*), that is, within the macro structure of the whole book there are many stories that have their own structure. All the characters are vividly presented by the author in the General Prologue and with the tales told by them. One of the most outstanding characteristics of Chaucer's writing is his subtle irony and mild satire, which is so skillfully maneuvered in the tales that one could not but smile gently. We should also bear in mind that Chaucer is the grand master of Middle English which is a mixture of different dialects based on the London dialect in a time when Norman lords spoke French daintily and the Christian monks spoke Latin austerely.

The Canterbury Tales

(The General Prologue)

When the sweet showers of April fall and shoot
Down through the drought[1] of March to pierce the root[2],
Bathing every vein in liquid power[3]
From which there springs[4] the engendering[5] of the flower,
When also Zephyrus[6] with his sweet breath
Exhales an air in every grove[7] and heath[8]
Upon the tender shoots, and the young sun[9]
His half-course in the sign of the Ram has run[10],
And the small fowls[11] are making melody
That sleep away the night with open eye
(So nature pricks them and their heart engages[12])
Then people long to go on pilgrimages
And palmers[13] long to seek the stranger strands[14]
Of far-off saints, hallowed[15] in sundry lands,
And specially from every shire's end[16]
In England, down to Canterbury[17] they wend[18]
To seek the holy blissful martyr[19], quick
In giving help to them when they were sick.
It happened in that season that one day
In Southwark, at *The Tabard*[20], as I lay
Ready to go on pilgrimage and start
For Canterbury, most devout at heart,
At night there came into that hostelry[21]
Some nine and twenty in a company
Of sundry[22] folk happening then to fall
In fellowship, and they were pilgrims all
That towards Canterbury meant to ride.
The rooms and stables of the inn were wide[23];

They made us easy, all was of the best.

And shortly, when the sun had gone to rest,

By speaking to them all upon the trip

I was admitted to their fellowship

And promised to rise early and take the way

To Canterbury, as you heard me say.

But none the less, while I have time and space,

Before my story takes a further pace

It seems a reasonable thing to say

What their condition was, the full array

Of each of them, as it appeared to me.

According to profession and degree[24],

And what apparel[25] they were riding in;

* * *

There also was a Nun, a Prioress[26]

Simple her way of smiling was and coy.[27]

Her greatest oath was only 'By St Loy[28]!'

And she was known as Madam Eglantyne[29].

And well she sang a service, with a fine

Intoning through her nose, as was most seemly[30],

And she spoke daintily[31] in French, extremely,

After the school of Stratford-atte-Bowe[32],

French in the Paris style she did not know.

At meat her manners were well taught withal[33];

No morsel[34] from her lips did she let fall,

Nor dipped her fingers in the sauce too deep;

But she could carry a morsel up and keep

The smallest drop from falling on her breast.

For courtliness[35] she had a special zest.

And she would wipe her upper lip so clean

That not a trace of grease was to be seen

Upon the cup when she had drunk; to eat,

She reached a hand sedately[36] for the meat.
She certainly was very entertaining[37],
Pleasant and friendly in her ways, and straining
To counterfeit[38] a courtly kind of grace,
A stately bearing[39] fitting to her place,
And to seem dignified in all her dealings.
As for her sympathies and tender feelings,
She was so charitably solicitous[40]
She used to weep if she but saw a mouse
Caught in a trap, if it were dead or bleeding.
And she had little dogs she would be feeding
With roasted flesh, or milk, or fine white bread.
Sorely she wept if one of them were dead
Or someone took a stick and made it smart[41]
She was all sentiment and tender heart.
Her veil was gathered in a seemly way,
Her nose was elegant, her eyes glass-grey;
Her mouth was very small, but soft and red,
And certainly she had a well-shaped head,
Almost a span[42] across the brows, I own[43];
She was indeed by no means undergrown[44].
Her cloak, I noticed, had a graceful charm.
She wore a coral trinket[45] on her arm,
A set of beads, the gaudies[46] tricked[47] in green,
Whence[48] hung a golden brooch of brightest sheen[49]
On which there first was graven[50] a crowned A[51],
And lower, *Amor vincit omnia*[52].

Notes

1. drought: *n.* a long period of time with little or no rain
2. to pierce the root: (the sweet shower of April) piercing to the root of plants; notice that the General Prologue and most tales are written in heroic couplet.

3. vein: *n.* the thin tubes that form the frame of a leaf; bathing every vein in liquid power: the sweet April rain running through the tubes of leaves and giving power to the plants

4. spring: *v.* bring

5. engendering: (formal) making to happen or coming into being (Here it means the blooming of flowers.)

6. Zephyrus: the west wind, which is said to be prevalent in the spring according to tradition

7. grove: *n.* (literary) a piece of land with trees

8. heath: *n.* an open land that is covered with wild grass and plants (or without trees)

9. young sun: the sun is in its early stage in a yearly course; notice the use of personification here.

10. Ram (公羊座): the first sign of the Zodiac (黄道十二宫), which is a diagram designed to show the positions of the planets and stars diving into 12 parts to figure out the influence of the planets and stars on people's lives; Ram's course is from March 21st to April 21st.

11. fowls: *n.* birds

12. So nature pricks them and their hearts engages: So nature pricks them and engages their hearts; prick: stimulate; engage: attract

13. palmers: wide-ranging and experienced pilgrims

14. strange strands: foreign shores or coasts, especially of holy places; here notice that there is the use of alliteration, which is also a common phenomenon in Middle English literature though in Chaucer the use of ending rhyme is getting more and more popular.

15. hallowed: honored or made sacred

16. every shire's end: every farthest place (of England)

17. Canterbury: a town in the southeast of London that is located in Kent; there is a famous cathedral in it.

18. wend: (archaic or literary) to go or travel

19. the holy blissful martyr: Here it means the saint St. Thomas Becket, who was a friend to Henry II since childhood and later became the Chancellor of England and

Archbishop of Canterbury. But he was murdered in 1170 in Canterbury Cathedral by knights sent by Henry II in defending the church's power while the latter wanted to break it. He was canonized in 1172 and his shrine in Canterbury Cathedral became the object of most popular pilgrimage.

20. *The Tabard*: the name of an inn in Southwark, in Chaucer's time a suburb of London, south of the Thames River; it was a real inn and later burned down in the 17th century.

21. hostelry: inn

22. sundry: various; it could be used to refer to places and people.

23. wide: *adj.* with large room or space

24. degree: social rank

25. apparel: (old fashioned or formal) clothing, especially those worn on a formal occasion

26. Prioress: the head of a group of nuns in a covenant

27. coy: shyly reserved or affectedly shy; here it can be a pun to show Chaucer's subtle irony on this Prioress.

28. St Loy was the name of a well-known French goldsmith in the 6th century and here is another of Chaucer's subtle irony because on the one hand, a prioress should not make swear, on the other hand, this prioress did swear, only with an exotic name whose oath had no effect at all.

29. Eglantyne: meaning "sweetbriar" which sounds like a romantic and elegant name; notice the meaning of her name and her manners at the table (elegantly) and bear in mind Chaucer's gentle satire.

30. seemly: properly; on the one hand, the prioress was singing softly to attract attention from the male audience and on the other hand, it is also common or proper in Chaucer's time to sing like that.

31. daintily: (trying to be) elegantly or delicately

32. Stratford-atte-Bowe: a suburb of London; notice here the irony made by Chaucer in hinting that the prioress is speaking French with a London accent, not standard Parisian French.

33. withal: (archaic) and also

34. morsel: a small piece or amount of something (such as food)

35. courtliness: courtly conduct; proper behaviors in court

36. sedately: calmly and slowly

37. entertaining: attracting or holding the attention of the people present

38. counterfeit: to imitate (the court manners) or to deceive (the people present)

39. bearing: figure or shape

40. solicitous: generous, caring and attentive

41. made it smart: hit it (the dog)

42. span: the distance between one's thumb and little finger when the hand is outstretched; here notice the irony that on the one hand, a prioress was not supposed to expose her forehead while on the other hand, this prioress did expose hers by folding her headdress specially to attract attention.

43. I own: I guess

44. Here it is an irony and the writer actually means that the prioress is a big and strong female.

45. trinket: a piece of jewelry or decorative object

46. gaudies: A gaudy is a large bead that is usually put in every ten smaller beads in a rosary (usually worn in Roman Catholicism) for counting prayers.

47. tricked: decorated

48. whence: (old use) from where

49. sheen: a soft smooth shiny quality

50. graven: engraved (cut or mark words on metal, wood, etc.)

51. a crowned A: the letter "a" in its capitalized form

52. *Amor vincit omnia*: It is a Latin sentence meaning "Love conquers all." Whether it is divine love or earthly love, it is not sure. Maybe a bit of both. Here it is the climax of ironies in the narration of this prioress.

Questions for Discussion

(1) Read the whole book or at least some typical sections of the poem in its original Middle English to discern the evolution from Middle English to Modern English.

(2) Identify the alliteration and the ending rhyming pattern in the selection that

shows Chaucer's contribution to perfecting the heroic couplet, which paved the way for the later poetic forms as sonnets.

(3) How did Chaucer narrate his characters in the poem? How did Chaucer describe these characters so vividly as round, not flat characters?

(4) What do Chaucer's narration and the general prologue reveal about the relationship between his personal experience and the historical rise of the capitalistic class?

(5) Try to complete reading Boccaccio's *Decameron* and compare it with Chaucer's *The Canterbury Tales*. Make out the influence of the former on the latter and discriminate Chaucer's unique contribution to English literature and even in European literature.

(6) Chaucer's time is about the early stage of the Ming Dynasty in China and we also have such important works as *San Yan Er Pai* (三言二拍), which are also collections of tales only to be in prose style. Compare the characterization in *The Canterbury Tales* and these tales in Chinese and their historical significance.

Suggested Reading

(1) Geoffrey Chaucer. *The Canterbury Tales: A Selection*. New York: Signet Classics, 2013.

(2) Geoffrey Chaucer. *The Canterbury Tales: Complete*. Cambridge: Wadsworth Publishing, 2000.

(3) Piero Boitani & Jill Mann. *The Cambridge Companion to Chaucer*. Shanghai: Shanghai Foreign Language Education Press, 2000.

(4) 乔叟：《坎特伯雷故事》，方重译，北京：人民文学出版社，2004年。

(5) 乔叟：《坎特伯雷故事》，黄杲炘译，上海：上海译文出版社，2011年。

(6) 肖明翰编选：《乔叟研究文集》，南京：译林出版社，2019年。

(7) 乔叟：《乔叟文集》，方重译，北京：商务印书馆，2020年。

(8) 李安：《乔叟文学思想研究》，广州：暨南大学出版社，2014年。

4. Popular Ballads

With significant historical events such as the Hundred Years' War, the War of the Roses and the 1381 Uprising, from the 14th to 16th century there appears a variety of folk narrative songs categorized as Popular Ballads. There are "border ballads", dealing with fierce strife between England and Scotland, "Robin Hood ballads", telling tales of the famous Sherwood Forest outlaw Robin Hood and his followers, and others with themes of daily life or supernatural paganism. One outstanding feature of these popular ballads is that the majority of them are from Scotland instead of England. It is also noteworthy that these ballads are handed by oral tradition down through generations. It was not until the 18th century that they were introduced to the world by Bishop Thomas Percy when he collected and published them in his collection *Reliques of Ancient English Poetry*. Almost 100 years later, F. J. Child published *English and Scottish Ballads* in 5 volumes with 305 ballads that mainly originate from the 15th century. Ballads have a far-reaching influence on later English and Scottish writers with such typical cases as Robert Burns' collections, Walter Scott's *Minstrelsy of the Scottish Border* (with his own adaptations and imitations) and Wordsworth and Coleridge's *Lyrical Ballads* (with their own interpretation and development of the term "ballad"). William Butler Yeats and Thomas Hardy and many others also obtain inspiration from ballads for their writing.

Artistically traditional popular ballads share some of the following common characteristics. Firstly, the themes in ballads are as various as war, love, daily life, etc., but mostly they hold a tragic atmosphere. Secondly, the structure of a ballad is often in stanzas of four lines, with four feet in each odd-numbered line and three feet in each even-numbered line. As often is the case, even-numbered lines are rhyming and there is a refrain (a repeated line) at the end of each stanza. Thirdly, the story in a ballad often starts abruptly to directly usher the audience into the scene and gradually develops itself into the episode climax by adding dramatic elements. Simple but terse dialogues are often used in a ballad to advance the story along with strong actions. Because of its exclusively oral tradition, the modern version of ballads may appear differently from its Middle Ages version to some extent (in some cases to a great extent). What is presented in this chapter is mostly in its modern version, that is, they are standardized to some degree, either in spelling or in presenting the refrain.

Get up and Bar the Door

It fell about the Martinmas[1] time,
And a gay time it was then[2],
When our goodwife[3] got puddings to make,
And she's boild[4] them in the pan.

The wind so cold blew south and north.
And blew into the floor;
Quoth[5] our goodman to our goodwife,
"Go out and bar the door."

"My hand is in my hussyfskap[6],
Goodman, as ye[7] may see;
If it shoud[8] not be barr'd[9] this hundred year,
It's not be barr'd by me."

They made a paction[10] 'tween[11] them two,
They made it firm and sure,
That the first word whoe'er[12] should speak,
Should rise and bar the door.

Then by there came two gentlemen,[13]
At twelve o'clock at night,
And they could neither see house nor hall,
Nor coal, nor candle-light,

"Now whether is this a rich man's house,
or whether is it a poor?"

But ne'er a word would one of them speak,
For barring of the door.

And first they ate the white puddings,
And then they ate the black;
Tho'[14] much thought the goodwife to herself,
Yet ne'er[15] a word she spake[16].

Then said the one unto the other,
"Here, man, take ye my knife;
Do ye take off the old man's beard,
And I'll kiss the goodwife."

"But there's no water in the house,
And what shall we do then?"
"what ails ye at the pudding-broth[17],
That boils into the pan?"

O, up then started[18] our Goodman,
An angry man was he:
"Will ye kiss my wife before my eye?
And scald[19] me with pudding-broth?"

O, up then started our goodwife,
Made three skips[20] on the floor:
"Goodman, you've spoken the foremost word[21],
Get up and bar the door."

Notes

1. Martinmas: the feast day to memorize St Martin, which is on 11th November
2. As in other forms of poetry, an inverted order or mixed order is often used;

here the normal sentence order should be "And it was a gay time then"; gay: happy

3. goodwife: the wife, hostess or mistress of a house; as in the following lines, "goodman" means the husband, host or the master of a house.

4. boild: boiled; notice usually in poems some words are shortened and abbreviated or some letters are omitted, but it should be easy for readers to find out.

5. quoth: said

6. hussyfskap: sometimes shortened as "hussy"; the small basket or case for needles and thread and so on

7. ye: you

8. shoud: should

9. barr'd: barred

10. paction: a pact, or an agreement or a bet

11. 'tween: between

12. whoe'er: whoever

13. Notice the irony here: these two are thieves actually; the whole ballad is a comic one with the reflection of daily people's lives, including their argument and reconciliation and their resentment on the surface and profound love deep within.

14. Tho': though

15. ne'er: never

16. spake: spoke; notice that there are various spellings in ballads that are not standardized English.

17. What ails ye at the pudding-broth: why not use the pudding-broth (to shave off the beard of the goodman); ails: troubles; broth: a thick soup made by boiling meat or vegetables

18. started: jumped

19. scald: to burn with hot liquid or steam

20. skips: stamping of the foot

21. you've spoken the foremost word: you have been the first (between the two of us) to speak out any word

The Three Ravens

There were three ravens sat on a tree,
Down a down, hey down, hey down,[1]
They were as black as they might be,[2]
With a down, derry, derry, derry down, down.

The one of them said to his mate,
"Where shall our breakfast take?"

"Down in yonder[3] green field,
There lies a knight slain 'neath[4] his shield.

His hounds they lie down at his feet,
So well they do their master keep.[5]

His hawks they fly so eagerly,
There's no other fowl dare come him nigh[6]."

Down there comes a fallow[7] doe[8],
As great with young as might she go.

She lifted up his bloody head,
And kissed his wounds that were so red.

She got him up upon her back,
And carried him to earthen lake[9].

She buried him before the prime[10];
She was dead herself ere evensong[11] time,

God send every gentleman,[12]

Such hawks, such hounds, and such a leman[13].

Notes

1. This sentence and line four in this stanza are typical refrains which are sung by the chorus. In this ballad, these refrains are meaningless words that are just for singing effect. The refrains are omitted in the following stanzas.

2. They were as black as they might be: They were just so black

3. yonder: (old use or dialect) over there

4. 'neath: beneath; under

5. So well they do their master keep: They do guard their master so well

6. nigh: near

7. fallow: reddish brown

8. doe: a female deer; Here it is a figure of speech to refer to the knight's mistress or lover; notice in this ballad the chivalry spirit such as faithful love and loyalty.

9. earthen lake: a lake that is made of earth; a pit or a hole; this may ring a bell of kenning in Old English literature.

10. prime: early morning or sunrise

11. evensong: songs or hymns sung at the evening prayer service

12. God send every gentleman: May God send every gentleman

13. leman: sweetheart; lover or mistress

Sir Patrick Spens

The King sat in Dunfermline[1] town
Drinking of the blood red wine.
"Where can I get a good sea captain
To sail this mighty ship of mine?"

Then up there spak[2] an elder knight
Sat at the King's right knee,
"Sir Patrick Spens is the best sailer[3]

That ever sails upon the sea."

The King has written a braid[4] letter
And signed it with his hand,
And sent it to Sir Patrick,
Was walking on the sand.

The first line that Sir Patrick read,
A loud lauch lauched[5] he;
The next line that Sir Patrick read,
The tear blinded his ee[6].

"O wha[7] is this has done this deed,
This ill deed done to me,
To send me out this time o' the year,
To sail upon the sea?

"Make haste, make haste, my mirry[8] men all,
Our guid[9] ship sails the morn[10]."
"O say na sae[11], my master dear,
For I fear a deadly storm.

"Last night I saw the new moon
With the old moon in her arm,
And I fear, I fear, my dear master,
That we will come to harm."

O our Scots nobles were richt laith[12]
To weet[13] their cork-heeled shoon[14],
But lang owre a' the play were played[15]
their hats they swam aboon[16].

O lang, lang may their ladies sit,
Wi' their fans into their hand,
Or e'er[17] they see Sir Patrick Spens,
Come sailing to the land.

O lang, lang may the ladies stand,
With their gold kembs[18] in their hair,
Waiting for their ain[19] dear lords,
For they'll see thame na mair[20].

Half o'er, half o'er[21] to Aberdeen[22]
It's fifty fadom[23] deep.
And there lies guid Sir Patrick Spens
Wi' the Scots lords at his feet.

Notes

1. Dunfermline: the capital of Scotland in the 13th century and before that; this ballad is quite an old Scottish ballad, so the words are mainly Scottish English.

2. spak: spoke

3. sailer: sailor

4. braid: broad; long

5. lauch: laugh; notice here the dramatic effect: in the beginning Sir Spens is laughing (maybe because the King praises his deed and gives him a mission) and then he cries loud (he reads the date of the mission when it is deadly to sail).

6. ee: eye

7. wha: who

8. mirry: merry

9. guid: good

10. the morn: the next morning

11. say na sae: do not say so

12. richt laith: loathe rightly (what the sailor said is correct)

13. weet: wet

14. shoon: shoes

15. lang: long; owre: over (before); a': all; play: action; the whole line means "before all actions can be taken"/ "before their journey is over".

16. aboon: above (on the surface of the water); here "wet their shoes" and "their hats swam above" indicate that these sailors met terrible storms and were drowned.

17. e'er: ever; or e'er: before (they could see…), meaning also they will never see their husbands or masters again

18. kembs: combs

19. ain: own

20. see thame na mair: see them no more

21. half o'er: half over, that is, half way over (There are other fuller versions saying that Sir Spens is to seek marriage for his King to the court of Norway.)

22. Aberdeen: a coast city in northeast Scotland

23. fadom: fathom; unit for measuring the depth of water, which is equal to 6 feet or 1.8 meters

Questions for Discussion

(1) How are popular ballads similar to and different from Middle English poetry as romance poems and Chaucer's poems?

(2) Why are Scottish ballads an indispensable part of popular ballads? What are the historical backgrounds of this phenomenon?

(3) Besides the poets mentioned in the introduction, are there any more such poets that are related to ballads or are under the influence of popular ballads? Compare their poems with popular ballads, in style and craftsmanship.

(4) One of the most significant features of popular ballads is their oral tradition, in that most or even all of them can be sung (the word "ballad" itself is derived from the Latin "ballare", meaning to "dance" as in "ballet"). Read every ballad you encounter as carefully as possible and ponder on how the "singing" qualities of a ballad are achieved.

(5) In Chinese, we also enjoy a treasure house of popular ballads, some of which

are still sung in places such as mountainous areas or the countryside. Find some representative Chinese ballads and compare them with English and Scottish ballads, either in themes, metrical techniques or in rhetorical devices and singing features.

Suggested Reading

(1) Francis James Child. *The English and Scottish Popular Ballads: Complete Set*. Dover: Dover Publications Inc., 2003.

(2) Judith M. Bennett, C. Warren Hollister. *Medieval Europe: A Short History*. Beijing: Peking University Press, 2007.

(3) John Gillingham, Ralph A. Griffiths. *Medieval Britain: A Very Short Introduction*. Beijing: Foreign Languages Teaching and Research Press, 2007.

(4) 沈弘选译：《英国中世纪诗歌选集》，杭州：浙江大学出版社，2019年。

(5) J. A. 伯罗：《中世纪作家和作品：中古英语文学及其背景(1100—1500)》(修订版)，沈弘译，北京：北京大学出版社，2007年。

(6) 王宏印选译：《英国诗歌选译：从中古民谣到现代诗歌》，北京：外语教学与研究出版社，2018年。

Part Two

The English Renaissance

5. Edmund Spenser

Edmund Spenser (c. 1552–1599) was born into a relatively poor family, but he acquired an excellent humanistic education by attending the Merchant Taylors' School and Pembroke Hall, Cambridge under the influence of Renaissance spirit. The two inspiring figures he came to know in these two institutions became the Archbishop of Canterbury and Bishop of Rochester respectively, and their religious views formed Spenser's ideas of religion throughout his life time. Later he was introduced to some important aristocrats, including Sir Philip Sydney to whom Spenser dedicated his early representative work *Shepheardes Calender*. After working as secretary to several lords he began to undertake the post of lord deputy in Ireland. Because of the sharp conflicts between England and Ireland, Edmund Spenser was inevitably and profoundly involved in the tense and complicated relationship between them. Generally, he was on the side of suppressing the Irish uprisings and his living quarter in Ireland–Kilcolman Castle in Cork County–was acquired in the English settlement of Munster (the southern part of Ireland). In the autumn of 1589, Spenser came back to England along with Sir Walter Raleigh and he dedicated the first three books of his masterpiece *The Faerie Queene* to Queen Elizabeth I, thus being given a pension of 50 pounds for life. Spenser continued to write the rest of the books and to manage affairs in Ireland, which were getting worse and worse and finally resulted in the burning of Kilcolman Castle in a sudden insurrection of local people. Fleeing back to London, Spenser died in poverty and distress and he was buried in Poets' Corner of

Westminster Abbey, next to his favorite poet–Geoffrey Chaucer.

The most prominent contribution made by Spenser to English literature is his invention of the Spenserian stanza, which consists of eight lines in iambic pentameter and the last line of iambic hexameter. The ending rhyme pattern for the Spenserian stanza is ababbcbcc. Spenser employed it to write his most influential work *The Faerie Queene*, and he also used it to write other forms of poetry such as sonnets. Edmund Spenser and William Shakespeare are the two most important poets who wrote a large number of sonnets and their respective unique stanzas are epitome of the genre in English literature. His tombstone are engraved such words as "the prince of poets in his time", which is so precise to describe his undeniable influence on later poets, especially John Milton and John Keats.

Sonnet 75

One day I wrote her name upon the strand[1],
But came the waves and washed it away:
Agayne[2] I wrote it with a second hand[3],
But came the tyde, and made my payns his pray[4].
"Vayne man[5]", said she, "that doest[6] in vaine assay[7]
A mortall[8] thing so to immortalize,
For I my selve[9] shall lyke to this decay[10],
And eek[11] my name bee[12] wyped[13] out lykewise.[14]"
"Not so," quod[15] I, "let baser things[16] devize[17]
To dy[18] in dust[19], but you shall live by fame[20]:
My verse your vertues rare shall eternize[21],
And in the heavens wryte[22] your glorious name.
Where whenas[23] Death shall all the world subdew[24],
Our love shall live, and later life renew[25]."

Notes

1. strand: beach; sand

2. agayne: again

3. with a second hand: in a second time

4. tyde: tide; my payns: my work, my efforts; pray: prey, the object in a hunting game; made my payns his pray: made my efforts in vain; my work became the victim of (the tide)

5. vayne man: vain man; man with illusions

6. doest: does in its Middle English form

7. vaine assay: vain assay; try in vain

8. mortall: mortal; earthly

9. my selve: myself

10. lyke: like; shall lyke to this decay: shall decay like this

11. eek: eke; also

12. bee: be

13. wyped: wiped

14. lykewise: likewise

15. quod: quoth; said

16. baser things: more humble objects in nature

17. devize: devise; contrive

18. dy: die

19. in dust: an allusion to biblical texts–for dust thou art, and unto dust shalt thou return (Genesis 3: 19)

20. fame: great and beautiful reputation; you shall live by fame: you shall be immortal with your great reputation; Spenser and his contemporaries think that art (including poetry) can make people immortal because the poet's poetry will be handed down generations by generations and the praised person in the poetry will be eternal along with the poetry. The same theme can be found in Shakespeare's sonnet 18 and sonnet 55.

21. verse: poem; vertues: virtues; My verse your vertues rare shall eternize: My poem shall eternize your rare virtues.

22. wryte: write

23. whenas: whereas; although

24. subdew: subdue; conquer

25. later life renew: renew later life, renew the future generations; Spenser holds that love is to end in marriage, which can result in offspring (thus renewing the body), and that the offspring's soul can go to heaven and be eternal (thus renewing the soul). In this sense, it equals "love conquers all" (The Prioress, "General Prologue", *The Canterbury Tales*).

Questions for Discussion

(1) Note the special form of the stanza in Edmund Spenser's *Shepheardes Calender* and sections of *The Faerie Queene*. Compare them with the poems in the previous sections and show the developing track of poetry in English literature.

(2) In the previous chapters, the selections are translated into modern English, whereas in this chapter Spenser's "Sonnet 75" is entirely in its original form. Based on your reading of books on the history of the English language, how are these words or expressions different from modern English, and how is Middle English evolving into Modern English?

(3) What are the similarities and differences between Spenser's sonnets and Shakespeare's sonnets?

Suggested Reading

(1) Edmund Spenser. *The Faerie Queene*. London: Penguin Classics, 1979.

(2) Andrew Hadfield. *Edmund Spenser: A Life*. New York: Oxford University Press, 2012.

(3) R. M. Cummings, ed. *Edmund Spenser: The Critical Heritage*. London: Routledge, 1996.

(4) Liu Lihui. *Harmony of Life: A Study of the Underlying Argument in Spenser's The Faerie Quenne*. Beijing: Foreign Language Teaching and Research Press, 2005.

(5) 埃德蒙·斯宾塞：《斯宾塞诗歌选集：十四行组诗及其他》，胡家峦译，杭州：浙江大学出版社，2018 年。

(6) 埃德蒙·斯宾塞：《小爱神——斯宾塞十四行诗集》，曹明伦译，保定：河北大学出版社，2008 年。

6. Christopher Marlowe

Christopher Marlowe was born into a shoemaker's family in Canterbury in 1564, received an education at King's School in the town, and went to Corpus Christi College, Cambridge where he obtained his Bachelor of Arts degree in 1584 and Master of Arts degree in 1587. He was closely related to the University Wits, a group of writers who were educated either at Oxford University or Cambridge University, (comparing that to Shakespeare's receiving little education in youth), although he was not the key player in the circle. To some extent, Marlowe demonstrated the significant dual characteristics of humanistic cultivation in Renaissance in England: on one hand, he acquired an excellent classical attainment; on the other hand, he was full of rebellious, violent or even criminal temperament. He might have been profoundly involved with certain secret political and diplomatic missions, whereas he also undertook some dangerous individual adventures and tasks. His intimacy with such University Wits dramatists as Kyd created a tendency towards atheism or even blasphemy. In May 1593, Marlowe was stabbed to death after a quarrel in a London tavern, while others guessed that he may have fallen victim to some malicious political conspiracies or maneuvers.

Marlowe was a versatile writer. He translated and published poems of Ovid and other classical writers, he wrote roughly-structured but influential plays such as *Tamburlaine*, *The Jew of Malta* and *The Tragical History of Doctor Faustus*, and he was also an important poet. His plays influenced significantly Shakespeare's early plays with Shakespeare paying tribute to Marlowe with the "dead shepherd" in *As You Like It*. Marlowe preferred and perfected the blank verse (unrhymed iambic pentameter), which became the major form used by Shakespeare in his plays. Another Renaissance writer Ben Jonson praised Marlowe's writing as "Marlowe's mighty line". Marlowe's plays are like the playwright himself, fraught with imagination, reflective power, sensuous passion, varying pace and emotion, while his poetry is full of such classical qualities as graveness and unified beauty. Though living a short life, Marlowe is a genius and a representative of the rising capitalistic class being imbued with Renaissance spirit. His life resonates with the vicissitudes of his time and his works embodies his versatility and overwhelming knowledge, being "the mighty pen" along with an actual mighty sword.

The Passionate Shepherd to His Love[1]

Come live with me and be my love,
And we will all the pleasures prove[2]
That valleys, groves, hills, and fields,
Woods, or steepy mountain yields[3].

And we will sit upon rocks,
Seeing the shepherds feed their flocks,
By shallow rivers to whose falls[4]
Melodious birds sing madrigals[5].

And I will make thee beds of roses
And a thousand fragrant posies[6],
A cap of flowers, and a kirtle[7]
Embroidered all with leaves of myrtle[8];

A gown made of the finest wool
Which from our pretty lambs we pull;
Fair lined slippers for the cold,
With buckles[9] of the purest gold;

A belt of straw and ivy buds,
With coral clasps[10] and amber studs;[11]
And if these pleasures may thee move,
Come live with me, and be my love.

The shepherd swains[12] shall dance and sing
For thy delight each May morning:

If these delights thy mind may move,

Then live with me and be my love.

Notes

1. The poem is in the form of pastoral poetry (牧歌, a special form of poetry that idealizes the beautiful country scene and pleasure, especially the love between a shepherd and shepherdess). There are two famous poems that are responding to or continuation of this poem: Walter Raleigh's "The Nymph's Reply to the Shepherd" and John Donne's "The Bait".

2. prove: (archaic) test; experience

3. yields: gives; the normal order for these lines should be: we will prove all the pleasures that ...steepy mountain yields

4. falls: Here it means both waterfalls and the sound of these waterfalls.

5. madrigals: pastoral songs (usually love songs) for several singers popular in the 16th century; the first two stanzas describe the beauty of the country scene.

6. posies: small bunches or bouquets of flowers; here also means the poems.

7. kirtle: long dress or gown for female

8. myrtle: a bush with shiny leaves, pink or white flowers and bluish-black berries 香桃木; it is said to be the sacred plant of the Venus, Goddess of Love.

9. buckles: a piece of metal or plastic for holding a part of a shoe or bag

10. clasp: the device to fasten the ends of a belt; stud: the metal or plastic object to be fixed on the surface of a belt or shoe

11. The above lines are showing scenes of the country festival or playing games and the decoration of the shepherdess reminds of the queen of May Day celebration in the British countryside.

12. swain: (old use) a young lover, especially in the countryside; this last line in the last stanza is resounding the first line in the first stanza; notice that there are two versions of this poem and in another version, there is one more stanza before the last one and the spellings and words are different.

Questions for Discussion

(1) Compare the spelling of this poem with that of Spenser's poems. What does it reveal about the development of the English language from the 15th century to the 16th century?

(2) How do the three masterpieces of Marlowe's plays compare with the structure of his poems? Discern the use of blank verse and the development of the plot in his plays and their influence on Shakespeare's plays.

(3) How does Marlowe's life experience in the Elizabethan age and society affect his writing?

(4) How does Raleigh's "The Nymph's Reply to the Shepherd" respond to and Donne's "The Bait" continue the description of Marlowe? Do the similarities and differences reflect any historical significance?

(5) The responding or continuing writing is also or even more popular in ancient Chinese literature (和诗或奉和诗). Identify the similarities and differences between some of these Chinese poems and those in English literature.

Suggested Reading

(1) Constance Brown Kuriyama. *Christopher Marlowe: A Renaissance Life*. Ithaca: Cornell University Press, 2002.

(2) Christopher Marlowe. *The Complete Poems and Translations*. London: Penguin Classics, 2007.

(3) Christopher Marlowe. *The Complete Plays*. London: Penguin Classics, 2003.

(4) 克里斯托弗·马洛:《马洛戏剧全集》(全两册), 华明译, 北京: 商务印书馆, 2020年。

(5) 冯伟:《克里斯托弗·马洛的传记研究》, 开封: 河南大学出版社, 2013年。

(6) 傅浩:《窃火传薪: 英语诗歌与翻译教学实录》, 上海: 上海外语教育出版社, 2011年。

7. William Shakespeare

William Shakespeare (1564–1616) is the greatest playwright in European Renaissance and English history. In 1564, he was born into a well-off merchant family in Stratford-upon-Avon, a small town to the northwest of London. This is why he was called "the bard of Avon". Shakespeare is widely regarded as the greatest writer in the English language and the world's greatest dramatist. He created thirty-seven plays from 1590 to 1616. His plays encompass history plays, comedies and tragedies. His earliest tragedy is *Titus Andronicus* (1593), but *Romeo and Juliet* revealed his distinguished skill in tragedies. In 1601, his best-known tragedy *Hamlet* demonstrated his remarkable exploration of human perplexities and enlightened countless readers with the eternal question "To be, or not to be–that is the question", from which each reader is endowed with a unique interpretation of this tragedy. As for Shakespeare's comedies, *A Midsummer Night's Dream* (1595) and *The Merchant of Venice* (1596) have been the most widespread and discussed. *A Midsummer Night's Dream* is a romantic fairy-tale; it shows people's unrelenting pursuit of true love and female's resistance against patriarchy.

William Shakespeare is also an extraordinary poet in Elizabethan Age. His sonnets with abundant themes enjoyed worldwide popularity, especially the "Sonnet 18". In his lifetime, he had written one hundred and fifty-four sonnets and two narrative poems. In 1616, Shakespeare died in his hometown. "Sonnet 18" is a typical Elizabethan sonnet. Generally, a sonnet in this genre has fourteen lines, points to unnamed subjects and follows a specific rhyme–the iambic pentameter. The beginning of "Sonnet 18" employs the literary device–metaphor, implying the brilliant beauty of this noble young man. His flawless complexion is incomparable but "more lovely and more temperate". By virtue of complimenting a man's beauty, Shakespeare stressed the essence of humanism.

Sonnet 18

Shall I compare thee[1] to a summer's day?

Thou art[2] more lovely and more temperate[3]:
Rough winds do shake the darling buds of May,
And summer's lease[4] hath[5] all too short a date:
Sometime too hot the eye of heaven shines,
And often is his gold complexion dimm'd[6];
And every fair[7] from fair[8] sometime declines,
By chance or nature's changing course untrimm'd[9]
But thy eternal summer shall not fade
Nor lose possession of that fair thou owest[10];
Nor shall Death brag thou wander'st in his shade,
When in eternal lines[11] to time thou growest:
So long as men can breathe or eyes can see,
So long lives this and this gives life to thee.

Notes

1. thee: the objective case of "thou"

2. thou art: you are

3. temperate: moderate

4. summer's lease: the time held by summer

5. hath: has

6. dimm'd: dimmed; faded; less bright

7. fair: beauty

8. fair: beautiful look

9. untrimm'd: untrimmed, stripped of beauty; By chance or nature's changing course untrimm'd: everything in the world will be stripped of beauty by chance or by natural changes

10. owest: own

11. eternal lines: eternal poems

Questions for Discussion

(1) Which figurative language does the first line "Shall I compare thee to a

summer's day?" employ, simile or metaphor? What is the real meaning?

(2) Identify the alliteration used in this sonnet (e.g. line 8, line 14) and explain its definition with those examples.

(3) Why does the poet think the young man's beauty is eternal when it is universally accepted that human beings are mortal? How can it be preserved according to the poet?

(4) "Summer" is a frequent image in Shakespeare's sonnet. Why is Shakespeare so keen on describing summer?

(5) Compare this sonnet with Shakespeare's other sonnets on their subjects and themes, like "Sonnet 29" and "Sonnet 30".

Suggested Reading

(1) William Shakespeare. *The Complete Sonnets and Poems*, New York: Oxford University Press, 2002.

(2) Hilton Landry. *New Essays on Shakespeare's Sonnets*, New York: AMS Press, 1976.

(3) Stanley Wells. *Shakespeare Studies,* Shanghai: Shanghai Foreign Language Education Press, 2000.

(4) E. Faas. *Shakespeare's Poetics*, Cambridge: Cambridge University Press, 1986.

(5) 莎士比亚：《莎士比亚十四行诗》，屠岸译，北京：外语教学与研究出版社，2012 年。

(6) 罗益民编著：《莎士比亚十四行诗名篇详注》，北京：中国人民大学出版社，2010 年。

Hamlet

Hamlet or *The Tragedy of Hamlet, the Prince of Denmark* is a revenge tragedy. This play is set in Denmark. Hamlet is summoned home because his father, the king, is dead. However, when he discovers his uncle Claudius has become the new king of Denmark and even has got married to his mother, queen Gertrude, within a month,

Hamlet is astonished and angry. One night, a ghost is approaching Hamlet, telling Hamlet that his father is murdered. This ghost is believed to be the old king. Based on the ghost's explanation, Hamlet is aware of the filthy conspiracy conducted by his uncle, Claudius. Hamlet resolves to avenge his father's death. With his friend Horatio's loyal assistance, Hamlet hatches an intricate plan. He feigns madness and organizes a court performance which reproduces the crimes committed by his uncle to verify if his uncle is guilty. Hamlet is capable of killing the villain, Claudius, but he defers his decision all the time during which so many innocent people are accidentally victimized, including his beloved Ophelia and his mother Gertrude. On the other hand, it is Hamlet's hesitation renders this play a great tragedy. In this play, Hamlet's soliloquies disclose his struggle, caution, perplexities and uncertainties in this character. (Act III, Scene I, excerpt, A Room in the Castle)

Hamlet's Soliloquy

To be, or not to be[1]–that is the question:
Whether 'tis nobler in the mind to suffer
The slings[2] and arrows of outrageous fortune,
Or to take arms[3] against a sea of troubles[4],
And by opposing end them;[5] to die: to sleep–
No more, and by a sleep to say we end
The heartache and the thousand natural shocks
That flesh is heir to: 'tis a consummation[6]
Devoutly to be wish'd–to die: to sleep–
To sleep, perchance to dream[7]–ay, there's the rub[8],
For in that sleep of death what dreams may come
When we have shuffled off this mortal coil[9],
Must give us pause[10]: there's the respect[11]
That makes calamity of so long life[12].
For who would bear the whips and scorns of time[13],
Th' oppressor's wrong, the proud man's contumely[14],
The pangs of despised love[15], the law's delay,

The insolence of office and the spurns[16]
That patient merit of th' unworthy takes[17],
When he himself might his quietus make[18]
With a bare bodkin.[19] Who would fardels[20] bear
To grunt[21] and sweat under a weary life
But that the dread of something after death
(The undiscovered country[22] from whose bourn[23]
No traveller returns) puzzles the will[24]
And makes us rather bear[25] those ills we have
Than fly to others[26] that we know not of.
Thus conscience does make cowards–
And thus the native hue of resolution[27]
Is sicklied o'er with[28] the pale cast of thought,
And enterprises of great pitch[29] and moment
With this regard their currents turn awry[30]
And lose the name of action[31]. Soft you now,
The fair Ophelia! Nymph, in thy orisons
Be all my sins remembered.

Notes

1. To be, or not to be: To live, or to die

2. slings: a device for holding or lifting heavy objects

3. arms: weapons

4. a sea of troubles: numerous troubles

5. And by opposing end them: fight against and end all the troubles

6. a consummation: a perfect and happy ending of something

7. perchance to dream: perhaps to dream

8. rub: problems and difficulties

9. shuffled off this mortal coil: freed from all the troubles in this life; they are like coils encircling us.

10. pause: to stop and hesitate

11. respect: consideration

12. calamity of so long life: disaster in such a long time

13. the whips and scorns of time: the lash and contempt from contemporaries

14. the proud man's contumely: the proud man's rudeness and scorn

15. despised love: love with disdain

16. The insolence of office and the spurns: the scornful officials and kicks

17. That patient merit of th' unworthy takes: the man of merit receives the kicks from the unworthy, those who do not deserve the respect

18. his quietus make: make his quietus; end his life

19. a bare bodkin: a mere dagger

20. fardels: burdens

21. grunt: groan

22. The undiscovered country: a country that has not been found; the world after death

23. bourn: limit; boundary

24. puzzles the will: baffles the decision to act

25. rather bear: would rather bear

26. fly to others: seek for other ills or evils

27. the native hue of resolution: the original color of resolution

28. is sicklied o'er with: is covered with sickly color

29. pitch: importance; height

30. their currents turn awry: turn awry their currents, change their course or purpose

31. And lose the name of action: the action cannot be accomplished with the purpose changed

Questions for Discussion

(1) In Hamlet's soliloquy, he is struggling to make a decision. What is the cause of his hesitation?

(2) How do you interpret Hamlet's revenge? Can his revenge be justified?

(3) In order to kill Claudius, Hamlet feigns madness. Does his madness work

well? Why or why not?

(4) What is the core of Hamlet's tragedy? His hesitation or his action?

(5) Does Hamlet really love Ophelia? Are female characters marginalized in this play? How do you understand the tragedy of female characters?

(6) Compare *Hamlet* with a Chinese Drama *The Orphan of Chao* in their themes.

Suggested Reading

(1) William Shakespeare. *Hamlet*. New York: Oxford University Press, 2008.

(2) A.C. Bradley. *Shakespearean Tragedies*. New York: St. Martin's Press, 1957.

(3) Peter Mercer. *Hamlet and the Acting of Revenge*. Iowa City: University of Iowa Press, 1987.

(4) H.G. Hunter. *English Drama, 1586–1642: The Age of Shakespeare*. Oxford: Clarendon Press, 1997.

(5) 威廉·莎士比亚：《哈姆雷特》，朱生豪译，南京：译林出版社，2013年。

(6) 《解读〈哈姆雷特〉：莎士比亚原著汉译及详注》，黄国彬译注，北京：清华大学出版社，2013年。

(7) 张沛：《哈姆雷特的问题》，北京：北京大学出版社，2006年。

8. *Francis Bacon*

Francis Bacon (1561–1626) was the son of Lord Keeper in Elizabeth I's reign. He was closely related to the court and aristocracy since his childhood. Like Christopher Marlowe, Bacon also went to Cambridge and received education there, only in a different college–Trinity College. Law was his major in college studies and after graduation his career was invariably involved with the legal field, first being admitted to Gray's Inn and then made a barrister in 1582. Two years later he was elected as a member of Parliament. His career did not flourish much in the Queen's reign. One reason is his intimacy with Lord Essex who was the Queen's favorite in the beginning and who started a rebellion later. It was not until James I taking the throne that Bacon's career took off. He was appointed Solicitor-General in 1613, Lord Keeper in 1617 and eventually Lord Chancellor (the highest judicial position in the kingdom) in 1618. However, his life took a dramatic turn in 1621 when he was charged with 23 counts of corruption and accepting bribes. Bacon admitted to it claiming that in taking the bribery his judgment was not compromised. Consequently, he was fined heavily, imprisoned for a short time in the Tower of London and disqualified from Parliament. Bacon spent the rest of his life writing and doing experiments that had been his two favorite interests long before his "retirement", along with his zeal for political involvement.

In a broad sense, Bacon's reputation in cultural history lies in three aspects: his experiential philosophy, his activation and promotion of learning by experiment and induction, and his remarkable contribution to the development of the English essay. Bacon believed in the scientific method in promoting human knowledge, thus bringing forward *The Advancement of Learning* in 1605. He further emphasized the importance of induction in his Latin works *Novum Organum* (*The New Instrument of Learning*) in 1620. He even introduced the Utopian idea when he wrote *New Atlantis* in 1627. Different from his French predecessor Michel de Montaigne (蒙田 , 1533—1592), who proposes that essays should be tentative in structure, witty and reflective in style and intimate in tone, Francis Bacon holds that essay's structure should be definitive, style be curt and brusque and tone be largely objective. His first edition of essays collected in 1597 has only ten short pieces, he enlarged it into a bigger collection in 1612 with thirty-eight essays, and finally in 1625 he completed the popular version with fifty-eight longer, smoother, more aphoristic and unified essays with various figures of speech. The themes of these essays are diverse, including public life, moral issues, love, truth, etc., but a majority of them are concerned about the interests, issues and public virtues of the historical period from Elizabeth I to James I.

Of Studies

Studies serve for delight[1], for ornament[2], and for ability. Their chief use for delight, is in privateness[3] and retiring[4]; for ornament, is in discourse[5]; and for ability, is in the judgment, and disposition of business[6]. For expert men[7] can execute, and perhaps judge of particulars, one by one; but the general counsels[8], and the plots[9] and marshalling[10] of affairs, come best from those that are learned. To spend too much time in studies is sloth[11]; to use them too much for ornament is affectation[12]; to make judgment wholly by their rules is the humor[13] of a scholar. They perfect nature, and are perfected by experience: for natural abilities are like natural plants, that need proyning[14] by study; and studies themselves do give forth directions too much at large[15], except they be bounded in by experience. Crafty men[16] contemn[17] studies, simple men[18] admire them, and wise men use them; for they teach not their own use; but that is a wisdom without[19] them, and above them, won by observation. Read not to contradict and confute; nor to believe and take for granted; nor to find talk and discourse; but to weigh and consider. Some books are to be tasted, others to be swallowed, and some few to be chewed and digested; that is, some books are to be read only in parts; others to be read, but not curiously[20]; and some few to be read wholly, and with diligence and attention. Some books also may be read by deputy[21], and extracts[22] made of them by others; but that would be only in the less important arguments[23], and the meaner[24] sort of books, else distilled books are like common distilled[25] waters, flashy[26] things. Reading maketh[27] a full man; conference a ready man; and writing an exact man. And therefore, if a man write little, he had need have a great memory; if he confer little, he had need have a present wit[28]; and if he read little, he had need have much cunning[29], to seem to know that he doth[30] not. Histories make men wise; poets, witty[31]; the mathematics, subtile[32]; natural philosophy, deep; moral, grave; logic and rhetoric, able to contend. *Abeunt studia in mores*[33]. Nay[34], there is no stond[35] or impediment in the wit, but may be wrought out[36] by fit studies, like as diseases of the body may have appropriate exercises. Bowling is good for the stone and reins[37], shooting for the lungs and breast, gentle walking for the stomach, riding for the head, and the like. So if a man's wit be wandering[38], let him study the mathematics; for in demonstrations[39], if his wit be called away never so little[40], he must begin again. If his wit be not apt to distinguish or find differences, let him study the schoolmen[41], for they are *cymini sectores*[42]. If he be not apt to beat over matters[43] and to call up one thing to prove and illustrate another, let him study the lawyers' cases. So every defect of the mind may have a special receipt[44].

Part Two The English Renaissance 49

Notes

1. delight: personal satisfaction
2. ornament: vivid and beautiful usage of one's language and style
3. privateness: private life, or being alone
4. retiring: living in recluse or alone
5. discourse: conversation or discussion
6. disposition of business: dealing with or management of worldly affairs
7. expert men: men with certain skills or techniques
8. counsel: advice or suggestion
9. plot: plan
10. marshalling: arrangement or dealing with
11. sloth: laziness, especially in the religious context
12. affectation: fake or unnatural emotion or manner
13. humor: the personality, the character or the temperament
14. proyning: pruning; cutting down redundant twigs or leaves of a tree
15. at large: too many directions; too general; not concentrated
16. crafty men: men with certain crafts or techniques
17. contemn: look down upon; despise
18. simple men: men with little knowledge; ignorant men
19. without: (old use) outside; not within (the studies) themselves
20. curiously: carefully; with meticulous attention
21. by deputy: by an agent; by another person
22. extract: excerpt; abstracted information
23. argument: (old use) topic; theme
24. meaner: less important or significant
25. distill: to take the filtration process in wine making
26. flashy: bright and shiny on the surface while meaningless or empty inside
27. maketh: (Middle English) makes
28. a present wit: a quick mind in speech or action
29. cunning: trick or skill in deception
30. doth: does

31. witty: able to write or say clever, smart things

32. subtile: the archaic spelling of "subtle"; good at finding distinction or difference

33. *Abeunt studia in mores*: (Latin) whatever one studies, they will be formed into one's character and manners; the sentence is from Ovid's *Heroides*.

34. Nay: No

35. stond: something that hinders; stoppage

36. wrought out: fixed; removed

37. stone and reins: gallstone and kidneys

38. wandering: cannot concentrate

39. demonstrations: (usually in mathematics) the process of proving a conclusion by doing the calculation step by step

40. never so little: just a little; even a little

41. the schoolmen: the scholars that belong to Scholastic School (经院哲学), who hold to the Medieval philosophies or ideas

42. *cymini sectores*: (Latin) people who can find the smallest distinction or difference; fault-finders

43. beat over matters: discuss a subject thoroughly

44. receipt: a cure or a prescription; here Bacon compares the shortcomings of reading or studies to the diseases or problems of our body.

Questions for Discussion

(1) Compare and contrast the language and style Francis Bacon uses in his essays with the ones by the writers of the previous chapters. Identify the unique characteristics of this essay genre.

(2) How does Bacon employ rhetorical devices such as parallelism, simile, metaphor, personification, and quotation to achieve the particular effect or power of his essays?

(3) Why does Bacon pay special attention to the close relationship between science and learning (as in experiential philosophy), particularly in the Elizabethan and Jacobean reigns from the end of the 16th century to the beginning of the 17th

century?

(4) Read some essays by Montaigne in English translation or the French original, and compare that with Bacon's style and language. Are there any influences from the French writer on Bacon? Note their similarities (if there are any) and differences.

(5) How is Bacon's quoting classical Latin in English essays similar to modern Chinese essays using some classical phrases, sentences or quotations (文言文)?

(6) Chinese literature also enjoys a wonderful tradition of essays with such prominent essayists such as Han Yu, Ouyang Xiu and others in the Tang and Song Dynasties. Read some classical and modern Chinese essays and draw comparisons between Bacon's and Chinese essays.

Suggested Reading

(1) Francis Bacon. *The Major Works*. New York: Oxford University Press, 2002.

(2) Francis Bacon. *The Essays*. London: Penguin Classics, 1985.

(3) Francis Bacon. *Essays*. Beijing: Foreign Language Teaching and Research Press, 1998.

(4) 培根：《培根经典散文选》，曹明伦译，北京：外语教学与研究出版社，2020 年。

(5) 弗·培根：《培根论说文集》，水天同译，北京：商务印书馆，1958 年。

(6) 培根：《培根随笔全集》，蒲隆译，南京：译林出版社，2011 年。

Part Three

The Seventeenth Century

9. John Donne

John Donne (1572–1631) was the most outstanding metaphysical poet who lived during the reigns of Queen Elizabeth I and King Charles I. He was born into a Catholic family. His father died when he was only four years old. He received education at Oxford and Cambridge. Because of his Catholic religion, he couldn't get a degree from either university. Later he studied law at Lincoln's Inn, but never practiced it. As an adventurous young man, he travelled on the Continent, joining the expedition to Cadiz and Azores with Lord Essex. Some of his poems tell about his experiences during these trips. In 1598 Donne became the secretary of Sir Thomas Egerton, Lord Keeper of the Great Seal. But because of his secret marriage with Egerton's niece, he lost his job and was imprisoned for a short time. After his release, he lived in poverty with his growing family for many years. During this time, he wrote many beautiful lines, many of which were written to his beloved wife. In 1615 he abandoned his Catholic faith and took orders in the Anglican Church, where he became the most famous preacher of his time. Later in 1621 he was appointed dean of Saint Paul's Cathedral and held his post till his death in 1631. In his famous works, such as *Songs and Sonnets*[①](1633), *Devotions upon Emergent Occasions* (1624), and *Holy Sonnets*, he shows his strong interest in such themes as love, body and soul, and life and death. Donne's poems were not conventional in ideas and forms. His love

---

① *Songs and Sonnets*: a collection of love lyrics, written early but published posthumously in 1633, including *Go and Catch a Falling Star* and *The Flea*.

lyrics often challenged the sentimental exaggeration of Elizabethan love sonnets. His use of various forms was also shocking. He never allowed the form to constrain his emotion and gave nearly each theme a unique stanza form. He was also famous for using conceits[①] to express his ideas in a sharp and direct manner. Donne's poems, prose writings, and religious sermons demonstrate his intellectual wit and imaginative power.

Donne's religious poems concern the search for soul, death, and eternal life in Christianity. The poem "Death, Be Not Proud" is from Donne's *The Holy Sonnets* which contains a series of nineteen poems. The poem is an Italian sonnet with the rhyme pattern in the octave (abba, abba) and the sextet (cddc ee). All the lines share the same iambic pentameter with the exceptions of the first line "Death, be/ not proud,/ though some/ have called thee", which is tetrameter, and line 9 "Thou'art/ slave to/ fate, chance,/ kings, and/ despe/rate men", which is hexameter. The poem expresses the poet's detached and bold attitude towards death. For many people, death is "mighty and dreadful," but for the poet, there is nothing terrible about it. He sees death as sleep, rest for their body and freedom for their mind, and also as the path to "eternal awakening." For a religious man, death is instantaneous, while life after death is eternal. Death is just a beginning of eternal life. The last line "And death shall be no more; Death, thou shalt die," combining Donne's Christian faith with a paradox, reinforces his contempt for death.

Death, Be Not Proud

Death, be not proud, though some have called thee[1]
Mighty[2] and dreadful, for thou[3] are not so;
For those whom thou think'st thou dost overthrow[4]
Die not, poor Death, nor yet canst thou kill me.
From rest and sleep, which but thy[5] pictures be,[6]
Much pleasure; then from thee much more must flow,

---

① conceits: figures of speech that establish a striking parallel, usually ingeniously elaborate, between two very dissimilar things or situations

And soonest our best men with thee do go,
Rest of their bones, and soul's delivery.[7]
Thou'art slave to[8] fate, chance, kings, and desperate men[9],
And dost with poison, war, and sickness dwell[10],
And poppy[11] or charms[12] can make us sleep as well
And better than thy stroke[13]; why swell'st thou then?[14]
One short sleep past, we wake eternally[15],
And death shall be no more; Death, thou shalt die.

Notes

1. thee: *pron.* archaic or dialect form of "you", as the singular object of a verb or proposition

2. mighty: *adj.* powerful

3. thou: *pron.* archaic or dialect form of "you", as the singular subject of a verb

4. overthrow: *v.* conquer; defeat

5. thy: *pron.* (also "thine" before a vowel) archaic or dialect form of "your"

6. From rest and sleep, which but thy pictures be: Rest and sleep is just pictures of death.

7. Rest of their bones, and soul's delivery: With death, they can find rest for their body and freedom ("delivery") for their souls.

8. Thou'art slave to: You are dominated by

9. desperate men: people who committed suicide

10. dwell: *v.* live

11. poppy: *n.* opium

12. charms: *n.* an act or words believed to have magic power; spell

13. thy stroke: It refers to the scythe of the Grim Reaper (an imaginary figure who represents death). Here it means a fatal blow.

14. why swell'st thou then?: why do you swell with pride?

15. eternally: *adv.* forever

Questions for Discussion

(1) In "Death, Be Not Proud", how does John Donne use figures of speech, such as conceit, personification, metaphor, irony, and paradox to express the theme of the poem?

(2) Point out the differences between some love poems written by early Elizabethan poets like Sidney and Spenser, and compare them with John Donne's, in both theme and form. What are the distinctive characteristics of metaphysical poems?

(3) "Death, Be Not Proud" reflects Christian belief in death and eternity. In the poem, Donne shows his contempt and indifference towards death, which is similar to the Taoist Zhuangzi's artistic outlook on life and death. Compare these two different outlooks on life and death, and analyze their influence on Western and Chinese literature and philosophy.

Suggested Reading

(1) John Donne. *The Complete English Poems*. London: Penguin Classics, 1976.

(2) Smith, A.J, ed. *John Donne: the Critical Heritage*. New York: Routledge Publishing, 2002.

(3) Achsah Guibbory, ed. *The Cambridge Companion to John Donne*. Cambridge: Cambridge University Press, 2006.

(4) Molly Murray. *The Poetics of Conversion in Early Modern English Literature: Verse and Change from Donne to Dryden*. Cambridge: Cambridge University Press, 2009.

(5) 约翰·但恩：《约翰·但恩诗集》(修订本)，傅浩译，上海：上海译文出版社，2016年。

(6) 李正栓：《邓恩诗歌研究——兼议英国文艺复兴诗歌发展历程》，北京：商务印书馆，2011年。

(7) 李正栓：《邓恩诗歌思想与艺术研究》，北京：外语教学与研究出版社，2010。

(8) 胡小玲：《多恩爱情诗与神学诗研究》，成都：四川大学出版社，2020年。

(9) 吴笛：《英国玄学派诗歌研究》，北京：中国社会科学出版社，2013年。

10. John Milton

John Milton (1608–1674) was born into a staunch Puritan family, his father being a scrivener and an amateur composer. Milton felt enormous gratitude to his father for giving him a consolidated education in youth, especially on linguistic proficiency. Milton did attend excellent educational institutions such as St. Paul's and Christ's College, Cambridge, where he received his BA in 1629 and MA in 1632. After graduation, he stayed at his father's country dwelling for six years and then embarked on a journey on the European continent. In 1639 he returned to England immediately when he heard news of a possible civil war in England. During the civil war, Milton held various public service positions, the Secretary of Latin being the most important. Milton's influence and contribution are mainly on the spiritual level and his importance equals, or at least is no less than, to Oliver Cromwell on the military side. In the course of defending the parliamentary cause, Milton began to suffer the loss of sight and became totally blind by 1652. He continued to serve his people until the Restoration, when Charles II returned to England to claim the throne and to put the country into more Catholic atmosphere. Milton was imprisoned for a short period of time in prison and then released, spending the majority of his rest life composing his masterpieces as *Paradise Lost* and so on.

From an early age, Milton showed the promising talent of a poet when he wrote L' Allegro ("The Cheerful Man") and Il Penseroso ("The Pensive Man") in which he proved the title with fruitful production. His most important poems are the three epics that are related to biblical texts: *Paradise Lost*, *Paradise Regained* and *Samson Agonistes*. In these epics, Milton skillfully steered his creation genius with the form of blank verse that runs throughout the poems. In *Paradise Lost* Milton used the rebellious words of Satan, to show his profound hatred for the contemporary monarch—the restored Charles II. He did not mean to show Satan was the symbol of revolutionary spirit of the revolutionists led by Cromwell; on the whole Satan and his followers were condemned. Instead of using the usual English sentence order, Milton prefers to employ the elaborate Latin sentence structure, which usually runs on many lines. With frequent usage of inversion and allusions, Milton's particular writing style is generally acclaimed as "Miltonic style". Besides these epics, Milton also wrote sonnets and political pamphlets which resonate with his own personal life tragedies and public ups and downs during one of the most turbulent times in the history of England–the Revolution and Restoration period.

To Mr. Cyriack Skinner Upon His Blindness[1]

Cyriack, this three years' day[2] these eyes, though clear
To outward view of blemish or of spot[3];
Bereft of light[4] their seeing have forgot[5],
Nor to their idle orbs[6] doth sight appear[7]
Of Sun or Moon or Star throughout the year,
Or man or woman. Yet I argue not
Against heav'n's[8] hand or will, nor bate[9] a jot
Of[10] heart[11] or hope; but still[12] bear up[13] and steer
Right onward[14]. What supports me, dost thou ask?
The conscience[15], Friend, to have lost them overplied[16]
In liberty's defence[17], my noble task,
Of which all Europe talks from side to side.
This thought might lead me through the world's vain mask[18]
Content though blind, had I no better guide[19].

Notes

1. In some versions the title of this sonnet is "To Cyriack Skinner"; Cyriack Skinner is Milton's student and intimate friend. Besides this sonnet, Milton had written another sonnet deploring his own blindness – "On His Blindness"; the "His" in the title means Milton himself.

2. this three years' day: this day three years ago

3. clear/ To outward view of blemish or of spot: to outward view, clear of blemish or spot; on the surface, (there) are no mark or dot that are bad for the eyes; Milton's blindness might be caused by glaucoma (青光眼), so the eyes look like normal ones.

4. bereft of light: deprived of light, lost light; "bereft" is the past tense or past participle of "bereave".

5. their seeing have forgot: have forgotten their seeing; forgot: lost

6. idle orbs: useless eyeballs

7. doth: does; the normal order of this part should be: does (not) appear sight of (the Sun...)

8. heav'n's: heavens

9. bate: (shortened form of abate) decrease; diminish

10. a jot of: a bit; a small amount of

11. heart: courage

12. still: in poetry before modern times, "still" usually means "always"

13. bear up: keep up (the courage)

14. steer... right onward: steer (the ship of my life) to go forward rightly

15. conscience: consciousness

16. overplied: overworked

17. In liberty's defence: in defence of liberty; in 1651 Milton worked days and nights in writing the Latin pamphlet *Pro Populo Anglicano Defensio* (*The Defence of the English People*).

18. the world's vain mask: the futile or meaningless show of the world; it is common in Milton's time and before to compare the world to a show or a stage (As in Spenser's sonnet 54 and in Shakespeare's *As You Like It*: All the world's a stage).

19. had I no better guide: if I had no better guide; "guide" usually means "God"; here Milton says that even if there is no guidance from God, he would also be brave enough to fight for the liberty of English people and the commonwealth; Milton in this sonnet shows that even if his eyesight is lost he is not sad or depressed because he knows that he lost them for the defence of his people, so he is extremely proud of that and determines to go forward.

Areopagitica

(Excerpt)

Good and evil we know in the field of this world grow up together almost inseparably; and the knowledge of good is so involved and interwoven with the knowledge of evil, and in so many cunning resemblances[1] hardly to be discerned[2], that those confused seeds which were imposed on Psyche[3] as an incessant labor to cull out[4] and sort asunder[5] were not more intermixed. It was from out the rind of one apple tasted, that the knowledge of good and evil, as two twins cleaving together, leaped forth into the world.[6] And perhaps this is that doom which Adam fell into of knowing good and evil, that is to say of knowing good by evil.[7]

As therefore the state of man now is, what wisdom can there be to choose, what continence[8] to forbear[9], without the knowledge of evil? He that can apprehend and consider vice with all her baits and seeming pleasures, and yet abstain, and yet distinguish, and yet prefer that which is truly better, he is the true wayfaring Christian[10]. I can not praise a fugitive[11] and cloistered[12] virtue, unexercised and unbreathed[13], that never sallies out[14] and sees her adversary, but slinks[15] out of the race where that immortal garland[16] is to be run for, not without dust and heat. Assuredly we bring not innocence into the world, we bring impurity much rather: that which purifies us is trial, and trial is by what is contrary. That virtue therefore which is but a youngling[17] in the contemplation of evil, and knows not the utmost that vice promises to her followers, and rejects it, is but a blank virtue[18], not a pure; her whiteness is but an excremental whiteness[19]; which was the reason why our sage and serious poets Spenser (whom I dare be known to think a better teacher than Scotus or Aquinas[20]), describing true temperance under the person of Guyon[21], brings him in with his Palmer through the Cave of Mammon and the Bower of Earthly Bliss, that he might see and know, and yet abstain.

Since therefore the knowledge and survey of vice is in this world so necessary to the constitution of human virtue, and the scanning of error to the confirmation of truth, how can we more safely, and with less danger, scout[22] into the regions of sin and falsity than by reading all manner of tractates[23] and hearing all manner of reason? And this is the benefit which may be had of books promiscuously[24] read.

Notes

1. resemblance: (between A and B) likeness; the fact of being similar

2. discern: to recognize or understand something that usually is not obvious

3. Psyche: According to Roman Mythology tradition, Psyche and Cupid became lovers and then they were forced to separate by Venus, Cupid's mother. To find Cupid, Psych had to go through a great deal of trials set by Venus, one of which is to separate barley, wheat, bean, and so many others in a bundle of "confused seeds". Finally, the ants took pity on her and finished the job.

4. cull out: to choose or pick out one thing from many things

5. sort asunder: sort out in separate groups

6. rind: thick skin of fruits; cleave: (to) (literary) stick close to; this sentence is resounding the first sentence in pointing out that good and evil are in one apple that is eaten by Adam and Eve in the garden of Eden (Genesis). According to Biblical tradition, they come out to the world in that way.

7. doom: the fall from heaven to the earthly world; paradise lost; this sentence means that one can know good by knowing evil.

8. continence: control or the ability to control one's bowels or emotions

9. forbear: to control; to endure

10. baits: temptations, deceiving attractions; abstain: control oneself from (temptations); wayfaring: the truly faithful (usually of Christian pilgrims); notice that Milton prefers to use long sentence structures both in prose and poetry, an influence of his profound knowledge and proficiency about Latin.

11. fugitive: escaping

12. cloistered: isolated far away

13. unexercised and unbreathed: not forced to breathe hard

14. sally out: (literary or old fashioned) to leave a place determinedly

15. slink: move stealthily; creep

16. garland: a circle of flowers and leaves to wear on the head of the winner of the race; "the crown of life"

17. youngling: early stage

18. blank virtue: empty virtue; not pure virtue

19. excremental whiteness: faultlessness on surface

20. John Duns Scotus and Thomas Aquinas are two important Scholastic philosophers.

21. Guyon is the major character in Spenser's Book II of *Faerie Queene*; he is the symbol of temperance (self-control) and he successfully passes the Cave of Mammon (symbolic of all worldly goods and honours) and then the Bower of Earthly Bliss (the same to the previous cave).

22. scout: search; look for

23. tractate: a long argument written to discuss topics such as monarch and civil power, liberty and tyranny, education and church, etc. in Milton's time; the shorter one is called a "tract".

24. promiscuous: in a mixed state; the sentence means "that is the benefit in the reading of both good books and bad books".

Questions for Discussion

(1) What are the advantages of Milton's deliberate use of long sentences in expressing his argument logically and clearly?

(2) Like Bacon, Milton also wrote quite a few works on Latin. Except for the linguistic influence of Latin on his English, what are other features that show the influence of Latin in Milton's writing?

(3) Milton is a pious Puritan and although he wrote a powerful section in *Paradise Lost* to express Satan's rebellion, he still holds the fundamental idea of Christian tradition that Satan should be condemned. How are his religious ideas intertwined with his defence of liberty for common English people?

(4) *Beowulf* and Milton's *Paradise Lost* and his other two works are considered epics. What are the basic elements of an epic? What characteristics are special and different in Milton's epics?

(5) Milton's works are intimately reflective of his personal life tragedies (such as his loss of children and especially his loss of sight since middle age) and the turbulent historical events around him in the middle of the 17th century. How should we understand this intimacy and see through the essence of literature?

Suggested Reading

(1) Gordon Campbell, Thomas N. Corns. *John Milton: Life, Work, and Thought*. Oxford: Oxford University Press, 2008.

(2) Harold Bloom. *John Milton: Comprehensive Research and Study Guide*. London: Chelsea House Publications, 1999.

(3) John Milton. *The Major Works*. Oxford: Oxford University Press, 2008.

(4) 马克·帕蒂森：《弥尔顿传略》，金发燊、颜俊华译，北京：生活·读书·新知三联书店，2001年。

(5) 弥尔顿：《弥尔顿诗选》，朱维之译，北京：人民文学出版社，1998年。

(6) 沈弘：《弥尔顿的撒旦与英国文学传统》，北京：北京大学出版社，2010年。

11. John Bunyan

John Bunyan (1628–1688) was a devout Puritan writer and preacher. His father, a tinker, died when Bunyan was 16 and his mother remarried. Bunyan had to lead a life on his own. He joined the Parliamentary Army in 1644 and got married before 1649. With help from his wife, John Bunyan started forming religious beliefs that included frequent self-examination. Though he did not receive any formal education, John Bunyan made a great contribution to the field of religion. He advocated resolute religious beliefs and preached them with unremitting efforts, which also conforms to a fundamental element in his writing. In his lifetime, John Bunyan was jailed twice for unauthorized preaching, but he never retreated in the face of those hardships in life. He actually wrote more than nine books in his first twelve-year imprisonment, including a spiritual autobiography *Grace Abounding to the Chief of Sinners*, in which Bunyan exposed his own sins and made pious confessions. During his second imprisonment, John Bunyan composed his masterpiece, *The Pilgrim's Progress*, establishing him as a famous writer.

The Pilgrim's Progress is an immortal prose allegory in the English language;

it consists of two parts—Part I (1678) and Part II (1684). Part I is set in a dream. Christian, the hero of this allegory, sets out from the City of Destruction to the destination, the Celestial city in order to seek the salvation of his soul. Under the guidance of Evangelist, Christian leaves his family behind and heads for the Celestial City. On his journey, he encounters a lot of difficulties and temptations. In the Slough of Despond, Christian is saved by a man named Help. He is offered a sealed scroll after his burdens fall from his shoulders. But he accidentally loses his scroll when he falls asleep in the Hill Difficulty. Then he fights the monster Apollyon in the Valley of Humiliation and continues to pass through the Valley of Shadow of Death. After that, he catches up with a company, Faithful. In Vanity Fair, Christian is put into prison but escapes afterward. When he leaves Vanity, Christian meets a new company named Hopeful. They go astray while trying to cross the plain of Ease. Later, Christian and Hopeful are prisoned in the Doubting Castle, where Christian unlocks the door with the key Promise. Before they are finally admitted into the Celestial city, they experience a series of tests and trials on the way. Part II depicts the journey of Christian's wife and their children, who make great efforts to arrive at the Celestial city and reunite with Christian. Stories in Part II are much similar to those in Part I. Hence, Part I is more classical and impressive.

  The most realistic part of *The Pilgrim's Progress* is Vanity Fair epitomizing England society at that time. In Vanity Fair, everything can be sold and exchanged, including souls, crimes and lusts. Through this absurd picture, John Bunyan sought to expose the social ills of his time. The influence of this allegory is profound, rendering it a prominent work in English history.

The Pilgrim's Progress

(Vanity Fair)

  Then I[1] saw in my dream, that when they[2] were got out[3] of the wilderness[4], they presently saw a town before them, and the name of that town is Vanity; and at the town there is a fair[5] kept, called Vanity Fair: it is kept all the year long. It beareth[6] the name of Vanity Fair because the town where it is kept is lighter than vanity; and, also because all that is there sold, or that cometh thither, is vanity. As is the saying of the wise, "all that cometh is vanity.[7]"

This fair is no new-erected business, but a thing of ancient standing; I will show you the original[8] of it. Almost five thousand years agone[9], there were pilgrims walking to the Celestial City[10], as these two honest persons are: and Beelzebub, Apollyon, and Legion[11], with their companions, perceiving by the path that the pilgrims made, that their way to the city lay through this town of Vanity, they contrived here to set up a fair; a fair wherein, should be sold all sorts of vanity, and that it should last all the year long: therefore at this fair are all such merchandise sold, as houses, lands, trades, places, honours, preferments[12], titles, countries, kingdoms, lusts, pleasures, and delights of all sorts, as whores, bawds[13], wives, husbands, children, masters, servants, lives, blood, bodies, souls, silver, gold, pearls, precious stones, and what not[14].

And, moreover, at this fair there is at all times to be seen juggling cheats, games, plays, fools, apes[15], knaves, and rogues[16], and that of every kind. Here are to be seen, too, and that for nothing[17], thefts, murders, adulteries, false swearers, and that of a blood-red colour.

And as in other fairs of less moment[18], there are the several rows[19] and streets, under their proper[20] names, where such and such wares are vended[21]; so here likewise you have the proper places, rows, streets, (viz.[22] countries and kingdoms), where the wares[23] of this fair are soonest to be found. Here is the Britain Row, the French Row, the Italian Row, the Spanish Row, the German Row, where several sorts of vanities are to be sold. But, as in other fairs, some one commodity is as the chief of all the fair, so the ware of Rome[24] and her merchandise is greatly promoted in this fair; only our English nation, with some others, have taken a dislike[25] thereat[26].

Now, as I said, the way to the Celestial City lies just through this town where this lusty[27] fair is kept; and he that will go to the city, and yet not go through this town, must needs[28] go out of[29] the world.

The Prince of princes[30] himself, when here[31], went through this town to his own country, and that upon a fair day too; yea, and as I think, it was Beelzebub, the chief lord[32] of this fair, that invited him to buy of his vanities; yea[33], would have made him lord of the fair, would he but[34] have done him reverence[35] as he went through the town.

Yea, because he was such a person of honour, Beelzebub had him from street to street, and showed him all the kingdoms of the world in a little time, that he might, if possible, allure the Blessed One[36] to cheapen[37] and buy some of his vanities; but he had no mind to the merchandise, and therefore left the town, without laying out[38] so much as one farthing[39] upon these vanities. This fair, therefore, is an ancient thing, of long standing, and a very great fair.

Now these pilgrims, as I said, must needs go through this fair. Well, so they did: but, behold, even as they entered into the fair, all the people in the fair were moved[40], and the town itself as it were in a hubbub[41] about them; and that for several reasons.

Notes

1. I: the author himself; John Bunyan

2. they: The hero Christian and his company Faithful, who is killed in this town

3. were got out: (old use) "were" here is an auxiliary verb to complete the past perfect tense.

4. wilderness: It refers to their early experience in the wild area.

5. fair: a kind of market where people sell and buy goods

6. beareth: old use of third person singular, equals "bears"

7. all that cometh is vanity: a saying from the *Bible*, "cometh" equals "comes".

8. original: origin

9. agone: (old English) ago

10. Celestial City: Heaven

11. Beelzebub, Apollyon, and Legion: Beelzebub, Hebrew, the devil and "the lord of flies"; Apollyon, the destroyer and the ruler of the abyss; Legion, the group of demons in the *Bible*; They are fallen devils, the followers of Satan.

12. preferments: being promoted to a higher rank

13. bawds: women who are in charge of prostitutes in a brothel

14. and what not: and so on

15. apes: mimics

16. rogues: dishonest people

17. for nothing: free of charge

18. of less moment: less important; of moment = very important

19. rows: roads or alleys

20. their proper: their own

21. vended: sold

22. viz. : (Latin) videlicet, equals "namely"

23. wares: goods selling on the market

24. the ware of Rome: an ironic symbol against the Roman Catholic Church

25. dislike: an unpleasant attitude

26. thereat: at it

27. lusty: vigorous; full of strength

28. needs: used as an adverb here to stress the necessity

29. go out of: die

30. The Prince of princes: Jesus Christ

31. when here: when he was here

32. the chief lord: a position in charge of managing the fair and solving disputes there

33. yea: yes

34. would he but: if only he would

35. done him reverence: pay reverence to somebody

36. the Blessed One: referring to Jesus Christ

37. cheapen: buy

38. laying out: spending money

39. farthing: one-quarter of an old penny that has been withdrawn in 1961

40. moved: restless

41. hubbub: chaos

Questions for Discussion

(1) Vanity Fair is a place that sells various uncommon goods. Why does John Bunyan create such an unusual fair on such a holy journey?

(2) Is the character Christian a devout follower of Christianity? How do we define his salvation beyond the context of religion?

(3) Of Christian's companies Pliable, Faithful and Hopeful on his journey to the Celestial, only Hopeful and Christian make it in the end; what is the trial Faithful meets in Vanity Fair?

(4) Read in its entirety *The Pilgrim's Progress* and identify more biblical images and allusions in this allegory.

(5) Compare this book with the Chinese classic by Wu Cheng'En in the 16th century—*Journey to the West* on main characters, themes and endings. Figure out their similarities and differences.

(6) What is the relationship between Bunyan's allegory *The Pilgrim's Progress* and William Makepeace Thackeray's *Vanity Fair*?

(7) William Makepeace Thackeray, a British novelist, wrote a novel named *Vanity Fair* in the 19th century. Try to figure out its relation to this allegory.

Suggested Reading

(1) John Bunyan. *The Pilgrim's Progress*. New York: Oxford University Press, 1998.

(2) J. Brown. *John Bunyan: His life, Times, and Works*. London: The Hulbert Publishing Company.

(3) Henry Talon. *John Bunyan: The Man and His Works*. London: Salisbury Square, 1951.

(4) 约翰·班扬：《天路历程》，黄文伟译，武汉：长江文艺出版社，2006年。

(5) 王军：《东西方神话比较研究》，北京：现代出版社，2008年。

(6) 刘意青：《〈圣经〉的文学阐释——理论与实践》，北京：北京大学出版社，2004年。

Part Four

The Eighteenth Century

12. Daniel Defoe

Daniel Defoe (1660–1731), a prolific novelist and pamphleteer, is called "the father of the English novel". Daniel Defoe was born in 1660, the same year of the Restoration, to a butcher's family. His father, James Foe, is a Nonconformist, which hindered Defoe from receiving formal college education. Defoe went to an academy in Newington Green where his father had hoped Defoe become a clergyman in the future. However, Defoe was reluctant to follow his father's will. He started his own business after apprenticeship and gained a lot of opportunities to travel across Europe. At the age of thirty-two, Defoe went bankrupt and then rebuilt his career with trades and writing. This decision proved that Defoe is a versatile journalist and writer. He is adept at narrating a story in the first-person perspective with realistic and accurate language. In politics, he once openly opposed the Tories in his article for its unfair policy against dissenters and appealed to the public to reflect upon the legal rights of women, like education and vocation. Due to Defoe's bold opinions against authority, he was put into prison in 1703. Afterward, his talent was noticed by a politician who enabled the development of Defoe's periodical *The Review*. Over the span of twenty decades, Defoe created hundreds of articles for various publishing agencies. Besides, he accomplished several books and guide pamphlets, such as *The Family Instructor* (1715) and *Tour Through the Whole Island of Great Britain* (1724–1726). In 1719, as an excellent journalist, Defoe found an attractive story in real life. He had come to learn about a sailor named Alexander Selkirk who lived in an isolated island for five years before being rescued. Defoe was keen on good stories. Fusing it with his fertile imagination, Defoe weaved this story into an adventure novel, that became his masterpiece novel *The Life and Adventures of Robinson Crusoe*, or *Robinson Crusoe*(1719). This publication successfully ushered in Defoe's new literary achievements. Although there are more adventure novels in the following years such as *The Fortunes and Misfortunes of Moll Flanders*(1722), none of them could transcend the significance and popularity of *Robinson Crusoe*.

Robinson Crusoe is a great success not only for Defoe but for the rise of the novel in the eighteenth century. Accompanied by the accumulation of social wealth, English novelists were endowed with a unique opportunity to introduce England to the rest of the world. *Robinson Crusoe* undoubtedly is the most crucial one. It tells of how the hero, Robinson Crusoe, having survived a shipwreck had lived on a desolate island alone. In the beginning, he is at a loss in the face of all these adversities and difficulties. But soon after, he recovers from enormous panic and sets out to live in a rational way. First, he succeeds in finding some useful goods in the wrecked ship. Then he builds a simple hut as his shelter and makes a lot of tools by himself. After finding ways to meet his basic needs, Crusoe gradually grows accustomed to the life on the island. He has to learn to rely on the guidance of God, which renders him confident and dogged when encountering hardships. One day, Crusoe discovers the sign of natives on the island. He saves a native and names him Friday. From then on, Friday becomes Crusoe's loyal servant and helper. After thirty years, Crusoe finally returns to England. This novel encompasses multiple meanings. While traveling with Defoe's picturesque depiction, readers could be enlightened from different perspectives.

Robinson Crusoe

(Chapter XXIII)

He was a comely[1], handsome fellow, perfectly well made, with straight strong limbs, not too large; tall and well-shaped, and, as I reckon, about twenty-six years of age. He had a very good countenance[2], not a fierce and surly aspect; but seemed to have something very manly in his face, and yet he had all the sweetness and softness of an European in his countenance too, especially when he smiled. His hair was long and black, not curled like wool; his forehead very high and large; and a great vivacity and sparkling sharpness in his eyes. The color of his skin was not quite black, but very tawny; and yet not of an ugly, yellow, nauseous[3] tawny, as the Brazilians and Virginians, and other natives of America are; but of a bright kind of a dun[4] olive color that had in it something very agreeable, though not very easy to describe. His face was round and plump; his nose small, not flat like the Negroes; a very good mouth, thin lips, and his fine teeth well set, and white as ivory. After he had slumbered[5], rather than slept, about half an hour, he waked again, and comes out of the cave to me; for I had been milking my goats, which I had in the enclosure just by. When he espied[6] me, he came running to me, laying himself down again upon the ground, with all the possible signs of an humble, thankful disposition, making a many antic[7] gestures to show it. At last he lays his head flat upon the ground, close to my foot, and sets my other foot upon his head, as he had done before; and after this, made all the signs to me of subjection, servitude, and submission imaginable, to let me know how he would serve me as long as he lived; I understood him in many things and let him know I was very well pleased with him; in a little time I began to speak to him and teach him to speak to me; and first, I made him know his name should be Friday, which was the day I saved his life; I called him so for the memory of the time; I likewise taught him to say Master, and then let him know that was to be my name; I likewise taught him to say Yes and No and to know the meaning of them; I gave him some milk in an earthen pot and let him see me drink it before him and sop my bread in it; and I gave him a cake of bread to do the like, which he quickly complied with, and made signs that it was very good for him.

  I kept there with him all that night; but as soon as it was day, I beckoned to him to come with me; and let him know I would give him some clothes, at which he seemed very glad, for he was stark naked. As we went by the place where he had buried the two men, he pointed exactly to the place and showed me the marks that he had made to find them again, making signs to me that we should dig them up again and eat them; at this I appeared very angry, expressed my abhorrence[8] of it, made as if I would vomit at the thoughts of it, and beckoned with my hand to him to come away, which he did immediately, with great submission. I then led him up to the top of the hill, to see if his enemies were gone; and pulling out my glass⁹, I looked, and saw plainly the place where they had been, but no appearance of them or of their canoes; so that it was plain they were gone and had left their two comrades behind them, without any search after them.

But I was not content with this discovery; but having now more courage, and consequently more curiosity, I took my man Friday with me, giving him the sword in his hand, with the bow and arrows at his back, which I found he could use very dexterously, making him carry one gun for me, and I two for myself. and away we marched to the place where these creatures had been; for I had a mind now to get some fuller intelligence of them. When I came to the place, my very blood ran chill in my veins and my heart sunk within me at the horror of the spectacle. Indeed it was a dreadful sight, at least it was so to me, though Friday made nothing of it. The place was covered with human bones, the ground dyed with their blood, great pieces of flesh left here and there, half eaten, mangled and scorched; and in short, of all the tokens of the triumphant feast they had been making there, after a victory over their enemies. I saw three skulls, five hands, and the bones of three or four legs and feet, and abundance of other parts of the bodies; and Friday, by his signs, made me understand that they brought over four prisoners to feast upon; that three of them were eaten up and that he, pointing to himself, was the fourth; that there had been a great battle between them and their next king, whose subjects it seems he had been one of; and that they had taken a great number of prisoners, all which were carried to several places by those that had taken them in the fight, in order to feast upon them, as was done here by these wretches upon those they brought hither.

I caused Friday to gather all the skulls, bones flesh, and whatever remained, and lay them together on a heap and make a great fire upon it and burn them all to ashes. I found Friday had still a hankering stomach¹⁰ after some of the flesh, and was still a cannibal in his nature; but I discovered so much abhorrence at the very thoughts of it and at the least appearance of it that he durst not discover it; for I had by some means let him know that I would kill him if he offered it.

When we had done this, we came back to our castle, and there I fell to work for my man Friday; and first of all, I gave him a pair of linen drawers¹¹, which I had out of the poor gunner's chest I mentioned, and which I found in the wreck; and which with a little alteration fitted him very well; then I made him a jerkin[12] of goat's skin, as well as my skill would allow, and I was now grown a tolerable good tailor; and I gave him a cap, which I had made of a hare-skin, very convenient and fashionable enough; and thus he was clothed for the present tolerably well; and was mighty well pleased to see himself almost as well clothed as his master. It is true, he went awkwardly in these things at first; wearing the drawers was very awkward to him, and the sleeves of the waistcoat galled his shoulders and the inside of his arms; but a little easing them where he complained they hurt him and using himself to them, at length he took to them very well.

The next day after I came home to my hutch with him, I began to consider where I should lodge him; and that I might do well for him and yet be perfectly easy myself, I made a little tent for him in the vacant place between my two fortifications[13], in the inside of the last and in the outside of the first; and as there was a door or entrance there into my cave, I made a formal framed door-case, and a door to it of boards, and set it up in the passage, a little within the entrance; and causing the door to open on the inside, I barred it up in the night, taking in my ladders too; so that Friday could no way come at me in the inside of my innermost wall without making so much noise in getting over that it must needs waken me; for my first wall had now a complete roof over it of long poles, covering all my tent and leaning up to the side of the hill, which was again laid across with smaller sticks instead of laths, and then thatched[14] over a great thickness with the rice-straw, which was strong like reeds; and at the hole or place which was left to go in or out by the ladder I had placed a kind of trapdoor, which, if it had been attempted on the outside, would not have opened at all, but would have fallen down and made a great noise; and as to weapons, I took them all into my side every night.

But I needed none of all this precaution; for never man had a more faithful, loving, sincere servant than Friday was to me; without passions, sullenness, or designs, perfectly obliged and engaged; his very affections were tied to me, like those of a child to a father; and I dare say he would have sacrificed his life for the saving mine upon any occasion whatsoever; the many testimonies he gave me of this put it out of doubt and soon convinced me that I needed to use no precautions as to my safety on his account.

This frequently gave me occasion to observe, and that with wonder, that however it had pleased God, in His providence, and in the government of the works of His hands, to take from so great a part of the world of His creatures the best uses to which their faculties and the powers of their souls are adapted, yet that He has bestowed upon them the same powers, the same reason, the same affections, the same sentiments of kindness and obligation, the same passions and resentments of wrongs, the same sense of gratitude, sincerity, fidelity, and all the capacities of doing good and receiving good that He has given to us; and that when He pleases to offer to them occasions of exerting these, they are as ready, nay, more ready to apply them to the right uses for which they were bestowed than we are. And this made me very melancholy sometimes, in reflecting, as the several occasions presented, how mean a use we make of all these, even though we have these powers enlightened by the great lamp of instruction, the Spirit of God, and by the knowledge of His Word, added to our understanding; and why it has pleased God to hide the like saving knowledge from so many millions of souls, who, if I might judge by this poor savage, would make a much better use of it than we did.

From hence, I sometimes was led too far to invade the sovereignty of Providence and, as it were, arraign[15] the justice of so arbitrary a disposition of things that should hide that light from some and reveal it to others, and yet expect a like duty from both. But I shut it up and checked my thoughts with this conclusion; first, that we did not know by what light and law these should be condemned; but that as God was necessarily, and by the nature of His being, infinitely holy and just, so it could not be but that if these creatures were all sentenced to absence from Himself, it was on account of sinning against that light which, as the Scripture[16] says, was a law to themselves, and by such rules as their consciences would acknowledge to be just, though the foundation was not discovered to us. And second, that still, as we are all the clay in the hand of the Potter[17], no vessel could say to Him, "Why hast Thou formed me thus?"

But to return to my new companion: I was greatly delighted with him and made it my business to teach him everything that was proper to make him useful, handy, and helpful; but especially to make him speak and understand me when I spake[18]; and he was the aptest[19] scholar that ever was, and particularly was so merry, so constantly diligent, and so pleased when he could but understand me or make me understand him that it was very pleasant to me to talk to him; and now my life began to be so easy that I began to say to myself that could I but have been safe from more savages, I cared not if I was never to remove from the place while I lived.

After I had been two or three days returned to my castle, I thought that, in order to bring Friday off from his horrid way of feeding and from the relish of a cannibal's stomach, I ought to let him taste other flesh; so I took him out with me one morning to the woods. I went, indeed, intending to kill a kid[20] out of my own flock and bring him home and dress[21] it. But as I was going, I saw a she-goat lying down in the shade and two young kids sitting by her; I catched hold of Friday. "Hold," says I, "stand still"; and made signs to him not to stir; immediately I presented my piece, shot and killed one of the kids. The poor creature, who had at a distance, indeed, seen me kill the savage, his enemy, but did not know or could imagine how it was done, was sensibly surprised, trembled and shook, and looked so amazed that I thought he would have sunk down. He did not see the kid I had shot at, or perceive I had killed it, but ripped up his waistcoat to feel if he was not wounded, and, as I found presently, thought I was resolved to kill him; for he came and kneeled down to me and, embracing my knees, said a great many things I did not understand; but I could easily see that the meaning was to pray me not to kill him.

I soon found a way to convince him that I would do him no harm and, taking him up by the hand, I laughed at him and pointed to the kid which I had killed, beckoned to him to run and fetch it, which he did; and while he was wondering and looking to see how the creature was killed, I loaded my gun again, and by and by I saw a great fowl[22], like a hawk[23], sit upon a tree, within shot; so, to let Friday understand a little what I would do, I called him to me again, pointed at the fowl, which was indeed a parrot, though I thought it had been a hawk; I say, pointing to the parrot and to my gun and to the ground under the parrot, to let him see I would make it fall, I made him understand that I would shoot and kill that bird; accordingly I fired and bade him look, and immediately he saw the parrot fall, he stood like one frighted[24] again, notwithstanding all I had said to him; and I found he was the more amazed because he did not see me put anything into the gun; but thought that there must be some wonderful fund of death and destruction in that thing, able to kill man, beast, bird, or anything near or far off; and the astonishment this created in him was such as could not wear off for a long time; and I believe, if I would have let him, he would have worshiped me and my gun. As for the gun itself, he would not so much as touch it for several days after; but would speak to it and talk to it as if it had answered him, when he was by himself; which, as I afterwards learned of him, was to desire it not to kill him.

Notes

1. comely: attractive; pleasant-looking
2. countenance: facial expression
3. nauseous: disgusting
4. dun: dark
5. slumber: fall into a deep sleep
6. espy: see
7. antic: funny and odd
8. abhorrence: hatred
9. glass: telescope
10. a hankering stomach: a stomach longing for human flesh
11. a pair of linen drawers: a pair of trousers made of linen
12. jerkin: a type of jacket without sleeves
13. fortification: wall to defend the inside areas
14. thatched: covered with dried straws
15. arraign: doubt and denounce
16. the Scripture: the *Bible*
17. the Potter: The *Bible* says God is the potter and people are the clay.
18. spake: the old use of "spoke"
19. aptest: the most intelligent
20. a kid: a lamb
21. dress: prepare the food before cooking
22. fowl: a bird
23. hawk: a large bird of prey
24. frighted: scared

Questions for Discussion

(1) Why does Robinson Crusoe have Friday call him "Master"? Is there any implicit meaning taking British colonial history into account?

(2) How do you understand Friday's response to the gun? Is his loyalty to Robinson out of his own free will or out of fear?

(3) Read the novel in its entirety, and determine why Robinson is so keen on marine travel. What does his travel bring him in the end?

(4) Why does Friday change his habits of eating and dressing under Crusoe's guidance? How do you define Crusoe's guidance from the perspective of colonialism?

(5) Compare *Robinson Crusoe* with Jonathan Swift's *Gulliver's Travels* in the category of island literature.

Suggested Reading

(1) Daniel Defoe. *Robinson Crusoe*. New York: Oxford University Press, 2008.

(2) Greif Martin. *The Conversion of Robinson Crusoe*. Houston: Rice University Press, 1996.

(3) Ian Watt. *The Rise of the Novel: Studies in Defoe, Richardson and Field*. Berkeley: California University Press, 1957.

(4) 丹尼尔·笛福：《鲁滨孙飘流记》，郭建中译，南京：译林出版社，2010年。

(5) 塞昌槐：《西方小说与文化帝国》，武汉：武汉大学出版社，2004年。

(6) 弗朗兹·法侬：《黑皮肤，白面具》，万冰译，南京：译林出版社，2005年。

13. Jonathan Swift

Jonathan Swift (1667–1745) is a celebrated Irish satirist; he was born in Dublin, the capital of Ireland. His father died before his birth, so Jonathan Swift was raised by his uncle for most of his childhood. Due to his uncle's generosity in his education,

Swift finally gained access to Trinity College, Dublin. Nevertheless, he failed to achieve his academic career smoothly. After the Glorious Revolution in 1688, the political chaos forced Swift to leave Ireland for England and live with his mother. During his stay in England, Swift's genius was noticed by Sir William Temple who later introduced him to the King. Then Swift became Temple's secretary, which allowed him to write poems and prose. From 1691 to 1694, Swift created several poems, but his poems were not as noticeable as his prose satire. Swift is proficient in manipulating political satire with a humorous tone. His first prose satire *The Battle of Books* was anonymously published in 1704. Later, Swift continued this feature in another work *The Tale of a Tub* where he criticized religious corruptions with satirical wit. After the death of Sir William Temple, Swift served as a pamphleteer for political parties, first the Whigs and then the Tories. In 1714, Swift returned to Ireland, where he started to focus on the people who lived under the oppression of England landlords. As a way of exposing the cruel deeds of the English government, Swift conveyed his anger through his works, including "Drapier's Letters" (1724) and "A Modest Proposal" (1729). In "A Modest Proposal", Swift employed incisive satire to mock the rich, who imposed enormous burdens on the Irish people. However, *Gulliver's Travels* is no doubt his masterpiece. By virtue of depicting an imaginative journey, Swift satirized the English government through Gulliver's experience. This novel in form resembles Daniel Defoe's *Robinson Crusoe* but they were created for totally different reasons. What Jonathan Swift had done for the Irish people has made him a real hero in Ireland.

"A Modest Proposal" is actually a vehement criticism of the English government. In this satire prose, Jonathan Swift proposed that Irish people should have more children who later would be served on English people's dining tables. This proposal, while appalling was the harsh reality imposed on the Irish people set against the historical background of this period. In 1729, apart from famine, the Irish had to endure the aftermath of religious, political as well as social conflicts. Swift attempted to attack the evil English society with his sharp satire. This proposal not "modest" at all, is in fact, quite violent, explicit and thought-provoking. With Swift's perfect satire, more and more readers would notice the hideous crime committed by the English government. It was Swift's heartfelt sympathy that awakened the heartless attitudes, and eventually led to the easing of the common people's plight.

A Modest Proposal

(For Preventing The Children of Poor People in Ireland from Being A Burden to Their Parents or Country; and for Making Them Beneficial to The Public.)

It is a melancholy object[1] to those who walk through this great town[2] or travel in the country, when they see the streets, the roads, and cabin doors, crowded with beggars of the female sex, followed by three, four, or six children, all in rags and importuning every passenger[3] for an alms[4]. These mothers, instead of being able to work for their honest livelihood, are forced to employ all their time in strolling to beg sustenance[5] for their helpless infants: who as they grow up either turn thieves for want of work, or leave their dear native country to fight for the Pretender in Spain[6], or sell themselves to the Barbadoes[7].

I think it is agreed by all parties[8] that this prodigious[9] number of children in the arms, or on the backs, or at the heels of their mothers, and frequently of their fathers, is in the present deplorable state of the kingdom a very great additional grievance; and, therefore, whoever could find out a fair, cheap, and easy method of making these children sound[10], useful members of the commonwealth, would deserve so well of the public[11] as to have his statue set up for a preserver of the nation[12].

But my intention is very far from being confined to provide only for the children of professed beggars[13]; it is of a much greater extent, and shall take in the whole number of infants at a certain age who are born of parents in effect[14] as little able to support them as those who demand our charity in the streets.

As to my own part, having turned my thoughts for many years upon this important subject, and maturely weighed[15] the several schemes of other projectors[16], I have always found them grossly mistaken in the computation[17]. It is true, a child just dropped from its dam[18] may be supported by her milk for a solar year[19], with little other nourishment; at most not above the value of 2 shillings, which the mother may certainly get, or the value in scraps[20], by her lawful occupation of begging; and it is exactly at one year old that I propose to provide for them in such a manner as instead of being a charge upon their parents or the parish, or wanting food and raiment[21] for the rest of their lives, they shall on the contrary contribute to the feeding, and partly to the clothing, of many thousands.

There is likewise another great advantage in my scheme, that it will prevent those voluntary abortions, and that horrid practice of women murdering their bastard children[22], alas! too frequent among us! sacrificing the poor innocent babes[23] I doubt[24] more to avoid the expense than the shame, which would move tears and pity in the most savage and inhuman breast.

The number of souls[25] in this kingdom being usually reckoned one million and a half, of these I calculate there may be about two hundred thousand couple whose wives are breeders[26]; from which number I subtract thirty thousand couples who are able to maintain their own children, although I apprehend there cannot be so many, under the present distresses of the kingdom; but this being granted[27], there will remain a hundred and seventy thousand breeders. I again subtract fifty thousand for those women who miscarry[28], or whose children die by accident or disease within the year. There only remains one hundred and twenty thousand children of poor parents annually born. The question therefore is, how this number shall be reared and provided for, which, as I have already said, under the present situation of affairs, is utterly impossible by all the methods hitherto[29] proposed. For we can neither employ them in handicraft or agriculture; we neither build houses (I mean in the country) nor cultivate land: they can very seldom pick up a livelihood by stealing, till they arrive at six years old, except where they are of towardly parts[30], although I confess they learn the rudiments[31] much earlier, during which time, they can however be properly looked upon only as probationers[32], as I have been informed by a principal gentleman in the county of Cavan, who protested to me[33] that he never knew above one or two instances under the age of six, even in a part of the kingdom so renowned for the quickest proficiency in that art.

I am assured by our merchants, that a boy or a girl before twelve years old is no salable[34] commodity; and even when they come to this age they will not yield above three pounds, or three pounds and half-a-crown[35] at most on the exchange; which cannot turn to account[36] either to the parents or kingdom, the charge of nutriment and rags[37] having been at least four times that value.

I shall now therefore humbly propose my own thoughts, which I hope will not be liable to the least objection.

I have been assured by a very knowing American[38] of my acquaintance in

London, that a young healthy child well nursed is at a year old a most delicious, nourishing, and wholesome food, whether stewed, roasted, baked, or boiled; and I make no doubt that it will equally serve in a fricassee or a ragout[39].

I do therefore humbly offer it to public consideration that of the hundred and twenty thousand children already computed, twenty thousand may be reserved for breed, whereof only one-fourth part to be males; which is more than we allow to sheep, black cattle or swine; and my reason is, that these children are seldom the fruits of marriage, a circumstance not much regarded[40] by our savages, therefore one male will be sufficient to serve four females. That the remaining hundred thousand may, at a year old, be offered in the sale to the persons of quality and fortune through the kingdom; always advising the mother to let them suck plentifully in the last month, so as to render them plump and fat for a good table. A child will make two dishes at an entertainment[41] for friends; and when the family dines alone, the fore or hind quarter[42] will make a reasonable dish, and seasoned with[43] a little pepper or salt will be very good boiled on the fourth day, especially in winter.

I have reckoned upon a medium that a child just born will weigh 12 pounds, and in a solar year, if tolerably nursed, increaseth[44] to 28 pounds.

I grant this food will be somewhat dear, and therefore very proper for landlords, who, as they have already devoured[45] most of the parents, seem to have the best title[46] to the children.

Infant's flesh will be in season[47] throughout the year, but more plentiful in March, and a little before and after; for we are told by a grave author[48], an eminent French physician, that fish being a prolific[49] diet, there are more children born in Roman Catholic countries about nine months after Lent[50] than at any other season; therefore, reckoning a year after Lent, the markets will be more glutted than usual, because the number of popish infants is at least three to one in this kingdom: and therefore it will have one other collateral[51] advantage, by lessening the number of papists[52] among us.

I have already computed the charge of nursing a beggar's child (in which list I reckon all cottagers[53], laborers, and four-fifths of the farmers) to be about two shillings per annum[54], rags included; and I believe no gentleman would repine to give ten shillings for the carcass of a good fat child, which, as I have said, will make four dishes of excellent nutritive meat, when he hath only some particular friend or his own family to dine with him. Thus the squire will learn to be a good landlord, and grow popular among his tenants; the mother will have eight shillings net profit, and be fit for work till she produces another child.

Those who are more thrifty (as I must confess the times require) may flay the carcass; the skin of which artificially dressed will make admirable gloves for ladies, and summer boots for fine gentlemen.

As to our city of Dublin, shambles[55] may be appointed for this purpose in the most convenient parts of it, and butchers we may be assured will not be wanting; although I rather recommend buying the children alive, and dressing[56] them hot from the knife, as we do roasting pigs.

A very worthy person, a true lover of his country, and whose virtues I highly esteem, was lately pleased in discoursing on this matter to offer a refinement[57] upon my scheme. He said that many gentlemen of this kingdom, having of late destroyed their deer, he conceived that the want of venison might be well supplied by the bodies of young lads and maidens, not exceeding fourteen years of age nor under twelve; so great a number of both sexes in every country being now ready to starve for want of work and service; and these to be disposed of by their parents, if alive, or otherwise by their nearest relations. But with due deference to so excellent a friend and so deserving a patriot, I cannot be altogether in his sentiments[58]; for as to the males, my American acquaintance assured me, from frequent experience, that their flesh was generally tough and lean, like that of our schoolboys by continual exercise, and their taste disagreeable; and to fatten them would not answer the charge. Then as to the females, it would, I think, with humble submission[59] be a loss to the public, because they soon would become breeders themselves; and besides, it is not improbable that some scrupulous people might be apt to censure such a practice (although indeed very unjustly), as a little bordering upon[60] cruelty; which, I confess, hath always been with me the strongest objection against any project, however so well intended.

But in order to justify my friend, he confessed that this expedient was put into his head by the famous Psalmanazar[61], a native of the island Formosa, who came from thence[62] to London above twenty years ago, and in conversation told my friend, that in his country when any young person happened to be put to death, the executioner sold the carcass to persons of quality as a prime dainty; and that in his time the body of a plump girl of fifteen, who was crucified for an attempt to poison the emperor, was sold to his imperial majesty's prime minister of state, and other great mandarins[63] of the court, in joints from the gibbet[64], at four hundred crowns. Neither indeed can I deny, that if the same use were made of several plump young girls in this town, who without one single groat to their fortunes[65] cannot stir abroad without a chair[66], and appear at playhouse and assemblies in foreign fineries[67] which they never will pay for, the kingdom would not be the worse.

Some persons of a desponding spirit are in great concern about that vast number of poor people, who are aged, diseased, or maimed[68], and I have been desired to employ my thoughts what course may be taken to ease the nation of so grievous an encumbrance[69]. But I am not in the least pain upon that matter, because it is very well known that they are every day dying and rotting by cold and famine, and filth and vermin, as fast as can be reasonably expected. And as to the young laborers, they are now in as hopeful a condition; they cannot get work, and consequently pine away[70] for want of[71] nourishment, to a degree that if at any time they are accidentally hired to common labor, they have not strength to perform it; and thus the country and themselves are happily delivered from the evils to come.

I have too long digressed[72], and therefore shall return to my subject. I think the advantages by the proposal which I have made are obvious and many, as well as of the highest importance.

For first, as I have already observed, it would greatly lessen the number of papists, with whom we are yearly overrun[73], being the principal breeders of the nation as well as our most dangerous enemies; and who stay at home on purpose with a design to deliver the kingdom to the Pretender, hoping to take their advantage by the absence of so many good protestants, who have chosen rather to leave their country than stay at home and pay tithes[74] against their conscience to an episcopal curate[75].

Secondly, the poorer tenants will have something valuable of their own, which by law may be made liable to distress[76] and help to pay their landlord's rent, their corn and cattle being already seized, and money a thing unknown.

Thirdly, whereas the maintenance of an hundred thousand children, from two years old and upward, cannot be computed at less than ten shillings apiece per annum, the nation's stock[77] will be thereby increased fifty thousand pounds per annum, beside the profit of a new dish introduced to the tables of all gentlemen of fortune in the kingdom who have any refinement in taste. And the money will circulate among ourselves, the goods being entirely of our own growth and manufacture.

Fourthly, the constant breeders, beside the gain of eight shillings sterling per annum by the sale of their children, will be rid of the charge of maintaining them after the first year.

Fifthly, this food would likewise bring great custom[78] to taverns; where the vintners will certainly be so prudent as to procure the best receipts for dressing it to perfection, and consequently have their houses frequented by all the fine gentlemen, who justly value themselves upon their knowledge in good eating: and a skilful cook, who understands how to oblige his guests, will contrive to make it as expensive as they please.

Sixthly, this would be a great inducement to marriage, which all wise nations have either encouraged by rewards or enforced by laws and penalties. It would increase the care and tenderness of mothers toward their children, when they were sure of a settlement for life[79] to the poor babes, provided in some sort by the public, to their annual profit instead of expense. We should see an honest emulation[80] among the married women, which of them could bring the fattest child to the market. Men would become as fond of their wives during the time of their pregnancy as they are now of their mares in foal, their cows in calf, their sows when they are ready to farrow[81]; nor offer to beat or kick them (as is too frequent a practice) for fear of a miscarriage.

Many other advantages might be enumerated. For instance, the addition of some thousand carcasses in our exportation of barreled beef, the propagation of swine's flesh, and improvement in the art of making good bacon, so much wanted among us by the great destruction of pigs, too frequent at our tables; which are no way comparable in taste or magnificence to a well-grown, fat, yearling child, which roasted whole will make a considerable figure[82] at a lord mayor's feast or any other public entertainment. But this and many others I omit, being studious of[83] brevity.

Supposing that one thousand families in this city, would be constant customers for infants flesh, besides others who might have it at merry meetings, particularly at weddings and christenings, I compute that Dublin would take off annually about twenty thousand carcasses; and the rest of the kingdom (where probably they will be sold somewhat cheaper) the remaining eighty thousand.

I can think of no one objection, that will possibly be raised against this proposal, unless it should be urged, that the number of people will be thereby much lessened in the kingdom. This I freely own[84], and 'twas indeed one principal design in offering it to the world. I desire the reader will observe, that I calculate my remedy for this one individual Kingdom of Ireland, and for no other that ever was, is, or, I think, ever can be upon Earth. Therefore let no man talk to me of other expedients: Of taxing our absentees[85] at five shillings a pound: Of using neither cloaths, nor houshold furniture, except what is of our own growth and manufacture: Of utterly rejecting the materials and instruments that promote foreign luxury: Of curing the expensiveness of pride, vanity, idleness, and gaming in our women: Of introducing a vein of parsimony, prudence and temperance: Of learning to love our country, wherein we differ even from Laplanders[86], and the inhabitants of Topinamboo[87]: Of quitting our animosities and factions, nor acting any longer like the Jews, who were murdering one another at the very moment their city was taken: Of being a little cautious not to sell our country and consciences for nothing: Of teaching landlords to have at least one degree of mercy towards their tenants. Lastly, of putting a spirit of honesty, industry, and skill into our shop-keepers, who, if a resolution could now be taken to buy only our native goods, would immediately unite to cheat and exact upon us in the price, the measure, and the goodness, nor could ever yet be brought to make one fair proposal of just dealing, though often and earnestly invited to it.

Therefore I repeat, let no man talk to me of these and the like expedients, 'till he hath at least some glympse of hope, that there will ever be some hearty and sincere attempt to put them into practice.

But, as to my self, having been wearied out for many years with offering vain, idle, visionary thoughts, and at length utterly despairing of success, I fortunately fell upon this proposal, which, as it is wholly new, so it hath something solid and real, of no expence and little trouble, full in our own power, and whereby we can incur no danger in disobliging England. For this kind of commodity will not bear exportation, and flesh being of too tender a consistence, to admit a long continuance in salt, although perhaps I could name a country, which would be glad to eat up our whole nation without it[88].

After all, I am not so violently bent upon my own opinion as to reject any offer proposed by wise men, which shall be found equally innocent, cheap, easy, and effectual. But before something of that kind shall be advanced in contradiction to my scheme, and offering a better, I desire the author or authors will be pleased maturely to consider two points. First, as things now stand, how they will be able to find food and raiment for an hundred thousand useless mouths and backs. And secondly, there being a round[89] million of creatures in human figure[90] throughout this kingdom, whose whole subsistence put into a common stock would leave them in debt two millions of pounds sterling, adding those who are beggars by profession to the bulk of farmers, cottagers, and laborers, with their wives and children who are beggars in effect: I desire those politicians who dislike my overture, and may perhaps be so bold as to attempt an answer, that they will first ask the parents of these mortals, whether they would not at this day think it a great happiness to have been sold for food, at a year old in the manner I prescribe, and thereby have avoided such a perpetual scene of misfortunes as they have since gone through by the oppression of landlords, the impossibility of paying rent without money or trade, the want of common sustenance, with neither house nor clothes to cover them from the inclemencies of the weather, and the most inevitable prospect of entailing the like or greater miseries upon their breed for ever.

I profess, in the sincerity of my heart, that I have not the least personal interest in endeavoring to promote this necessary work, having no other motive than the public good of my country, by advancing our trade, providing for infants, relieving the poor, and giving some pleasure to the rich. I have no children by which I can propose to get a single penny; the youngest being nine years old, and my wife past child-bearing.

Notes

1. a melancholy object: a miserable scene

2. this great town: the capital of Ireland, Dublin

3. importuning every passenger: begging and asking each passer-by for something

4. alms: money and food that are given to the poor

5. substance: necessities

6. the Pretender in Spain: referring to the son of James II, James Stuart
7. the Barbadoes: an island in the West Indies, one of the British colonies at the time
8. all parties: all the people involved
9. prodigious: impressive; large
10. sound: healthy
11. deserve so well of the public: the man who has made great achievements deserves the gratitude of the public
12. a preserver of the nation: the defender and dedicator of the nation
13. professed beggars: people who take begging as a job
14. in effect: actually
15. maturely weighed: carefully thought over
16. projectors: people who propose new methods
17. computation: calculation
18. dam: mother
19. a solar year: a whole year
20. in scraps: in pieces
21. raiment: clothing
22. bastard children: children born of wedlock
23. babes: babies
24. I doubt: I believe
25. souls: people
26. breeders: fertile women
27. this being granted: after reaching this condition
28. miscarry: give birth to children before they are able to live
29. hitherto: until now
30. towardly parts: master the skill of stealing at a very young age
31. rudiments: the basic skills of theft
32. probationers: interns
33. protest to me: tell me seriously
34. salable: able to be sold
35. half-a-crown: Crown is equal to five shillings.
36. turn to account: take advantage of something

37. nutriment and rags: nourishment and torn clothes
38. a very knowing American: an American who knows something beforehand
39. fricassee or a ragout: stewed meat and vegetables
40. not much regarded: not seriously valued
41. entertainment: treat
42. the fore or hind quarter: the fore or hind leg of a child
43. seasoned with: add flavor to food
44. increaseth: increases
45. devour: use up or destroy greatly
46. title: the legal right
47. in season: the right time of the year
48. a grave author: referring to Francois Rabelais, a famous French writer
49. prolific: plants or animals that produce a lot of creatures and fruits
50. Lent: a period lasting forty days before Easter for the Christians to memorize Jesus's sacrifice
51. collateral: extra
52. papist: an offensive address for Catholics
53. cottager: tenant farmer
54. per annum: (Latin) each year
55. shambles: places to butcher animals for meat
56. dressing: preparing food before cooking
57. refinement: improvement
58. sentiments: opinions
59. humble submission: asking for correction in a humble way
60. bordering upon: approaching; coming very close to something
61. Psalmanazar: George Psalmanazar (1679?–1763), an impostor who claimed he was the first man from Taiwan to visit Europe
62. thence: that place
63. mandarins: government officials
64. gibbet: a wooden structure to hang criminals
65. without one single groat to their fortunes: own no money; groat: an old silver coin

66. stir abroad without a chair: go abroad without a sedan chair

67. fineries: elegant clothing

68. maimed: damaged or disabled

69. encumbrance: burden

70. pine away: become sick or weak day by day

71. want of: lack of

72. digress: stray from the original subject

73. overrun: in large numbers

74. tithes: a fixed amount of tax paid to the Church

75. episcopal curate: the clergyman in the Anglican Church

76. distress: sell the valuable things of the poorer tenants as a pledge

77. stock: money available for use

78. custom: business

79. settlement for life: the expenditure life

80. emulation: the action to surpass or equal each other

81. their mares in foal, their cows in calf, their sows when they are ready to farrow: mares in foal: female pregnant horses; cows in calf: female pregnant cows; sows… to farrow: female pregnant pigs

82. make a considerable figure: become quite noticeable

83. being studious of: being diligent to do something

84. own: admit

85. absentee: landlord who lived outside of Ireland

86. Laplanders: natives of Lapland

87. Topinamboo: a district in Brazil

88. although perhaps I…nation without it.: a coy reference to England

89. a round: a whole number, usually ending in 0 or 5

90. creatures in human figure: an ironic reference to the poor people

Questions for Discussion

(1) What are "projectors" according to Jonathan Swift? What kind of role do they play at the time?

(2) Offering a healthy child as food sounds inhumane, so how do you interpret Swift's proposal through literary devices?

(3) According to Swift, the Irish people seem to have degraded into cannibalism. What has caused such a horrible scene?

(4) Is it true that Irish landlords devour children and their parents? Who has endowed them with such a privilege?

(5) Compare "A Modest Proposal" with Lu Xun's "Dairy of a Madman" in terms of writing motive and style.

(6) Ireland gained its independence in the 20th century. How do you understand its relationship with Great Britain?

Suggested Reading

(1) Jonathan Swift. *A Modest Proposal and Other Satirical Works*. New York: Dover Publications, 1996.

(2) Claude Rawson. *Swift's Angers*. Cambridge: Cambridge University Press, 2014.

(3) David Oakleaf. *A Political Biography of Jonathan Swift*. London: Pickering & Chatto, 2008.

(4) 叶普·列尔森：《欧洲民族思想变迁：一部文化史》，周明圣、骆海辉译，上海：上海三联书店，2013年。

14. Samuel Johnson

When Samuel Johnson (1709–1784) was born his parents were quite elderly. He spent his childhood and youth in a relatively poor situation, receiving education at Lichfield Grammar School in his home town and Pembroke College, Oxford for only 14 months without taking a degree. Even after being married to his considerably elder wife who brought with her a small amount of dowry, Johnson still lived an economically backward life and failed in several attempts to change his fortune by starting a private school and running his own newspaper. He constantly contributed essays and articles to journals, newspapers and magazines and exerted his utmost to compile the first complete English language dictionary, a work that took nine years to finish after being rejected by Lord Chesterfield patronage. The publication of the dictionary established Johnson's firm reputation and brought a degree from Oxford University. After being granted a 300-pound yearly pension from the court, Johnson ceased doing the diligent and hard work of writing essays and articles in enormous amounts. The rest of Johnson's life was spent in talking casually with eloquence in coffee shops, visiting trustworthy friends, editing Shakespeare's works and writing on the lives of English poets, which were recorded faithfully in *The Life of Samuel Johnson* by his friend and disciple James Boswell.

Johnson's important work in his early career is the poem "The Vanity of Human Wishes", which was published in 1749, renowned for its grave moral seriousness and powerful but well structured generalizations. His most influential contribution to the English language, undoubtedly, is his compilation of *A Dictionary of the English Language* with the aim to fix the English pronunciation and to facilitate its attainment. For the dictionary, Johnson wrote definitions for over 40,000 items and explained and illustrated them with about 114,000 quotations that he took from almost every field of learning since the 16th century. In 1759, he published *Rasselas, Prince of Abyssinia*, a romance prose with themes resonating with his early work *The Vanity of Human Wishes*–happiness is almost impossible to obtain. When still in his youth, Johnson began to write on the lives of poets he knew, then in 1777 with the request from publishers, he commenced to write as a serious collection of lives of poets–*The Lives of English Poets*. Johnson's writing is like the man himself–powerful, brilliant, generous, humanistic, pertinent, knowledgeable, insightful, profound, even sometimes eccentric or striking. In a word, Johnson is the genius and "giant" of his time, literately and culturally.

Samuel Johnson's Letter to Lord Chesterfield[1]

(7th February 1755)

To The Right Honourable The Earl of Chesterfield

My Lord,

I have been lately informed, by the proprietor[2] of *The World*[3], that two papers, in which my Dictionary is recommended to the public, were written by your Lordship. To be so distinguished[4], is an honour, which, being very little accustomed to favours from the great[5], I know not[6] well how to receive, or in what terms to acknowledge.[7]

When, upon some slight encouragement, I first visited your Lordship, I was overpowered[8], like the rest of mankind, by the enchantment of your address[9], and could not forbear to wish[10] that I might boast myself *Le vainqueur du vainqueur de la terre*[11]; — that I might obtain that regard for which I saw the world contending; but I found my attendance[12] so little encouraged, that neither pride[13] nor modesty[14] would suffer[15] me to continue it. When I had once addressed your Lordship[16] in public, I had exhausted all the art of pleasing which a retired and uncourtly scholar[17] can possess. I had done all that I could; and no man is well pleased to have his all neglected[18], be it ever so little[19].

Seven years, my Lord, have now passed, since I waited in your outward rooms, or was repulsed[20] from your door; during which time I have been pushing on my work through difficulties, of which it is useless to complain, and have brought it, at last, to the verge of publication, without one act of assistance, one word of encouragement, or one smile of favour[21]. Such treatment I did not expect, for I never had a Patron before.

The shepherd in Virgil grew at last acquainted with Love, and found him a native of the rocks.[22]

Is not a Patron, my lord, one who looks with unconcern on a man struggling for life in the water, and, when he has reached ground, encumbers him with help?[23] The notice which you have been pleased to take of my labours, had it been early, had been kind;[24] but it has been delayed till I am indifferent, and cannot enjoy it; till I am solitary, and cannot impart it; till I am known, and do not want it.[25] I hope it is no very cynical asperity not to confess obligations where no benefit has been received, or to be unwilling that the Public should consider me as owing that to a Patron, which Providence has enabled me to do for myself.[26]

Having carried on my work thus far with so little obligation to any favourer of learning, I shall not be disappointed though I should conclude it[27], if less be possible, with less;[28] for I have been long wakened from that dream of hope, in which I once boasted myself with so much exultation[29], my Lord,

your Lordship's most humble,

most obedient servant,

SAM. JOHNSON.[30]

Notes

1. Lord Chesterfield: the celebrated patron of art and literature in Johnson's time; Johnson once expressed his wish to be under the patronage of this lord in compiling the dictionary but was rejected the favor; but when the dictionary was going to be published, Lord Chesterfield wrote two articles to praise the deed.

2. proprietor: owner

3. *The World*: a popular newspaper published in London from 1753 to 1756

4. to be so distinguished: to be praised highly

5. being very little accustomed to favours from the great: because I seldom got favours or special attentions from the important people

6. I know not: I don't know

7. to acknowledge: to express (my thanks) to the favours (from the great)

8. overpowered: overwhelmed; won over

9. enchantment of your address: the eloquence or charm of your speech and talk

10. I could not forbear to wish: I could not help wishing

11. *Le vainqueur du vainqueur de la terre*: (French) conqueror of the conqueror of the earth; the phrase is from the 17th century French classicist Boileau's *L'Art poetique*, which again quotes from another contemporary French writer Georges de Scudery's *Alaric*; what Johnson means is that years before he compares Lord Chesterfield to the conqueror of the world (as important people do) and if Johnson himself could get the favour from the Lord he would become the conqueror of this Lord.

12. attendance: visiting; waiting upon

13. pride: self-respect; self-esteem

14. modesty: shyness; sensitiveness

15. suffer: allow

16. address your Lordship: express respect or pay tribute to you

17. a retired and uncourtly scholar: a man of studies who is isolated from others and doesn't know much about pleasing important people

18. his all: all that he can do (to please others); have his all neglected: when his action of pleasing others is neglected/rejected

19. be it ever so little: even if what he can do (to please others) is so little

20. repulsed: driven away; refused

21. Notice the powerful parallel structure used here: "act, word, smile" are concrete words, while "assistance, encouragement, favour" are abstract words; the contrast makes the rhetoric stronger in tone.

22. The sentence is an allusion to the Roman poet Virgil's *Eclogue*, which narrates that a shepherd is out of love and complains that Cupid, God of Love, is as hard as the rocks where he is born; in one way, Johnson compares himself to be the shepherd and Chesterfield to Love (out of favour); in another way, Johnson compares England to Rome, the civilized center, and if Love is not in Rome, a Patron (like Chesterfield) is not to be found in England.

23. Is not a Patron: (ironically) Is a Patron; Can we call such a man... as a Patron? unconcern: indifference; encumber...with: give

24. Notice the ironic tone in this sentence; had it been early, had been kind: if you give your notice of my labour (the Dictionary) much earlier, it would have been kind.

25. indifferent: not concerned; solitary: single (Johnson's wife died in 1752); impart: share; notice the mighty use of parallel structure again that clearly expresses his refusal to Chesterfield's notice and vividly reflects Johnson's most aloof and arrogant character.

26. cynical asperity: pessimistic, doubtful and fault-finding character; Providence: God; the whole sentence means: Since I did not receive benefit (the favour), I can not confess my obligations. I also do not wish the public to think that

my finishing the dictionary is owing to the support of a Patron, because I do not have a Patron. God guides and helps me in finishing the work. Maybe Chesterfield's writing of two papers is good-willed, but I have to make clear these facts and I hope the public will not think of me as a cynical person.

27. it: a usage of pun that can refer to the work (the Dictionary) and also the letter

28. if less be possible, with less: (I will conclude my work soon) with less obligation to Patron if less obligation is possible

29. exultation: great pride or happiness

30. Notice Johnson's clever use of his own signature and the usual greeting to end a letter to be combined with the last sentence of the letter.

Questions for Discussion

(1) What does Johnson's style–his diction, his sentence structure, and use of rhetorical devices–reveal his intentions?

(2) Johnson is often recognized as the most typical man of letters in Classicism in English literature, or in other words, he is the representative of classical writers. How do we understand the word "Classicism" after reading Johnson's works?

(3) *The Letter to Lord Chesterfield* is considered generally the declaration of independence for men of letters in English literature. Describe the relationship between a patron and a man of letters in the patronage system before and in Johnson's time (including Shakespeare).

(4) Like Bacon, Johnson also quotes from continental writers in Latin or French. What is the particular reason for English writers to do so? How is Johnson's writing normally taken as the model of classical English? What is his contribution to the development of the English language?

(5) To a certain extent, before the advent of modern electronic or digital technology, letters were the usual means to convey information used nearly every day by some writers. However, it seems that not all the letters of writers, even famous writers, are considered to be works of literary value. What is the reason for that? Have you read any other famous letters in English literature? What is the position of letters

in English literature?

(6) In Chinese literature, we also share a wonderful treasure house of letters such as *Letter to Ren'an* (《报任安书》). Read some of the typical letters famous in Chinese literature and compare them with Johnson's letter and renowned letters in English literature. See what sort of reflection you can reach.

Suggested Reading

(1) Samuel Johnson. *The Major Works*. Oxford: Oxford University Press, 2009.

(2) Peter Martin *Samuel Johnson: A Biography*. Cambridge: Belknap Press, 2008.

(3) James Boswell. *The Life of Samuel Johnson*. London: Penguin Classics, 2008.

(4) 塞缪尔·约翰逊：《饥渴的想象：约翰逊散文作品选》，叶丽贤译，北京：生活·读书·新知三联书店，2015 年。

(5) 塞缪尔·约翰生：《王子出游记》，水天同译，上海：上海译文出版社，2020 年。

(6) 叶丽贤：《塞缪尔·约翰逊〈诗人传〉对英诗经典的建构》，厦门：厦门大学出版社，2020 年。

15. Thomas Gray

Thomas Gray (1716–1771), together with Thomas Parnell, Edward Young, and Robert Blair, was called graveyard poets, who wrote melancholy poems, usually set in a graveyard and on the theme of human mortality. Gray is the most successful among them with his famous melancholy poem "Elegy Written in a Country Churchyard" (1751). He was born in England and received education at Eton and Cambridge. His unhappy childhood, domineering father, tension between his parents, and death of his beloved mother marked his life with melancholy, which is reflected in all his poems. Besides his masterpiece, he wrote many poems that display human emotion by describing nature, including "Ode on the Spring" (1742), "Ode on a Distant Prospect of Eton College" (1747), "Hymn to Adversity" (1742). Thomas Gray lived a quiet scholarly life. He spent most of his life teaching, writing, and studying poetry at Cambridge. In 1768 he was appointed professor of history and modern language. He was interested in ancient poetry, history, and science. In his last days, he gathered and translated Celtic and Icelandic poetry, and wrote many poems related to their history and legends. Gray died in 1771, and was buried in his hometown churchyard of Stoke Poges. Gray's poems, though, were consistent with Classicism in form, they were very distinctive in thought and language. In his poems, emotions played the most important role instead of rules and regulations. His fantastic imagination, combined with melancholy, created a romantic flavor, which laid a significant foundation for the later development of Romanticism.

"Elegy Written in a Country Churchyard", the best known and the most perfect poem in English literature, was sketched first in 1742, when Grey returned from his three-year tour on the European Continent and stayed for a short time at Stoke Poges. But it was finished nine years later. This poem has been recognized as the perfection of melancholy literature. Written in 128 lines quatrains, the poem expresses Gray's sympathy towards the common people who are buried in a churchyard. He pays respect to their humble way of life, and at the same time, criticizes the rich people who abuse their wealth and power. In the end, he shows his attitude toward human life and death that no matter how different people's lives may be, they all come to one end–death. The epitaph with which Gray ends his "Elegy Written in a Country Churchyard" is engraved on the poet's own tombstone. In the epitaph, the speaker describes himself as a well-educated and melancholy young man with generosity and sincerity. He shows sympathy for the miserable people, as a reward, he receives friendship from man and God. He asks passersby (readers) not to consider his merits and flaws, as they should be left to God's judgement.

The Epitaph[1]

Here rests his head upon the lap of Earth
A youth[2] to Fortune and to Fame unknown.

Fair Science³ frown'd⁴ not on his humble birth,
And Melancholy⁵ mark'd him for her own.

Large was his bounty⁶, and his soul sincere,
Heav'n did a recompense⁷ as largely⁸ send:
He gave to Misery⁹ all he had, a tear¹⁰,
He gain'd from Heav'n ('twas all he wish'd) a friend.

No farther seek his merits to disclose,
Or draw his frailties¹¹ from their dread abode¹²,
(There they¹³ alike in trembling hope repose¹⁴)
The bosom of his Father and his God.

Notes

1. Epitaph: *n.* an inscription on the tombstone, which the poet wrote for himself

2. A youth: Here it refers to the poet himself.

3. Science: *n.* knowledge in general

4. frown'd: *v.* disapproved of, looked down upon

5. Melancholy: *n.* a deep, pensive, and long-lasting sadness

6. bounty: *n.* generosity

7. recompense: *n.* reward

8. largely: *adv.* generously

9. Misery: miserable people

10. a tear: sympathy

11. frailties: *n.* weakness; flaws

12. dread abode: the dread place where the dead people go

13. they: Here it refers to the merits and frailties.

14. repose: *v.* a state of rest, sleep or feeling calm

Questions for Discussion

(1) Gray's view of life and death mostly came from the *Bible*, especially from

the New Testament. How is the poet's Christian faith reflected in "Elegy Written in a Country Churchyard"?

(2) While Gray uses Gothic elements in "Elegy Written in a Country Churchyard", unlike other Gothic poems, his poem doesn't give readers terrors and thrills. Instead, it creates a melancholic atmosphere. Identify the Gothic elements used in the poem, and the importance or the necessity of using them.

(3) In "Elegy Written in a Country Churchyard", Gray shows a strong sense of humanistic care toward common people. What factors prompt this to happen in the 18th century of English Literature?

(4) Thomas Gray is regarded as the pioneer of Romantic movements flourishing at the end of the 18th century and the beginning of the 19th century. Based on the distinctive characteristics of Romanticism reflected in Gray's poems, what are the differences between Neoclassicism and Romanticism both on theme and form?

Suggested Reading

(1) Thomas, Gray. *Elegy Written in a Country Churchyard and Other Poems*. London: Penguin Classics, 2009.

(2) Robert L. Mack. *Thomas Gray: A Life*. New Haven: Yale University Press, 2000.

(3) William Hutchings & William Ruddick. *Thomas Gray: Contemporary Essays*. Chicago: Chicago University Press, 1993.

(4) 托马斯·格雷：《墓畔挽歌》，文爱艺译，艾格尼斯·米勒·帕克木刻插图，北京：中央编译出版社，2018年。

(5)《沫若译诗集》，郭沫若译，上海：乐华图书公司，1929年。

16. William Blake

William Blake(1757–1827) was one of the important poets of the late 18th century and the pioneer of Romanticism movement in England. His poems were full of imagination and deep feelings. In the early 21st century, Blake has come to be regarded as the earliest and most original of the Romantic poets.

William Blake, an English writer and engraver, was born in a hosier's family in London. He didn't receive much formal education, but he showed his talent in writing and painting at a young age. When he was 10 years old, his parents sent him to study at a drawing school. But a few years later the increasing expense of art was no longer affordable for the family, so he was apprenticed to an engraver at 14. He became a good student of the craft. By age 21, he completed his apprenticeship and enrolled for a time in the newly formed Royal Academy. Engraving thus became his lifelong occupation. In 1782, William Blake married Catherine Boucher, who gave him a lot of support in his career. He published his first book of poems *Poetical Sketches* in 1783 with the help of some friends. In this collection, he broke with the neo-classical tradition both in form and content. His most famous poems are in the early two collections: *Songs of Innocence* (1789) and *Songs of Experience* (1794). They show "the two contrary states of the human soul". The poems collected in *Songs of Innocence* are mostly happy while the poems in *Songs of Experience* are bitter. Later on, he wrote some other important works including *The French Revolution* (1791), *America, A Prophecy* (1793), and *Milton* (1804–1808). William Blake's works have been greatly influenced by the dramatic changes of the society and he expressed his advocation through his poems. His works became known to people many decades later after he died in 1827.

Compared with the works of his contemporaries, William Blake's poems were original and full of imagination and mystery. He used the simplest language in his two collections: *Songs of Innocence* and *Songs of Experience*. In *Songs of Innocence*, the world is seen from the eyes of a child's imagination; in *Songs of Experience*, the atmosphere is no longer sunny but sad and gloomy. The poems in this collection show readers the misery of poor people and the unfair world they live in.

Laughing Song[1]

(From *Songs of Innocence*)

When the green woods laugh with the voice of joy,
And the dimpling[2] stream runs laughing by;
When the air does laugh with our merry wit,
And the green hill laughs with the noise of it;

When the meadows laugh with lively green,
And the grasshopper[3] laughs in the merry scene;
When Mary and Susan and Emily[4]
With their sweet round mouths sing 'Ha, Ha, He!'[5]

When the painted birds[6] laugh in the shade,
Where our table with cherries and nuts is spread:
Come live, and be merry, and join with me,
To sing the sweet chorus of 'Ha ha he!'

Notes

1. The poet wrote this poem before the French Revolution and expressed his positive attitude towards life even in the face of sorrow and suffering.

2. dimpling: *adj.* from dimple (*n.*), dimple means a small hollow place on the skin, especially one formed in the cheek when a person smiles; here dimpling means smiling stream.

3. grasshopper: *n.* jumping insect that makes a shrill chirping noise

4. Mary and Susan and Emily: These names refer to girls. The poet wants to show that the beauty of nature has brought the girls to sing.

5. Ha, Ha, He: expression of laughter

6. painted birds: colorful birds

The Chimney Sweeper[1]

(From *Songs of Innocence*)

When my mother died I was very young,
And my father sold me while yet my tongue
Could scarcely cry "'weep! 'weep!'weep!'weep!"[2]
So your chimneys I sweep & in soot[3] I sleep.

There's little Tom Dacre, who cried when his head
That curl'd[4] like a lamb's back, was shav'd[5], so I said,
"Hush, Tom! never mind it, for when your head's bare[6],
You know that the soot cannot spoil your white hair."

And so he was quiet, & that very night,
As Tom was a-sleeping he had such a sight!
That thousands of sweepers, Dick, Joe, Ned, & Jack,
Were all of them lock'd[7] up in coffins of black;

And by came an Angel who had a bright key,
And he open'd the coffin & set them all free;
Then down a green plain, leaping, laughing they run,
And wash in a river and shine in the Sun.

Then naked & white, all their bags left behind,
They rise upon clouds, and sport in the wind.
And the Angel told Tom, if he'd be a good boy,
He'd have God for his father & never want[8] joy.

And so Tom awoke; and we rose in the dark
And got with our bags & our brushes to work.
Tho'[9] the morning was cold, Tom was happy & warm;

So if all do their duty, they need not fear harm.

Notes

1. The Chimney Sweeper: children who were used for chimney sweeping due to their small size to fit into the very narrow and enclosed spaces that required cleaning inaccessible to an adult. In 18th century's London, a lot of children from poor families were sent by their parents to do this job. William Blake was shocked by this and he expressed his criticism to the government and society. He wrote two pieces of "The Chimney Sweeper": one from *Songs of Innocence*, another from *Songs of Experience*. The former one describes the miserable life of the chimney sweepers and ends with hope that angels would come to save them; whereas in the latter one, it seemed that the poet changed his attitude and pointed out that God could not save these poor children. The criticism is even stronger in the latter one.

2. 'weep: The child's lisping (they couldn't pronounce "s" clearly) attempt at the chimney sweeper's street cry, "Sweep! Sweep!"

3. soot: black powder which rises in the smoke from a fire and collects on the inside of chimneys

4. curl'd: *v.* curled

5. shav'd: *v.* shaved

6. bare: *adj.* not covered by anything

7. lock'd: *v.* locked

8. want: *v.* lack

9. tho': *conj.* though

The Chimney Sweeper

(From *Songs of Experience*)

A little black thing[1] among the snow,
Crying "'weep, 'weep," in notes of woe[2]!
"Where are thy father & mother? Say?"–
"They are both gone up to the church to pray.

"Because I was happy upon the heath[3],
And smil'd[4] among the winter's snow;
They clothed me in the clothes of death[5],
And taught me to sing the notes of woe.

"And because I am happy, & dance & sing[6],
They think they have done me no injury,
And are gone to praise God & his Priest & King,
Who make up a heaven of our misery."

Notes

1. A little black thing: a little boy who is a chimney sweeper

2. 'weep: the short form of "sweep"; it is said that these chimney sweepers would climb into the chimney to clean the soot, when they finished their work they would cry out loud "weep" ; woe: *n.* (literary) great sadness

3. heath: *n.* an area of open land where grass, bushes, and other small plants grow, especially in Britain

4. smil'd: *v.* smiled

5. clothes of death: It refers to the black clothes. In western culture, black is the color of mourning, death, and sadness.

6. because I am happy, & dance & sing: It is said that this refers to the scene during the May festival in Britain, when the chimney sweepers and milkers would dance on the street to please the philanthropists.

Questions for Discussion

Questions for "Laughing Song":

(1) In this poem, the poet presents the readers with a delightful picture full of laughing songs. Do you know where are they from?

(2) What is the rhyme scheme in this poem?

(3) Figures of speech are often used in poem-writing . Can you find the figures of

speech used in the poem?

(4) *To see a world in a grain of sand,*
And a heaven in a wild flower,
Hold infinity in the palm of your hand,
And eternity in an hour.

What's your understanding of these lines? Are there any similar expressions in Chinese?

Questions for "The Chimney Sweeper":

(1) What are the similarities and differences between "The Chimney Sweeper" from *Songs of Innocence* and "Laughing Song"? Describe what the chimney sweeper's life was like.

(2) What do you think the poet wants to criticize through these two poems?

(3) What symbols does the poet use in these two poems and what do they represent?

Suggested Reading

(1) Mary Lynn Johnson, John E. Grant. *Blake's Poetry and Designs: Illuminated Works, Other Writings, Criticism,* 2nd ed. New York: W.W. Norton & Co., 2008.

(2) William Blake. *Songs of Innocence and of Experience.* London: Macmillan Collectors, 2019.

(3) William Blake. *The Complete Poems of William Blake.* London: Penguin Classics, 1979.

(4) 布莱克：《布莱克诗选》(英汉对照)，袁可嘉、查良铮译，北京：外语教学与研究出版社，2011年。

(5) 威廉·布莱克：《天真与经验之歌》，杨苡译，北京：译林出版社，2002年。

17. Robert Burns

Unlike any of the writers in previous chapters, Robert Burns (1759–1796) was born into a farmer's family in Ayrshire, Scotland and his life, except for a short period of time in Edinburgh, was invariably involved with farming. However, his insightful father, though relatively poor in economic and educational means, was determined that his children would enjoy a solid education. So Robert Burns obtained a profound and consolidated schooling in English language and literature, doing extensive reading and tedious farming at the same time. When his father passed away, Burns and his brothers continued the strenuous efforts of farming but Burns never ceased writing poems, especially poems in English mixed with Scottish. At one time, Burns even contemplated migrating to Jamaica for work until the successful publication of his collection *Poems* granted him a stable financial income. With the publication, Burns came into the view of Edinburgh magazine and journal editors and reviewers where his special poetic skills and his seemingly "exotic" identity of "farmer" were acknowledged by the literary and aristocratic circles of Edinburgh. When a musical museum extended an invitation to collect traditional Scottish folk songs, he did so enthusiastically pro bono, because he considered it an act of patriotism for Scotland, a theme that runs through his poetry. He collected the songs with his own amendment, adaptation and rewriting even as he continued writing poems of his own. Burns was not free of farming life until 1791 when he was appointed as an excise officer almost two years ago. He died of rheumatic heart disease in 1796, a disease caused, largely by, long exposure to farming and country conditions.

Besides the brilliant work of collecting traditional Scottish songs, Robert Burns' main literary reputation lies in his unique poetry, a mixture of English and Scottish, an authentic and romantic reflection of Scottish landscapes and customs, and an enthusiastic passion for patriotism. Most of his poems are short, terse and musical, all of which show the influence of Scottish folk songs. Burns had a deep-rooted sympathy for the common people of Scotland and they in turn haled him as the national bard of Scotland. When he was younger, Burns had supported the French Revolution zealously and even sent guns to France, only to be intercepted by the customs and investigated by local authorities. But in his latter years, he changed his ideas and became suspicious of the events in France. These mixed feelings were evident in Burn's passionate love for Scotland.

A Man's a Man for A' That[1]

Is there for honest poverty
That hings his head, an' a' that?[2]
The coward slave, we pass him by[3],
We dare be poor for a' that!
For a' that an' a' that,
Our toils obscure[4], an' a' that,
The rank is but the guinea's stamp,
The man's the gowd for a' that.[5]

What though on hamely fare[6] we dine,
Wear hoddin grey[7], an' a' that?
Gie[8] fools their silks, and knaves[9] their wine–
A man's a man for a' that.
For a' that, an' a' that,
Their tinsel show[10], an' a' that,
The honest man, tho' e'er sae poor[11],
Is king o' men for a' that,

Ye[12] see yon[13] birkie[14] ca'd[15] a lord,
Wha[16] struts[17], an' stares, an' a' that;
Tho' hundreds worship at his word,
He's but a cuif[18] for a' that.
For a' that, an' a' that,
His ribband[19], star[20], an' a' that,
The man o' independent mind
He looks an' laughs at a' that.

A prince can mak[21] a belted knight[22]
A marquis, duke, an' a' that!
But an honest man's aboon his might[23] –
Guid faith[24], he mauna fa' that[25]!
For a' that, an' a' that,
Their dignities, an' a' that
The pith o' sense[26] an' pride o' worth[27]
Are higher rank than a' that.

Then let us pray that come it may,
(As come it will for a' that,)
That sense and Worth o'er a' the earth
Shall bear the gree[28] an' a' that,
For a' that, an' a' that,
It's comin[29] yet for a' that,
That man to man the world o'er
Shall brithers[30] be for a' that.

Notes

1. Most of Burns' poems are influenced by Scottish folk songs or directly rewritten based on them, so usually there is no title for the song. Thus, some anthologies would take the first line as the title of the poem; notice that the poem is written with iambic pentameter, though it originated from a folk song.

2. The omission is often used in Scottish folk songs, so in this poem: an'=and; a'=all; an' a' that=and all that, for all that, in spite of that (ironic tone); they are also like refrains (复调) in a song; this sentence means: did you see any one who is in honest poverty hangs his head?

3. we pass him by: we despise him; we look down upon him

4. toils obscure: obscure toils; humble work

5. guinea: a gold coin worth 21 shillings in the past; stamp: the lines and engravings (on a guinea); gowd: gold; these two lines mean: the high position or the

title is only a surface value and what matters is the man (a common man).

6. hamely fare: homely fare; common daily food and drink

7. hoddin grey: coarse grey cloth (usually worn by farmers)

8. gie: give

9. knave: (old use) a dishonest man; rascal

10. their tinsel show: their worthless, valueless and affectation appearance

11. tho': though; e'er: ever; sae: so; tho' e'er sae poor: no matter how poor he is

12. ye: you

13. yon: yonder; over there

14. birkie: (sarcastic) a fellow

15. ca'd: called

16. wha: who

17. strut: walk with arrogance or in a pompous way

18. cuif: a fool

19. ribband: riband; ribbon; a girdle in a gown showing the aristocratic title or rank

20. star: star on the title medal

21. mak: make

22. a belted knight: a noble man with a belt on him to show his rank or title

23. aboon his might: above the prince's power

24. guid faith: good faith (words in cursing or swearing)

25. he mauna fa' that: he (the prince) must not claim that power (of an honest man)

26. pith o' sense: the essence of learning and knowing

27. pride o' worth: noble characters; these are the qualities of an honest man that contrasts with those who only have shiny appearances.

28. bear the gree: bear/win the prize

29. It's comin: It is coming; It does come

30. brithers: brothers; these last lines mean that may all the men of the world be brothers.

Scots Wha Hae[1]

Scots, wha hae wi' Wallace[2] bled,
Scots, wham[3] Bruce[4] has aften led,
Welcome to your gory bed[5]
        Or to victorie![6]

Now's the day, and now's the hour:
See the front o' battle lour,[7]
See approach proud Edward's power–
        Chains and slaverie![8]

Wha will be a traitor knave?
Wha can fill a coward's grave?
Wha sae base as be a slave?–[9]
        Let him turn, and flee!

Wha for Scotland's King and Law
Freedom's sword will strongly draw,
Freeman stand, or Freeman fa',[10]
        Let him follow me!

By[11] Oppression's[12] woes and pains,
By your sons in servile[13] chains,
We will drain our dearest veins[14],
        But they shall be free!

Lay the proud usurpers low![15]
Tyrants fall in every foe![16]
Liberty's in every blow!–[17]
        Let us do, or die![18]

Notes

1. wha: who; hae: have; the original title for this poem is *Robert Bruce's March to Bannockburn*, but most editors prefer to use the first three words in the first line; notice that in each stanza (or a quatrain in a song) the first three lines are end rhyming while the last line in each stanza rhyming in one vowel.

2. Sir William Wallace: (c. 1270–1305), the Scottish national hero who once defeated the English army with great victory and later was betrayed and dismembered.

3. wham: whom

4. Robert Bruce: (1274–1329), another Scottish national hero and the Scottish king who conquered the English army at Bannockburn in 1314; aften: often

5. gory bed: bloody bed; bed of blood in fighting

6. victorie: victory; the last syllable in "victorie" should be stressed as in "slaverie"; the special spelling is to make it rhyming with "slaverie", "flee", "me", "free" and "die" (/di:/).

7. lour: (old use) lower as a verb; look dark and threatening; this line means "the front-line in battle looks dark and threatening".

8. Here Edward refers to King Edward II of England (1284–1327) and the king whom Wallace had been fighting was Edward I; slaverie: slavery

9. base: cowardly; these two lines mean "who is so cowardly that he wants to be a slave?"

10. fa': fall, die; this line means "when we are alive we are freeman and we will fight and die as a free man".

11. By: It is used to begin an oath as "By George".

12. Oppression: the people who are being oppressed

13. servile: being in slavery

14. drain...veins: to shed our blood to the last drop

15. lay... low: kill to death; usurper: a person who steals power from another without any lawful right; the proud usurper here means Edward II.

16. Tyrants fall in every foe: Whenever we kill an enemy, we are killing a tyrant.

17. Liberty's in every blow: Whenever we give a blow to our enemy, we get a piece of more freedom.

18. Let us do, or die: Let us fight our enemies bravely or let us die in fighting for our country; "do" and "die" are alliteration; "die" /di:/ and "victorie", "slaverie" and so on are end rhyming.

A Red, Red Rose

O, my luve[1] is like a red, red rose,
That's newly sprung in June.[2]
O, my luve is like the melodie,
That's sweetly play'd in tune.[3]

As fair art thou[4], my bonnie[5] lass[6],
So deep in luve am I;
And I will love thee[7] still[8], my dear,
Till a'[9] the seas gang[10] dry.

Till a' the seas gang dry, my dear,
And the rocks melt wi' the sun![11]
I will luve thee still, my dear,
While the sands o' life shall run.[12]

And fare thee weel[13], my only luve!
And fare thee weel, a while!
And I will come[14] again, my luve,
Tho' it were ten thousand mile!

Notes

1. luve: love; lover; sweetheart

2. sprung: bloomed; because of the geographical features of Scotland (mainly with highlands) roses often bloom in June which is quite late compared to that in England.

3. melodie: melody; play'd: played; in tune: in harmony; notice that this poem is in traditional folk song metrical form, that is, the stanza is in four lines with the odd lines having four stresses syllables and the even lines having three stressed syllables; the even lines are end rhyming.

4. fair: beautiful; fair art thou: you are beautiful

5. bonnie: pretty

6. lass: girl, maiden

7. thee: "you" in the objective case

8. still: always; forever

9. a': all

10. gang: gone

11. wi': with; seas gone dry...rocks melt wi' the sun: Compare that to the Chinese phrase 海枯石烂.

12. sands o' life: the glass of sands to measure time; the sands o' life shall run: as long as the sand glass runs; as long as I am alive

13. fare thee weel: fare you well; say goodbye to you

14. come: come back; return

Questions for Discussion

(1) What evidence in "A Man's a Man for A' That" shows Robert Burns' strong support for the French Revolution? How does Burns express his condemnation and contempt against the rich, the ranked and the aristocrats, and his sympathy for the honest and the poor?

(2) How does Burns recreate the scene of the great battle led by Robert Bruce in his poem "Scots Wha Hae"? How is it different from the presentation of a novel or prose? Compared with the poems in previous chapters, what are the differences in spelling and the use of refrains?

(3) Normally "A Red, Red Rose" is considered a love poem. However, it can also be interpreted as a patriotic poem, if we render "my luve" as Scotland. What can we infer from this kind of reading and interpretation?

(4) How is the history of Scotland with its relation with England and Burns' own

personal experience reflected in the passionate patriotism of his poetry?

(5) Why do the compilers of literary works or anthologies group Robert Burns along with William Blake as Pre-Romanticism poets?

(6) Identify similarities and differences between Robert Burns' ballads and poems and Scottish popular ballads. What influence do they have in the development of ballads in England and Scotland?

Suggested Reading

(1) Robert Burns. *Burns: Complete Poems & Songs*. New York: Oxford University Press, 1971.

(2) Robert Burns. *Poems and Songs* (Dover Thrift Editions). London: Dover Publications, 1991.

(3) John Stuart Blackie. *The Life of Robert Burns*. Whitefish: Kessinger Legacy Reprints, 2010.

(4) 彭斯：《我爱人像红红的玫瑰》，袁可嘉译，北京：人民文学出版社，2008 年。

(5) 罗伯特·彭斯：《彭斯诗歌精选》（英汉对照），李正栓译注，北京：清华大学出版社，2016 年。

(6) 彭斯：《彭斯诗选》，王佐良译，北京：人民文学出版社，1985 年。

Part Five

The Romantic Period

18. William Wordsworth

When Robert Burns was cultivating the barren field in Ayrshire, not far away in the picturesque area of Lake District, William Wordsworth (1770–1850) was traveling through the brilliant lakes and wonderful landscapes finding a tone for his *Lyrical Ballads*. Born in Cumbria, Wordsworth went through a mixed childhood with joys and terrors. He grew up enjoying a relatively abundant family atmosphere in an area with spectacular views of lakes Windermere and Grasmere but suffered the loss of both his parents before he was 15. Fortunately, during his whole life, Wordsworth received legacies, pensions or rewards from relatives, friends and authorities so he did not have to work like Burns, allowing him to devote his energy and time to writing poetry from an early age. As a young man, Wordsworth, like Burns, firmly supported the causes of the French Revolution, even going to France to experience it for himself. Around his 30s, he formed a staunch yet uncertain relationship with Samuel Taylor Coleridge and a friendship with Robert Southey. Calling themselves the "Lake Poets" they inspired each other and wrote poems together. With a more stable living and income, Wordsworth began to lose his early sprite and jolly and even rebellious spirit. He also changed his attitude towards the French Revolution upon learning of the tyranny of the republican reign in France. His art and style, including diction and rhetoric, became more mature while the creativity was no longer fresh and stimulating. Wordsworth spent the majority of his life in Ambleside, editing and pruning his collection of poems. Seven years before his death he received the honor of poet laureate succeeding his friend Robert Southey.

Wordsworth and Coleridge are usually esteemed as the representatives of the first part of Romanticism and their work of cooperation–*Lyrical Ballads*–was the landmark of the beginning of Romanticism in English literature. Besides the short or somewhat long poems in this collection, Wordsworth also wrote quite a long poem titled "The Prelude". The declaration in the preface of *Lyrical Ballads* that "(all good) poetry is the spontaneous overflow of powerful feelings...that recollected in tranquility", influenced the writing of literary works of contemporary writers and those of later generations. However, when read meticulously the definition is more reflective of Wordsworth's own poetic writing. Nature has always been an endless source of inspiration for Wordsworth, while the would-be poet laureate took no less interest and concern for the social issues of his time. Besides the selection below, his renowned poems also include the five Lucy poems, "Tintern Abbey", "The Solitary Reaper" and various sonnets.

I Wandered Lonely as a Cloud

I wandered lonely as a cloud
That floats on high o'er[1] vales[2] and hills,
When all at once I saw a crowd,
A host, of[3] golden daffodils;
Beside the lake, beneath the trees,
Fluttering[4] and dancing in the breeze[5].

Continuous[6] as the stars that shine
And twinkle on the milky way[7],
They stretched in never-ending line
Along the margin[8] of a bay:
Ten thousand saw I at a glance,
Tossing their heads in sprightly[9] dance.

The waves beside them danced; but they

Out-did[10] the sparkling waves in glee[11]:
A poet could not but[12] be gay[13],
In such a jocund company:[14]
I gazed–and gazed–but little thought
What wealth the show[15] to me had brought:

For oft[16], when on my couch I lie
In vacant or in pensive mood,[17]
They flash upon that inward eye
Which is the bliss of solitude;[18]
And then my heart with pleasure fills,
And dances with the daffodils.[19]

Notes

1. o'er: over

2. vales: (poetic) valleys

3. host: large group; notice that in poetry, punctuation is also important for its form value; in this line, the comma between "host" and "of" can not be omitted because it is to leave a certain space in singing the poem (ballad).

4. fluttering: moving gently and quickly

5. breeze: soft and tender wind; notice that this poem consists of four stanzas and in each stanza it is with iambic meter and end rhyme pattern ababcc.

6. continuous: spreading or stretching

7. milky way: a galaxy in the sky 银河

8. margin: brink; verge

9. sprightly: full of life and energy

10. out-did: win over; surpass

11. glee: a feeling of happiness

12. could not but: could only

13. gay: happy

14. in...company: with...as friends; jocund: bright; happy and cheerful

15. show: scene; view

16. oft: (poetic) often

17. vacant: unoccupied; empty; in vacant mood: without thinking much, showing no signs of thinking or expression; in pensive mood: in thinking profoundly, in deep thinking

18. "that inward eye" is "imagination"; Wordsworth thinks that imagination is the bliss of solitude (being alone) and the natural scene recollected in solitude is the most beautiful.

19. Notice that in this poem "dance" appears three times and the first two refer to the dance of daffodils (outward view) and the last one refers to the dance of imagination (inward eye); so the word links the outside world, the sensational pleasure of body parts, and inside world, the spiritual pleasure felt inside; the transition from outside world to inside world is the creation of poetry by imagination.

Michael: A Pastoral Poem

If from the public way you turn your steps
Up the tumultucus[1] brook[2] of Greenhead Ghyll[3],
You will suppose that with an upright path
Your feet must struggle; in such bold ascent
The pastoral mountains front you, face to face.
But, courage! for around that boisterous[4] brook
The mountains have all opened out themselves,
And made a hidden valley of their own.
No habitation[5] can be seen; but they
Who journey thither[6] find themselves alone
With a few sheep, with rocks and stones, and kites[7]
That overhead are sailing in the sky.
It is in truth an utter solitude;
Nor should I have made mention of this Dell[8]
But for one object which you might pass by,
Might see and notice not. Beside the brook

Appears a straggling[9] heap of unhewn[10] stones!
And to that simple object appertains[11]
A story—unenriched[12] with strange events,
Yet not unfit, I deem, for the fireside,
Or for the summer shade. It was the first
Of those domestic tales that spake[13] to me
Of shepherds, dwellers in the valleys, men
Whom I already loved; not verily
For their own sakes, but for the fields and hills
Where was their occupation[14] and abode[15].
And hence this Tale, while I was yet a Boy
Careless of books, yet having felt the power
Of Nature, by the gentle agency
Of natural objects, led me on to feel
For passions that were not my own, and think
(At random and imperfectly indeed)
On man, the heart of man, and human life.
Therefore, although it be a history
Homely and rude, I will relate the same
For the delight of a few natural hearts;
And, with yet fonder feeling, for the sake
Of youthful Poets, who among these hills
Will be my second self when I am gone.[16]

Upon the forest-side in Grasmere Vale[17]
There dwelt a Shepherd, Michael was his name;
An old man, stout[18] of heart, and strong of limb[19].
His bodily frame had been from youth to age
Of an unusual strength: his mind was keen,
Intense, and frugal[20], apt for[21] all affairs,
And in his shepherd's calling he was prompt
And watchful more than ordinary men.

Hence had he learned the meaning of all winds,
Of blasts of every tone; and, oftentimes,
When others heeded not, he heard the South[22]
Make subterraneous[23] music, like the noise
Of bagpipers[24] on distant Highland[25] hills.
The Shepherd, at such warning, of his flock
Bethought him[26], and he to himself would say,
"The winds are now devising work for me!"
And, truly, at all times, the storm, that drives
The traveller to a shelter, summoned him
Up to the mountains: he had been alone
Amid the heart of many thousand mists,
That came to him, and left him, on the heights.
So lived he till his eightieth year was past.
And grossly that man errs[27], who should suppose
That the green valleys, and the streams and rocks,
Were things indifferent to the Shepherd's thoughts.[28]
Fields, where with cheerful spirits he had breathed
The common air; hills, which with vigorous step
He had so often climbed; which had impressed
So many incidents upon his mind
Of hardship, skill or courage, joy or fear;
Which, like a book, preserved the memory
Of the dumb animals, whom he had saved,
Had fed or sheltered, linking to such acts
The certainty of honourable gain;
Those fields, those hills—what could they less?[29] had laid
Strong hold on his affections, were to him
A pleasurable feeling of blind love,
The pleasure which there is in life itself.

His days had not been passed in singleness.

His Helpmate was a comely matron, old–
Though younger than himself full twenty years.
She was a woman of a stirring life,
Whose heart was in her house: two wheels she had
Of antique[30] form; this large, for spinning wool;
That small, for flax[31]; and if one wheel had rest
It was because the other was at work.
The Pair had but one inmate in their house,
An only Child, who had been born to them
When Michael, telling o'er his years, began
To deem that he was old, –in shepherd's phrase,
With one foot in the grave. This only Son,
With two brave sheep–dogs tried in many a storm,
The one of an inestimable worth,
Made all their household. I may truly say,
That they were as a proverb in the vale
For endless industry. When day was gone
And from their occupations out of doors
The Son and Father were come home[32], even then,
Their labour did not cease; unless when all
Turned to the cleanly supper-board, and there,
Each with a mess of pottage[33] and skimmed milk[34],
Sat round the basket piled with oaten cakes[35],
And their plain home-made cheese. Yet when the meal
Was ended, Luke (for so the Son was named)
And his old Father both betook themselves
To such convenient work as might employ
Their hands by the fireside; perhaps to card[36]
Wool for the Housewife's spindle, or repair
Some injury done to sickle[37], flail[38], or scythe[39],
Or other implement of house or field.

......

There is a comfort in the strength of love;
'Twill make a thing endurable, which else
Would overset[40] the brain, or break the heart:
I have conversed with more than one who well
Remember the old Man, and what he was
Years after he had heard this heavy news.
His bodily frame had been from youth to age
Of an unusual strength. Among the rocks
He went, and still looked up to sun and cloud,
And listened to the wind; and, as before,
Performed all kinds of labour for his sheep,
And for the land, his small inheritance.
And to that hollow dell from time to time
Did he repair, to build the Fold of which
His flock had need. 'Tis not forgotten yet
The pity which was then in every heart
For the old Man—and 'tis believed by all
That many and many a day he thither went,
And never lifted up a single stone.

There, by the Sheepfold, sometimes was he seen
Sitting alone, or with his faithful Dog,
Then old, beside him, lying at his feet.
The length of full seven years, from time to time,
He at the building of this Sheepfold wrought,[41]
And left the work unfinished when he died.
Three years, or little more, did Isabel
Survive her Husband: at her death the estate
Was sold, and went into a stranger's hand.
The Cottage which was named the EVENING STAR

Is gone–the ploughshare[42] has been through the ground
On which it stood; great changes have been wrought
In all the neighbourhood: –yet the oak is left
That grew beside their door; and the remains
Of the unfinished Sheepfold may be seen
Beside the boisterous brook of Greenhead Ghyll.

Notes

1. tumultuous: dashing, roaring loud and running wildly

2. brook: stream; small river

3. Greenhead Ghyll: name of a place near Grasmere lake

4. boisterous: noisy and energetic

5. habitation: living place; dwelling place

6. thither: (old use) over there

7. kites: hawks

8. Dell: here is a special name for a place; dell: (literary) a small valley with trees growing

9. straggling: untidy and messy

10. unhewn: have not been arranged in order/ have not been engraved

11. appertain (to): related to; linked to

12. unenriched: without addition; in its original

13. spake: spoke (to me); I have heard

14. occupation: job

15. abode: living place; house

16. These lines mean that even if "I" was gone, there are future poets to sing this story.

17. Grasmere Vale: the vale around Grasmere lake in Lake District

18. stout: firm and strong

19. limb: arms or legs

20. frugal: economic; thrift

21. apt for: good at; suitable for

Part Five　The Romantic Period　123

22. the South: the south wind

23. subterraneous: (formal) from underground

24. bagpiper: the player who plays the music on bagpipe, a special musical instrument in Scotland 风笛

25. Highland: the special geographical landscape in Scotland, especially in the northern and western parts 高地

26. Bethought him: he would think of (the flock)

27. err: to make mistakes

28. The meaning of these lines is: if anyone thinks that Michael, the old man, was indifferent to these things (valleys, brooks), then anyone is making a big mistake.

29. what could they less: and all other things in the valley

30. antique: very old

31. flax: a plant with blue flowers that is grown to use its stem to make thread and its seeds to make oil 亚麻

32. were come home: were coming home; in folk songs or in poems, in order to meet the metrical technique sometimes the irregular usage or grammatical mistake do happen.

33. pottage: soup or stew; a mess of pottage: some pottage

34. skimmed milk milk that is without fat

35. oaten cakes: cakes made of oats

36. card: *v.* to comb or clean wool with a machine or something

37. sickle: a tool with a curved blade and a short handle 镰刀

38. flail: a tool with a long handle and a stick hanging from the handle to be used to separate grains of wheat or rice 连枷

39. scythe: a tool with a long handle and a slightly curved blade 长柄大镰刀

40. overset: conquer; damage

41. The normal order of this line should be "wrought at the building of the Sheepfold"; wrought at: worked at

42. ploughshare: plowshare, the broad curved blade of a plough 犁铧

Questions for Discussion

(1) Wordsworth and Coleridge (mainly Wordsworth) in *Lyrical Ballads* define good poetry as "the spontaneous overflow of powerful feelings...recollected in tranquility". How are key concepts of nature, feelings, spontaneous, recollection expressed in "I Wandered Lonely as a Cloud"?

(2) Only the first three and the last two stanzas of "Michael: A Pastoral Poem" is chosen for consideration here. This is a long poem written almost in the original form of a folk song or ballad. Identify the oral and folk features of this poem and compare them to Burns' ballad poems or popular ballads. What is Wordsworth's contribution to the development of the ballad in English literature?

(3) Read the whole poem "Michael: A Pastoral Poem". How did the poet fulfill his definition of using common and simple language of common people in writing poetry?

(4) "Michael: A Pastoral Poem" is remarkably different from Wordsworth's lyrical poems. It is a poem that tells the stories of Michael, whose son went town bringing about the disintegration of countries. It also shows the problems of leaving elderly and lonely men in the country in the process of industrialization. Why did Wordsworth want to retell this true story? How is this poem related to the macro changes happening in history?

(5) How can "Michael: A Pastoral Poem" work as a commentary on contemporary issues such as industrialization and urbanization? What are our advantages in this process?

(6) Compare "Michael: A Pastoral Poem" with poems of Du Fu, the great master of poetry in the Tang Dynasty, such as "Three Ministers and Three Departing" ("三吏三别").

Suggested Reading

(1) John L. Mahoney. *William Wordsworth: A Poetic Life*. Fordham: Fordham University Press, 1996.

(2) Stephen Gill. *William Wordsworth: A Life*. New York: Oxford University Press, 1990.

(3) William Wordsworth. *The Collected Poems of William Wordsworth*. London: Wordsworth Editions Ltd., 1998.

(4) 华兹华斯：《华兹华斯诗选》，杨德豫译，北京：外语教学与研究出版社，2012年。

(5) 威廉·华兹华斯：《序曲：或一位诗人心灵的成长》，丁宏为译，北京：北京大学出版社，2017年。

(6) 丁宏为：《理念与悲曲：华兹华斯后革命之变》，北京：北京大学出版社，2002年。

19. George Gordon Byron

George Gordon Byron (1788–1824), one of the greatest Romantic poets of the 19th century, was born into an aristocratic family. When he was ten, he inherited the title of baron and a large estate upon the death of his granduncle. He first studied at Harrow, and later entered Cambridge. During his college life, he published his first collection of lyrical poems *Hours of Idleness* (1807), which received harsh criticism from *The Edinburgh Review*, a conservative literary journal. Provoked by the attack, he wrote his famous poem "English Bards and Scotch Reviewers", written in the manner of Alexander Pope, satirically challenged literary celebrities like Wordsworth, Coleridge, Southey and other Edinburgh critics. After two years of tour in Europe, he returned to England and published the first two cantos of *Childe Harold's Pilgrimage*, which was an overnight success. During 1813–1816, Byron wrote a series of legendary works on oriental stories, known as the "Oriental Narrative Poems". The heroes in these poems, who are mysterious, proud and rebellious figures of noble origin, are called Byronic heroes and were well-received in Europe. However, his unhappy marriage and love affairs caused scandals and forced him to leave England for good in 1816. Byron first went to Switzerland, where he met and became friends with Shelley. Soon he wrote his famous narrative poem "The Prisoner of Chillon" (1816). Later he went to Italy and Greece, where he devoted himself to the national independence movements of two countries. During this period, he finished *Childe Harold's Pilgrimage* (1816–1818), *The Vision of Judgement* (1822), and his satiric masterpiece *Don Juan* (1819–1824). On May 19, 1824, he died of fever in Greece. Byron exerted a great influence throughout Europe. His poems are based on his own experience, while his heroes are mostly reflection of himself or people he knew. His devotion to the ideals of democracy, freedom and national liberation is reflected in many of his literary works, which have great significance in historical progress and extremely high artistic value.

"Sonnet on Chillon" was published as a poetical introduction to Byron's long narrative poem *The Prisoner of Chillon*, which was dedicated to the memory of Geneva patriot and reformer François Bonnivard (1493–1570) who was imprisoned in the Castle of Chillon by Duke Charles III of Savoy. "Sonnet on Chillon" was written in praise of the fighters of liberty who remained faithful to their ideals in the face of persecution by their oppressors. By dramatizing the conflict between liberty and tyranny, this poem was a strong protest against the political oppression of that time. This poem contains fourteen lines in anapestic tetrameter. It is essentially in the style of the Italian or Petrarchan Sonnet, with slight changes in the rhyming pattern in the octave (abba, acca) and the sextet (dedede).

"She Walks in Beauty" is chosen from *Hebrew Melodies* (1815), a collection of melodies, with lyrics by Byron and music by Isaac Nathan (1792–1864). On June 11, 1814, Byron met his beautiful young cousin, Lady Wilmot Horton, who was dressed in a black mourning gown brightened with spangles. Struck by her beauty, he wrote this poem overnight. The poem consists of three six-line stanzas of iambic tetrameter, with a rhyme scheme of ababab cdcdcd efefef. The poet describes the beauty of Lady Wilmot Horton from her gait, appearance, eyes, hair, face to her smile and soul to show that the perfect combination of external beauty and internal beauty is the embodiment of ideal beauty. From the description of physical beauty to inner beauty, the poem reveals the poet's praise for the beauty and highlights his unique and superb aesthetic ability.

Sonnet on Chillon

Eternal Spirit of the chainless Mind[1]!
Brightest in dungeons[2], Liberty! thou art,
For there thy habitation[3] is the heart–
The heart which love of thee alone can bind;
And when thy sons to fetters[4] are consign'd[5]–
To fetters, and the damp vault's dayless gloom[6],
Their country conquers with their martyrdom[7],
And Freedom's fame finds wings on every wind[8].
Chillon! thy prison is a holy place,
And thy sad floor an altar[9]–for 'twas trod,
Until his very steps have left a trace
Worn, as if thy cold pavement were a sod[10],
By Bonnivard! May none those marks efface[11]!
For they appeal from tyranny to God.[12]

Notes

1. chainless Mind: unbounded mind; it suggests that the mind refuses to be enslaved even the body is in chains.

2. dungeons: *n.* a dark underground prison cell

3. habitation: *n.* living place

4. fetters: *n.* chains

5. consign'd: *v.* commit

6. the damp vault's dayless gloom: Here it refers to the underground prison which is damp and dark.

7. martyrdom: *n.* the death or suffering of a martyr

8. finds wings on every wind: spreads by wind

9. altar: *n.* a holy table in a church or temple

10. sod: *n.* the surface of the ground, with the grass growing on it

11. efface: *v.* erase

12. For they appeal from tyranny to God: because they are asking God for help under the tyranny

She Walks in Beauty

SHE walks in beauty, like the night
Of cloudless climes[1] and starry skies;
And all that's best of dark and bright
Meet in her aspect[2] and her eyes:
Thus mellow'd[3] to that tender light
Which heaven to gaudy day[4] denies

One shade[5] the more, one ray[6] the less,
Had half impair'd[7] the nameless grace[8]
Which waves in every raven tress[9],
Or softly lightens o'er her face;
Where thoughts serenely sweet express
How pure, how dear their dwelling-place[10].

And on that cheek, and o'er that brow,
So soft, so calm, yet eloquent[11],
The smiles that win,[12] the tints that glow[13],
But tell of days in goodness spent,[14]
A mind at peace with all below,[15]
A heart whose love is innocent!

Notes

1. climes: *n.* climates
2. aspect: *n.* appearance
3. mellow'd: *adj.* become soft and rich
4. gaudy day: bright day

5. shade: *n.* darkness

6. ray: *n.* brightness

7. had half impair'd : would have half damaged

8. nameless grace: indescribable elegance

9. raven tress: a lock of long, dark hair

10. their dwelling-place: the body

11. eloquent: *adj.* able to express a feeling

12. The smiles that win: The smile attracts people

13. the tints that glow: the reddish color that shines

14. But tell of days in goodness spent: Show that she has been living her life with kindness

15. A mind at peace with all below: She is kind to everything on earth.

Questions for Discussion

(1) Read some of Byron's typical oriental narrative poems, such as "The Giaour", "The Corsair", and "Lara", and identify the distinguished characteristics of Byronic heroes in these poems. Explain the enormous popularity of Byronic heroes in Europe at that time.

(2) "Sonnet on Chillon" is a Petrarchan or Italian sonnet. Compare and analyze the differences between this kind of sonnet and Shakespearean sonnet in form. What do these two forms contribute to English literature and even to European literature?

(3) Identify the alliteration and other figures of speech used in "She Walks in Beauty". How do they contribute to the appeal of the poem and achieve an artistic effect?

(4) As one of the most famous western poets, Byron occupied a unique position in Chinese literary history during the late Qing Dynasty and early Republican periods. Many writers and translators, including Liang Qichao, Ma Junwu, Su Manshu, and Lu Xun, introduced Byron's ideals of democracy, freedom and national liberation to China. Analyze the importance of Byron's influence on Chinese literature and writers of that time.

Suggested Reading

(1) Martin Garrett. *George Gordon, Lord Byron*. Shanghai: Shanghai Foreign Language Education Press, 2009.

(2) Lord Byron. *Selected Poems of Lord Byron*. London: Wordsworth Editions, 1994.

(3) Harold Bloom. *Bloom's Classic Critical View: George Gordon, Lord Byron*. New York: Infobase Publishing, 2009.

(4) 安·莫洛亚：《拜伦传》，裘小龙、王人力译，杭州：浙江文艺出版社，1985年。

(5) 拜伦：《拜伦诗选》，查良铮译，北京：人民文学出版社，2021年。

(6) 杨莉：《拜伦叙事诗研究》，南京：东南大学出版社，2017年。

(7) 倪正芳：《拜伦与中国》，西宁：青海人民出版社，2008年。

20. Percy Bysshe Shelley

Percy Bysshe Shelley (1792–1822), was a renowned English Romantic poet. Born in an aristocratic family in Sussex, Shelley was well-educated first in Sion House Academy and then in Eaton. His zeal had been transformed from chemistry to literature before he was admitted to Oxford in 1810. Before eighteen, Shelley even published a collection of poems. In Oxford, he composed a pamphlet named "The Necessity of Atheism", which caused his expulsion from Oxford. His father, an England baronet, claimed to renounce him. When Shelley was alone in London, he was attracted to a girl named Harriet Westbrook. They eloped together to Scotland but their hasty marriage just lasted for three years. During this period, Shelley accomplished his first important work *Queen Mab* (1813), which employed symbols to reveal the ills of monarchy, religion and so on. When Harriet drowned herself in 1816, Shelley soon got married to Mary Godwin, the daughter of William Godwin. Before their acquaintance, Shelley had been greatly influenced by William Godwin's ideas. It turned out that Mary Godwin was an ideal match, who promoted Shelley's literary achievements. For most of Shelley's works, he presented profound images with his brilliant imagination. In 1820, Shelley had written his two major works—*The Revolt of Islam* (1818) and *Prometheus Unbound* (1820). However, his radical opinions on society were not tolerated. Shelley was expelled from England and settled in Naples. While expressing his political views, Shelley also composed important romantic works, such as "Ode to the West Wind" (1819), "The Cloud" (1820) and "To a Skylark"(1820). Among them "Ode to the West Wind" was most spread and discussed. In this poem, Shelley placed great hope in the future with firm beliefs, implying a definite victory. Two years later, on his journey to Spezzia, Shelley died in an accident at the age of thirty.

"Ode to the West Wind" is an allegorical poem in which Shelley adopts the image of the west wind to reveal that humankind will witness the victory of a new world just like the seasonal cycles. This poem is composed in iambic pentameter and includes five stanzas. In this poem, Shelley points out that the destructive power of the west wind will absolutely smash the old world and usher in a new age. Shelley's staunch beliefs are easily found between lines, like "The trumpet of a prophecy" and the most famous line "If Winter comes, can Spring be far behind?" Besides, the last line also indicates that Shelley advocates natural changes instead of violence to generate victory.

Ode to the West Wind

I

O, WILD West Wind, thou breath of Autumn's being[1],
Thou, from whose unseen presence the leaves dead
Are driven, like ghosts from an enchanter fleeing,
Yellow, and black, and pale, and hectic red,
Pestilence-stricken[2] multitudes[3]: O, thou,
Who chariotest[4] to their dark wintry bed
The winged seeds, where they lie cold and low,
Each like a corpse within its grave, until
Thine azure[5] sister of the spring[6] shall blow

Her clarion[7] o'er the dreaming earth, and fill

(Driving sweet buds like flocks to feed in air[8])

With living hues and odours plain and hill:

Wild Spirit, which art[9] moving every where;

Destroyer and preserver; hear, O, hear!

II

Thou on whose stream, mid the steep sky's commotion,

Loose clouds like earth's decaying leaves are shed,

Shook from the tangled boughs of Heaven and Ocean,

Angels of rain and lightning[10]: there are spread

On the blue surface of thine airy surge,

Like the bright hair uplifted from the head

Of some fierce Maenad[11], even from the dim verge

Of the horizon to the zenith's height

The locks of the approaching storm. Thou dirge[12]

Of the dying year, to which this closing night

Will be the dome of a vast sepulchre[13],

Vaulted with all thy congregated might

Of vapours, from whose solid atmosphere

Black rain, and fire, and hail will burst: O, hear!

III

Thou who didst[14] waken from his summer dreams

The blue Mediterranean, where he lay,

Lulled[15] by the coil of his crystalline streams,

Beside a pumice isle[16] in Baiae's bay[17],

And saw in sleep old palaces and towers

Quivering within the wave's intenser day,

All overgrown with azure moss and flowers

So sweet, the sense faints picturing them! Thou

For whose path the Atlantic's level powers

Cleave themselves into chasms, while far below

The sea-blooms and the oozy woods which wear

The sapless foliage of the ocean, know

Thy voice, and suddenly grow grey with fear,

And tremble and despoil themselves: O, hear!

IV

If I were a dead leaf thou mightest bear;

If I were a swift cloud to fly with thee;

A wave to pant[18] beneath thy power, and share

The impulse of thy strength, only less free

Than thou, O, uncontrollable! If even

I were as in my boyhood, and could be

The comrade of thy wanderings over heaven,

As then[19], when to outstrip thy skiey speed[20]

Scarce seemed a vision; I would ne'er have striven

As thus with thee in prayer in my sore need.

O! lift me as a wave, a leaf, a cloud!

I fall upon the thorns of life[21]! I bleed!

A heavy weight of hours has chained and bowed

One too like thee: tameless, and swift, and proud.

V

Make me thy lyre[22], even as the forest is:

What if my leaves[23] are falling like its own!

The tumult of thy mighty harmonies

Will take from both a deep, autumnal tone,

Sweet though in sadness. Be thou, spirit fierce,

My spirit! Be thou me, impetuous one!

Drive my dead thoughts over the universe

Like withered leaves to quicken a new birth!

And, by the incantation of this verse,

Scatter, as from an unextinguished hearth

Ashes and sparks, my words among mankind!

Be through my lips to unawakened earth

The trumpet of a prophecy! O, wind,

If Winter comes, can Spring be far behind?

Notes

1. Autumn's being: Autumn's existence; autumn is a personification.

2. Pestilence-stricken: stricken by an infectious disease

3. multitudes: a multitude of leaves

4. chariotest: chariot, a vehicle pulled by horses

5. azure: the color of blue sky

6. West wind in the Mediterranean Sea is called the sister of Spring.

7. clarion: a kind of trumpet

8. Driving sweet buds like flocks to feed in air: Flocks(herd) are feeding in the air just like sweet buds, it is a metaphor here.

9. art: are

10. Angels of rain and lightning: clouds

11. Maenad: Dionysus, a female follower of the Greek God of wine, famous for her madness

12. dirge: a song sung at the funeral

13. sepulcher: a place to bury a dead person

14. didst: (old use) the past tense of "do"

15. lulled: be soothed to fall into sleep

16. a pumice isle: an island made of a kind of light stone

17. Baiae's bay: a resort in Naples

18. pant: to breathe loudly

19. as then: in my boyhood

20. outstrip thy skiey speed: to surpass your speed in the sky

21. the thorns of life: the facts of real life

22. lyre: a stringed instrument

23. my leaves: my dead thoughts

Questions for Discussion

(1) Shelley employs several literary devices in this poem, such as personification

and apostrophe (an address to absent persons). What is the topic in Shelley's "Ode to the West Wind"?

(2) What do the types of color in stanza two, canto one–"Yellow, and black, and pale, and hectic red" symbolize?

(3) Shelley calls the west wind "Wind". Why does Shelley use the capital letter?

(4) Once the "The trumpet of prophecy" is blown, what would happen next?

(5) According to Shelley, is "Spring" really coming? What is the relationship between "Winter" and "Spring"?

(6) Compare this poem with "The Song of the Stormy Petrel" by Maxim Gorky on their writing backgrounds and themes.

Suggested Reading

(1) Percy Shelley. *The Prose Works of Percy Bysshe Shelley*. New York: Oxford University, 1993.

(2) Harold Bloom. *Shelley's Mythmaking*. New Haven: Yale University Press, 1959.

(3) George Bornstein. *Yeats and Shelley*. Chicago: University of Chicago Press, 1970.

(4) Richard Cronin. *Shelley's Poetic Thoughts*. London: The Macmillan Press LTD,1981.

(5) 雪莱：《雪莱抒情诗选》，查良铮译，北京：人民文学出版社，1958 年。

(6) 张耀之：《雪莱》，长春：辽宁人民出版社，1981 年。

21. John Keats

John Keats(1785–1821) was one of the young Romantic poets (Byron and Shelley) of 19th-century Britain. He wrote some of the most beautiful odes in the English language and his intellectual and spiritual passion for beauty has influenced many poets after him.

John Keats, unlike Byron and Shelley, was born in London, of lowly origin. His father was a keeper of a stable and married his employer's daughter. As the eldest son of this family, Keats had a happy and peaceful life when he was young. Then his father died when he was eight and his mother died later when he was 14. His guardian was mean and crafty, who forced Keats to leave school at 15 and asked him to become an apprentice of a surgeon. Thus Keats began his medical training. He had written his first extant poem, "An Imitation of Spenser," in 1814 when he was 19. During this period, he continued to write poems and in 1816, he abandoned his profession choosing instead of becoming a poet. In 1817 he published his first collection of poems, and in 1818, he published his long allegorical poem "Endymion". Both these two collections incurred severe criticism from *Blackwood's Magazine*, which was said to have caused his illness. Keats finished most of his best poems from 1818 to 1821. In 1821, the poet died of tuberculosis at the age of 26.

In his short life, Keats created many memorable poems such as "Isabella", "The Eve of St. Agnes", and many beautiful odes like "Ode on a Grecian Urn", "To a Nightingale" and "To Autumn". His poetry always presented a beautiful world of imagination in contrast to the reality of his day. He would express beauty in all of his poems. "To Autumn" is the last of his six odes (which include "Ode to a Nightingale" and "Ode on a Grecian Urn"). The poem praises autumn, describing its abundance, harvest, and transition into winter, and uses intense, sensuous imagery to elevate the fleeting beauty of the moment.

On the Grasshopper and Cricket[1]

The poetry of earth is never dead:
When all the birds are faint[2] with the hot sun,
And hide in cooling trees, a voice will run
From hedge to hedge[3] about the new-mown mead[4]:
That is the Grasshopper's–he takes the lead[5]
In summer luxury[6], –he has never done[7]
With his delights, for when tired out with fun[8],
He rests at ease[9] beneath some pleasant weed.

The poetry of earth is ceasing never:
On a lone winter evening, when the frost[10]
Has wrought[11] a silence, from the stove there shrills[12]
The Cricket's song, in warmth increasing ever[13],
And seems to one in drowsiness[14] half lost,
The Grasshopper's[15] among some grassy hills.

Notes

1. cricket: *n.* a small jumping insect that produces short, loud sounds by rubbing its wings together

2. faint: *adj.* lacking strength

3. hedge: *n.* a row of bushes or small trees, usually along the edge of a garden, field, or road

4. mead: *n.* (literary) meadow; new-mown mead: recently cut meadow

5. take the lead: take the first place or position

6. in summer luxury: in hot summer

7. done: *v.* be content or satisfactory for

8. tired out with fun: exhausted after playing

9. at ease: free from pain or discomfort

10. frost: *n.* ice that looks white and powdery and covers things that are outside when the temperature is very cold

11. wrought: *v.* make it happen; here it means that the winter has made both the humans and animals silence.

12. shrill: *v.* to make a loud high unpleasant sound

13. The Cricket's song, in warmth increasing ever: The song of cricket gets louder as he finds more and more warmth indoor.

14. drowsiness: *n.* half sleep

15. the Grasshopper's: the grasshopper's song

To Autumn[1]

I

Seasons of mists and mellow[2] fruitfulness,
Close bosom-friend[3] of the maturing sun[4];
Conspiring[5] with him how to load and bless
With fruit[6] the vines that round the thatch-eves[7] run;
To bend with apples the moss'd[8] cottage-trees,
And fill all fruit with ripeness to the core;
To swell the gourd[9], and plump the hazel[10] shells
With a sweet kernel[11]; to set budding more,
And still more, later flowers for the bees,
Until they think warm days will never cease,
For Summer has o'er-brimm'd[12] their clammy cells[13].

II

Who hath not seen thee oft amid thy store[14]?
Sometimes whoever seeks abroad[15] may find
Thee sitting careless on a granary[16] floor,
Thy hair soft-lifted by the winnowing[17] wind;
Or on a half-reap'd furrow[18] sound asleep,
Drowsed with the fume of poppies[19], while thy hook[20]
Spares the next swath[21] and all its twined flowers[22]:
And sometime like a gleaner[23] thou dost keep
Steady thy laden head across a brook[24];
Or by a cider-press[25], with patient look,
Thou watchest[26] the last oozings[27] hours by hours.

III

Where are the songs of Spring? Ay, where are they?
Think not of them, thou hast thy music[28] too,
While barred clouds[29] bloom[30] the soft-dying day[31],

And touch the stubble-plains[32] with rosy hue[33];
Then in a wailful choir[34] the small gnats[35] mourn
Among the river sallows[36], borne aloft
Or sinking as the light wind lives or dies;
And full-grown lambs loud bleat[37] from hilly bourn[38];
Hedge-crickets sing; and now with treble[39] soft
The redbreast whistles from a garden-croft[40];
And gathering swallows twitter[41] in the skies.

Notes

1. This poem was written in 1819. Two days after Keats finished this poem, he wrote to his friend J. H. Reynolds: "I never liked stubble fields so much as now–Aye, better than the chilly green of the spring. Somehow a stubble plain looks warm–in the same way that some pictures look warm–this struck me so much in my Sundays walk that I composed upon it." From this, we can see the poet considers autumn not as a time of decay but as a season of warmth and harvest, and emphasizes that autumn is better than spring. The poem is divided into 3 stanzas with eleven lines in each of them. The rhyme scheme of each stanza is ababcdecdde.

2. mellow: *adj.* fully ripe in flavour or taste

3. bosom-friend: *n.* very close friend

4. the maturing sun: the sun that causes fruit to ripen

5. conspiring: *v.* make a plan to do something; here the poet uses personification to show that autumn and the sun are close friends and they plan to ripen the fruits and plants together

6. bless with fruit: here "bless" means "be blessed with", ripeness, swell, plump

7. thatch: *n.* a roof made of straw; eves: *n.* the projecting edge of the roof

8. moss'd: covered with moss

9. gourd: *n.* a round fruit whose outer shell can be used as a container

10. hazel: *n.* a small tree that produces nuts

11. kernel: *n.* the part of a nut or seed inside the shell

12. brim: *v.* overflow; here "o'er-brimm'd" should be "brimmed over".

13. clammy: *adj.* sticky; here "clammy cells" means overfilled honey makes the

beehive sticky.

    14. store: *n*. what is harvested; here "thee" and "thy" refer to the autumn.

    15. seek abroad: go out of one's house

    16. granary: *n*. a building which is used for storing grain

    17. winnow: *v*. remove the chaff (outer part of the grain) from grain

    18. furrow: *n*. a long cut in the ground made by a plow

    19. drowse: *v*. be half asleep; fume: *n*. a floral scent; poppy: *n*. a plant with a large, delicate flower, usually red in colour, common in Britain; The drug opium is obtained from one type of poppy. Here "Drowsed with the fume of poppies" means autumn becomes drowsy because of the smell of the poppies.

    20. hook: *n*. scythe, a curved tool for cutting or chopping

    21. swath: *n*. a row of cut grain or grass left by a scythe

    22. twined flowers: twisted flowers on the crop

    23. gleaner: *n*. one who gathers grain or other produce left by the reaper

    24. brook: *n*. a small stream

    25. cider-press: *n*. a piece of equipment used to put weight on something in order to make it flat or to force liquid out of it

    26. watchest: *v*. watched

    27. oozings: *n*. the slowly flowing down fluid that is squeezed from the fruit

    28. thy music: Here it refers to the sounds heard in autumn.

    29. barred clouds: clouds in the shape of bars

    30. bloom: *v*. make glowing and radiant

    31. soft-dying day: evening; "barred clouds bloom the soft-dying day" means the clouds illumined by the setting sun make the evening sky bright.

    32. stubble: *n*. short ends of grain stalks left in the ground after harvesting; stubble plains: fields covered with stubble

    33. hue: *n*. a color

    34. wailful: *adj*. expressing grief or pain

    35. gnat: *n*. a small flying insect that bites

    36. sallow: *n*. willow

    37. bleat: *v*. to make a sound that a sheep or a goat makes

    38. bourn: *n*. region

39. treble: *n.* high-pitched in tune

40. croft: *n.* a small piece of arable land, especially adjoining a dwelling

41. twitter: *v.* make a series of light short sounds; chirp

Questions for Discussion

Questions for "On the Grasshopper and Cricket":

(1) What does "the poetry of earth" refer to in this poem?

(2) Who sings the poetry of earth in the summer season? Who sings the poetry of earth in the winter season? What does the poet want to show by these?

(3) What is the tone of this poem?

(4) Do you know the poem "Requesting Mr. Liu, the Nineteenth" by Bai Ju-yi? Do you think the beauty of peace is the same in the two poems?

Questions for "To Autumn":

(1) Locate the several figures of speech in the poem.

(2) Show signs of progression of autumn with each stanza. Also, note the underlying questions in each stanza of "how," "who," and finally "where."

(3) What Chinese poems do the same comparison of autumn with spring as Keats does in "To Autumn"?

(4) Byron, Shelley and Keats were usually called the three young poets of the Romantic period in England and their names have been closely connected with Romanticism, but Keats' poems are much different from Baron's and Shelley's. Read their poems again and analyze the differences among them.

Suggested Reading

(1) John Keats. *John Keats Selected Poems*. London: Pan MacMillan, 2019.

(2) John Keats. *The Complete Poems of John Keats*. London: Penguin, 1977.

(3) 济慈：《济慈诗选》（英汉对照），屠岸译，北京：外语教学与研究出版社，2011年。

(4) 卢炜：《济慈与中国诗人——基于诗人译者身份的济慈诗歌中译研究》，上海：上海外语教育出版社，2020年。

(5) 徐玉凤：《济慈诗学观研究》，北京：光明日报出版社，2019年。

22. Jane Austen

Jane Austen (1775–1817), the most influential female writer in Western literature, was born in the village of Steventon, Hampshire. Jane Austen's father, the Reverend George Austen, was the rector of Steventon, and her mother, Cassandra Leigh, was distantly related to members of the landed gentry and the aristocracy. Therefore, the Austens enjoyed a comfortable and socially respectable life. Jane and her elder sister Cassandra were mainly educated at home. As a keen reader from earliest childhood, Jane began writing around the age of twelve, encouraged by her loving and cultured family. Jane lived a quiet and uneventful life. Aside from doing domestic chores and parish work, she spent most of her time writing and revising her novels. From 1811 until 1816, she published four of her major works. *Sense and Sensibility*, a reworking of *Elinor and Marianne*, was published in 1811, followed by *Pride and Prejudice*, a reworking of *First Impression*, in 1813, *Mansfield Park* in 1814, and *Emma* in 1815. All of her novels were published anonymously, including *Persuasion* and *Northanger Abbey*, which were published posthumously in 1818. As a careful observer of human motivation and social interaction, Austen presented the peaceful country life of common people and their daily life experiences. Her novels are mostly concerned with young women's self-discovery and their longing for freedom in marriage life. Austen's ability to create unique and lively characters, her incomparable sense of irony and wit, her brilliant dialogues and well-woven plots made her one of the most popular novelists in English literature.

Pride and Prejudice, initially entitled *First Impression*, is the most popular of Austen's novels. It was written early between October 1796 and August 1797, and published late, by Thomas Egerton (who paid £110 for the copyright, thanks to the success of *Sense and Sensibility*) in 1813. The main plot of *Pride and Prejudice* revolves around Mrs. Bennet's attempt to marry off her five daughters, and it centers on the marriage of her second daughter Elizabeth and wealthy landowner Mr. Darcy. Elizabeth is not the ideal woman to be Darcy's wife at first sight because she is "not handsome enough to tempt" him, but later he finds himself drawn to her intelligence and lively manners. Elizabeth, offended by Darcy's pride and blinded by her prejudice against him, turns down his first proposal. Throughout the progression of the plot, they both overcome their prejudice and misunderstanding, and finally fall in love with each other. *Pride and Prejudice* conveys Austen's view on love and marriage that marriage should be built on both love and solid financial conditions, and love should play the guiding role. The heroine Elizabeth, with her bold independence and insistence on placing love above economic motive in marriage, has been the most favorite character in Austen's novels.

Pride and Prejudice

(Chapter I)

It is a truth universally acknowledged, that a single man in possession of a good fortune, must be in want of a wife.[1]

However little known the feelings or views of such a man may be on his first entering a neighbourhood, this truth is so well fixed in the minds of the surrounding families, that he is considered the rightful[2] property of some one or other of their daughters.

"My dear Mr. Bennet," said his lady to him one day, "have you heard that Netherfield Park[3] is let[4] at last?"

Mr. Bennet replied that he had not.

"But it is," returned she; "for Mrs. Long has just been here, and she told me all about it."

Mr. Bennet made no answer.

"Do you not want to know who has taken it?" cried his wife impatiently.

"YOU want to tell me, and I have no objection to hearing it."

This was invitation enough.

"Why, my dear, you must know, Mrs. Long says that Netherfield is taken by a young man of large fortune from the north of England; that he came down on Monday in a chaise and four[5] to see the place, and was so much delighted with it, that he agreed with Mr. Morris immediately; that he is to take possession before Michaelmas[6], and some of his servants are to be in the house by the end of next week."

"What is his name?"

"Bingley."

"Is he married or single?"

"Oh! Single, my dear, to be sure! A single man of large fortune; four or five thousand a year. What a fine thing for our girls!"

"How so? How can it affect them?"

"My dear Mr. Bennet," replied his wife, "how can you be so tiresome! You must know that I am thinking of his marrying one of them.[7]"

"Is that his design[8] in settling here?"

"Design! Nonsense, how can you talk so! But it is very likely that he MAY fall in love with one of them, and therefore you must visit him as soon as he comes."

"I see no occasion for that. You and the girls may go, or you may send them by themselves, which perhaps will be still better, for as you are as handsome as any of them, Mr. Bingley may like you the best of the party."

"My dear, you flatter me. I certainly HAVE had my share of beauty, but I do not pretend to be anything extraordinary now. When a woman has five grown-up daughters, she ought to give over thinking of her own beauty."

"In such cases, a woman has not often much beauty to think of."

"But, my dear, you must indeed go and see Mr. Bingley when he comes into the neighbourhood."

"It is more than I engage for, I assure you."

"But consider your daughters. Only think what an establishment it would be for one of them. Sir William and Lady Lucas are determined to go, merely on that account, for in general, you know, they visit no newcomers. Indeed you must go, for it will be impossible for US to visit him if you do not.[9]"

"You are over-scrupulous[10], surely. I dare say Mr. Bingley will be very glad to see you; and I will send a few lines by you to assure him of my hearty consent to his marrying whichever he chooses of the girls; though I must throw in a good word for my little Lizzy."

"I desire you will do no such thing. Lizzy is not a bit better than the others; and I am sure she is not half so handsome as Jane, nor half so good-humoured as Lydia. But you are always giving HER the preference."

"They have none of them much to recommend them," replied he; "they are all silly and ignorant like other girls; but Lizzy has something more of quickness than her sisters."

"Mr. Bennet, how CAN you abuse your own children in such a way? You take delight in vexing[11] me. You have no compassion for my poor nerves."

"You mistake me, my dear. I have a high respect for your nerves. They are my old friends. I have heard you mention them with consideration these last twenty years at least."

Mr. Bennet was so odd a mixture of quick parts[12], sarcastic humour, reserve, and caprice[13], that the experience of three-and-twenty years had been insufficient to make his wife understand his character. HER mind was less difficult to develop. She was a woman of mean[14] understanding, little information, and uncertain temper. When she was discontented, she fancied herself nervous. The business of her life was to get her daughters married; its solace was visiting and news.[15]

Notes

1. This is a periodic sentence that has been deliberately structured to place the main idea at the end. Such a sentence is more carefully arranged, especially for the purpose of building climax and creating suspense, and it is more complex, emphatic, formal and literary. The first sentence of this novel clarifies and sets the tone of the whole novel. It suggests that marriage is the theme of this novel, and wealth and social status are the major considerations in the marriage market at that time.

2. rightful: *adj.* having a legitimate right to property, position, or status

3. Netherfield Park: the name of an estate in the Bennets, neighbourhood

4. let: *v.* allow someone to have the use of (a room or property) in return for regular payments; rent

5. a chaise and four: *n.* four-wheeled closed carriage

6. Michaelmas: the feast of St. Michael the archangel, celebrated on September 29

7. Mrs. Bennet insists on marrying her daughters to wealthy men, because the system of inheritance at that time was primogeniture, a system in which the oldest son

in a family inherits all the property when his father dies, and if there were no boys of their own, the property would be passed on to the male relatives. As a landed gentry, Mr. Bennet has no sons, so his property should be inherited by his nephew, not his five daughters.

8. design: *n.* purpose, planning, or intention that exists or is thought to exist behind an action, fact, or material object

9. This explains the etiquette and customs of the middle and upper-class society in England at that time. Unmarried men don't venture to call on unmarried women they don't know, and vice versa. The general social rule is that men should first introduce themselves to each other before their female family members can be introduced to men. In common courtesy, Mr. Bennet should visit the newcomer Mr. Bingley, who would then call on the Bennets and be introduced to the ladies.

10. scrupulous: *adj.* (of a person or process) diligent, thorough, and extremely attentive to details

11. vex: *v.* make (someone) feel annoyed, frustrated, or worried, esp. with trivial matters

12. quick parts: strong intellectual ability or other natural talents

13. caprice: *n.* a sudden and unaccountable change of mood or behavior

14. mean: *adj.* (of a person's mental capacity or understanding) inferior; poor

15. The last paragraph of the first chapter highlights the characteristics of Mr. and Mrs. Bennet, and effectively reveals the relationship between them: Mr. Bennett is a well-educated landed gentry, while Mrs. Bennet was born in a merchant family and enhanced her social status by her marriage. Mr. Bennet's cold manner and pitiless sarcasm did not soothe or assist his wife in improving her mind and behaviour, but increased her uneasiness and absurdity. This introduction also acts as a foreshadow of Mr Darcy's later opposition to his and Bingley's marriage with the Bennett sisters.

Questions for Discussion

(1) The first line of the novel was claimed by some scholars to be the most famous opening line of all fiction. This detached opening offers a statement about several major issues and themes explored in the novel. List some of the major issues

reflected in this sentence. What kind of literary device does the author use to convey her opinion?

(2) The application of irony is one of the characteristics of this novel. Identify the irony used in the text, and its importance in the presentation of the theme and character analysis.

(3) *Pride and Prejudice* is considered the most popular of Austen's novels. What is the source of its immense and enduring popularity?

(4) Politics and class conflicts are far removed from Austen's novels. She centered her novels on the people and events she was most familiar with. It is sometimes said that Austen's gift was to be a shrewd observer of her narrow social circle, and her limited world experience. How does that affect her novels?

(5) *Pride and Prejudice* and *A Dream of Red Mansions* are both literary works on the theme of love and marriage. Due to the influence of social, cultural, and historical factors, the two works reflect the differences between Western and Chinese concepts of love and marriage. Compare the two works and analyze the reasons contributing to their different views on love and marriage.

Suggested Reading

(1) Jane Austen. *The Complete Novels of Jane Austen*. Cambridge: Wordsworth Publishing, 2014.

(2) Jane Austen. *Pride and Prejudice*. New York: Signet Classics, 2008.

(3) Claire Tomalin. *Jane Austen: A Life*. London: Penguin Books Ltd., 2012.

(4) Susannah Carson, ed. *A Truth Universally Acknowledged: 33 Great Writers on Why We Read Jane Austen*. New York: Random House, 2009.

(5) 简·奥斯丁：《傲慢与偏见》，孙致礼译，南京：译林出版社，2008 年。

(6) 詹姆斯·爱德华·奥斯丁利：《简·奥斯丁传：嫁给文字的女人》，岳玉庆译，南昌：江西教育出版社，2014 年。

(7) 龚龑、黄梅编选：《奥斯丁研究文集》，韩敏中等译．南京：译林出版社，2019 年。

Part Six

The Victorian Literature

23. Charles Dickens

Charles Dickens (1812–1870) is one of the most remarkable representative novelists of the Victorian Age. He was born in Portsmouth. His father was a naval clerk but later in 1824 was imprisoned for debt. After four-year education, Dickens was forced to leave school and make a living on his own. He went to a shoe factory earning six shillings a week to support his poor family. Miserable working conditions in childhood became Dickens' lifelong nightmare, which recurred several times in his novels. The cruel realities and underworld of London became major issues in his works. After his father paid off all the debts by family inheritance, Dickens went back to school. Dicken's turning point in life came in 1827, when he dropped out of school and became an office clerk in London where he learned more about reading and writing. Then he published his first book *Sketches by Boz* in 1836 under his pseudonym "Boz". His second work *The Posthumous Papers of the Pickwick Club* was well-received, winning him great popularity among readers. One year later, *Oliver Twist* (1837) was published. In this novel, with the description of an orphan's vagrant living in London, Dickens delved into the realistic world and revealed the social injustices of the impoverished underclass. From 1849, his masterpiece *David Copperfield*, the most beloved novel, was created and published monthly. In the same year, Dickens and his wife Catherine Hogarth had their eighth child. Dickens was prolific in the following decade. His novels like *Bleak House* (1852–1853) and *Hard Times* (1854) attacked social ills in England, including injustice and issues in the industry. His *A Tale of Two Cities* (1859) was also a classical historical novel. However, his marital life was not as satisfying as his career. In 1858, Dickens separated from his wife and was involved in an affair with a young actress. After he died in 1870, Dickens was buried in Westminster Abbey.

As mentioned earlier, Dickens' favorite book is clearly *David Copperfield* where he traces his own childhood experience. The protagonist Copperfield, under the cruelty of his stepfather, is forced to live with his surrogate parents. Soon, he goes to a boarding school but fails to receive an education. After his birth mother dies, Copperfield has to work in a factory where he undergoes a lot of adversities with many homeless children. This major plot is closely linked to Dickens' own childhood when he worked in a shoe factory. Later, Things start to change when Copperfield is adopted by his aunt in Dover. Copperfield even gets married to Dora, a solicitor's daughter. He writes fictions to support the family. However, his beloved wife dies after a long illness, which is a heavy hit to Copperfield. In the end, Copperfield marries Agnes and finally becomes a novelist. Dickens related his own experiences in this novel, such as working under harsh conditions in the factory, struggling to receive an education and becoming a novelist. In this autobiographical novel, Dickens expresses his sympathy and concern for the poor, especially for the children working under oppressive conditions. Nevertheless, he shows that even under the dehumanizing effects of industrialism, there are still love and kindness.

David Copperfield

(Chapter IV)

This[1] was my only and my constant comfort. When I think of it, the picture always rises in my mind, of a summer evening, the boys at play in the churchyard, and I sitting on my bed, reading as if for life. Every barn in the neighbourhood, every stone in the church, and every foot of the churchyard, had some association of its own, in my mind, connected with these books, and stood for some locality made famous in them. I have seen Tom Pipes[2] go climbing up the church-steeple; I have watched Strap[3], with the knapsack on his back, stopping to rest himself upon the wicket-gate;

and I know that Commodore Trunnion[4] held that club with Mr. Pickle, in the parlour of our little village alehouse[5].

The reader now understands, as well as I do, what I was when I came to that point of my youthful history to which I am now coming again.

One morning when I went into the parlour with my books, I found my mother looking anxious, Miss Murdstone[6] looking firm, and Mr. Murdstone[7] binding something round the bottom of a cane–a lithe and limber[8] cane, which he left off binding when I came in, and poised and switched in the air.

'I tell you, Clara,' said Mr. Murdstone, 'I have been often flogged[9] myself .'

'To be sure; of course,' said Miss Murdstone.

'Certainly, my dear Jane,' faltered my mother, meekly. 'But–but do you think it did Edward good?'

'Do you think it did Edward harm, Clara?' asked Mr. Murdstone, gravely.

'That's the point,' said his sister.

To this[10] my mother returned[11], 'Certainly, my dear Jane,' and said no more.

I felt apprehensive[12] that I was personally interested in this dialogue, and sought[13] Mr. Murdstone's eye as it lighted on mine.

'Now, David,' he said–and I saw that[14] cast again as he said it–'you must be far more careful today than usual.' He gave the cane another poise, and another switch; and having finished his preparation of it, laid it down beside him, with an impressive look, and took up his book.

This was a good freshener[15] to my presence of mind, as a beginning. I felt the words of my lessons slipping off, not one by one, or line by line, but by the entire page; I tried to lay hold of them; but they seemed, if I may so express it, to have put skates on, and to skim away from me with a smoothness there was no checking[16].

We began badly, and went on worse. I had come in with an idea of distinguishing myself[17] rather, conceiving that I was very well prepared; but it turned out to be quite a mistake. Book after book was added to the heap of failures, Miss Murdstone being firmly watchful of us all the time. And when we came at last to the five thousand cheeses (canes he made it that day, I remember), my mother burst out crying.

'Clara!' said Miss Murdstone, in her warning voice.

'I am not quite well, my dear Jane, I think,' said my mother.

I saw him wink, solemnly, at his sister, as he rose and said, taking up the cane:

'Why, Jane, we can hardly expect Clara to bear, with perfect firmness, the worry and torment that David has occasioned her today. That would be stoical[18]. Clara is greatly strengthened and improved, but we can hardly expect so much from her. David, you and I will go upstairs, boy.'

As he took me out at the door, my mother ran towards us. Miss Murdstone said, 'Clara! are you a perfect fool?' and interfered. I saw my mother stop her ears then, and I heard her crying.

He walked me up to my room slowly and gravely—I am certain he had a delight in that formal parade of executing justice[19]—and when we got there, suddenly twisted my head under his arm.

'Mr. Murdstone! Sir!' I cried to him. 'Don't! Pray don't beat me! I have tried to learn, sir, but I can't learn while you and Miss Murdstone are by. I can't indeed!'

'Can't you, indeed, David?' he said. 'We'll try that.'

He had my head as in a vice[20], but I twined round him somehow, and stopped him for a moment, entreating him not to beat me. It was only a moment that I stopped him, for he cut me heavily an instant afterwards, and in the same instant I caught the hand with which he held me in my mouth, between my teeth, and bit it through. It sets my teeth on edge to think of it.

He beat me then, as if he would have beaten me to death. Above all the noise we made, I heard them running up the stairs, and crying out—I heard my mother crying out—and Peggotty[21]. Then he was gone; and the door was locked outside; and I was lying, fevered and hot, and torn, and sore, and raging in my puny[22] way, upon the floor.

How well I recollect, when I became quiet, what an unnatural stillness[23] seemed to reign[24] through the whole house! How well I remember, when my smart[25] and passion began to cool, how wicked[26] I began to feel!

I sat listening for a long while, but there was not a sound. I crawled up from the floor, and saw my face in the glass, so swollen, red, and ugly that it almost frightened me. My stripes[27] were sore and stiff, and made me cry afresh[28], when I moved; but they were nothing to the guilt I felt. It lay heavier on my breast than if I had been a most atrocious[29] criminal, I dare say.

It had begun to grow dark, and I had shut the window (I had been lying, for the most part, with my head upon the sill[30], by turns crying, dozing, and looking listlessly[31] out), when the key was turned, and Miss Murdstone came in with some bread and meat, and milk. These she put down upon the table without a word, glaring at me the while with exemplary firmness, and then retired[32], locking the door after her.

Long after it was dark I sat there, wondering whether anybody else would come. When this appeared improbable[33] for that night, I undressed, and went to bed; and, there, I began to wonder fearfully what would be done to me. Whether it was a criminal act that I had committed? Whether I should be taken into custody, and sent to prison? Whether I was at all in danger of being hanged?

I never shall forget the waking, next morning; the being cheerful and fresh for the first moment, and then the being weighed down[34] by the stale and dismal oppression of remembrance. Miss Murdstone reappeared before I was out of bed; told me, in so many words, that I was free to walk in the garden for half an hour and no longer; and retired, leaving the door open, that I might avail myself of that permission[35].

I did so, and did so every morning of my imprisonment, which lasted five days. If I could have seen my mother alone, I should have gone down on my knees[36] to her and besought[37] her forgiveness; but I saw no one, Miss Murdstone excepted, during the whole time—except at evening prayers in the parlour; to which I was escorted[38] by Miss Murdstone after everybody else was placed; where I was stationed, a young outlaw, all alone by myself near the door; and whence I was solemnly conducted by my jailer, before any one arose from the devotional posture[39]. I only observed that my mother was as far off from me as she could be, and kept her face another way so that I never saw it; and that Mr. Murdstone's hand was bound up in a large linen wrapper[40].

The length of those five days I can convey no idea of to any one. They occupy the place of years in my remembrance. The way in which I listened to all the incidents of the house that made themselves audible to me; the ringing of bells, the opening and shutting of doors, the murmuring of voices, the footsteps on the stairs; to any laughing, whistling, or singing, outside, which seemed more dismal than anything else to me in my solitude and disgrace—the uncertain pace of the hours, especially at night, when I would wake thinking it was morning, and find that the family were not yet gone to bed, and that all the length of night had yet to come–the depressed dreams and nightmares I had–the return of day, noon, afternoon, evening, when the boys played in the churchyard, and I watched them from a distance within the room, being ashamed to show myself at the window lest they should know I was a prisoner–the strange sensation of never hearing myself speak–the fleeting intervals of something like cheerfulness[41], which came with eating and drinking, and went away with it–the setting in of rain one evening, with a fresh smell, and its coming down faster and faster between me and the church, until it and gathering night seemed to quench me in gloom, and fear, and remorse–all this appears to have gone round and round for years instead of days, it is so vividly and strongly stamped on my remembrance. On the last night of my restraint[42], I was awakened by hearing my own name spoken in a whisper. I started up in bed, and putting out my arms in the dark, said:

'Is that you, Peggotty?'

There was no immediate answer, but presently I heard my name again, in a tone so very mysterious and awful, that I think I should have gone into a fit[43], if it had not occurred to me that it must have come through the keyhole.

I groped my way to the door, and putting my own lips to the keyhole, whispered: 'Is that you, Peggotty dear?'

'Yes, my own precious Davy,' she replied. 'Be as soft as a mouse, or the Cat'll hear us.'

I understood this[44] to mean Miss Murdstone, and was sensible of the urgency of the case; her room being close by.

'How's mama, dear Peggotty? Is she very angry with me?'

I could hear Peggotty crying softly on her side of the keyhole, as I was doing on mine, before she answered. 'No. Not very.'

'What is going to be done with me, Peggotty dear? Do you know?'

'School. Near London,' was Peggotty's answer. 'I was obliged to[45] get her to repeat it, for she spoke it the first time quite down my throat, in consequence of my having forgotten to take my mouth away from the keyhole and put my ear there; and though her words tickled me a good deal, I didn't hear them.

'When, Peggotty?'

'Tomorrow.'

'Is that the reason why Miss Murdstone took the clothes out of my drawers?' which she had done, though I have forgotten to mention it.

'Yes,' said Peggotty. 'Box.'

'Shan't I see mama?'

'Yes,' said Peggotty. 'Morning.'

Then Peggotty fitted her mouth close to the keyhole, and delivered these words through it with as much feeling and earnestness as a keyhole has ever been the medium of communicating, I will venture to assert: shooting in each broken little sentence in a convulsive little burst of its own[46].

'Davy, dear. If I ain't been azackly as intimate with you. Lately, as I used to be. It ain't because I don't love you. just as well and more, my pretty poppet. It's because I thought it better for you. And for someone else besides. Davy, my darling, are you listening? Can you hear?'

'Ye-ye-ye-yes, Peggotty!' I sobbed.

'My own!' said Peggotty, with infinite compassion[47]. 'What I want to say, is. That you must never forget me. For I'll never forget you. And I'll take as much care of your mama, Davy. As ever I took of you. And I won't leave her. The day may come when she'll be glad to lay her poor head. On her stupid, cross old Peggotty's arm again. And I'll write to you, my dear. Though I ain't no scholar[48]. And I'll–I'll–' Peggotty fell to kissing the keyhole, as she couldn't kiss me.

'Thank you, dear Peggotty!' said I. 'Oh, thank you! Thank you! Will you promise me one thing, Peggotty? Will you write and tell Mr. Peggotty and little Em'ly, and Mrs. Gummidge and Ham, that I am not so bad as they might suppose, and that I sent 'em all my love–especially to little Em'ly? Will you, if you please, Peggotty?'

The kind soul[49] promised, and we both of us kissed the keyhole with the greatest affection–I patted it with my hand, I recollect, as if it had been her honest face–and parted. From that night there grew up in my breast a feeling for Peggotty which I cannot very well define. She did not replace my mother; no one could do that; but she came into a vacancy in my heart, which closed upon her, and I felt towards her something I have never felt for any other human being. It was a sort of comical affection[50], too; and yet if she had died, I cannot think what I should have done, or how I should have acted out the tragedy it would have been to me.

In the morning Miss Murdstone appeared as usual, and told me I was going to school; which was not altogether such news to me as she supposed. She also informed me that when I was dressed, I was to come downstairs into the parlour, and have my breakfast. There, I found my mother, very pale and with red eyes: into whose arms I ran, and begged her pardon from my suffering soul.

'Oh, Davy!' she said. 'That you could hurt anyone I love! Try to be better, pray to be better! I forgive you; but I am so grieved[51], Davy, that you should have such bad passions in your heart.'

They had persuaded her that I was a wicked fellow, and she was more sorry for that than for my going away. I felt it sorely. I tried to eat my parting breakfast, but my tears dropped upon my bread-and-butter, and trickled into my tea. I saw my mother look at me sometimes, and then glance at the watchful Miss Murdstone, and than look down, or look away.

'Master Copperfield's box there!' said Miss Murdstone, when wheels were heard at the gate.

I looked for Peggotty, but it was not she; neither she nor Mr. Murdstone appeared. My former acquaintance, the carrier, was at the door. the box was taken out to his cart, and lifted in.

'Clara!' said Miss Murdstone, in her warning note.

'Ready, my dear Jane,' returned my mother. 'Good-bye, Davy. You are going for your own good. Good-bye, my child. You will come home in the holidays, and be a better boy.'

'Clara!' Miss Murdstone repeated.

'Certainly, my dear Jane,' replied my mother, who was holding me. 'I forgive you, my dear boy. God bless you!'

'Clara!' Miss Murdstone repeated.

Miss Murdstone was good enough to take me out to the cart, and to say on the way that she hoped I would repent[52], before I came to a bad end; and then I got into the cart, and the lazy horse walked off with it.

Notes

1. This: the collection of books left by my father
2. Tom Pipes: a character in *The Adventures of Peregrine Pickle* by British novelist Tobias Smollett (1721–1771)
3. Strap: a character in *The Adventures of Roderick Random* by Tobias Smollett
4. Commodore Trunnion: also a character in *The Adventures of Peregrine Pickle*
5. alehouse: tavern; a place selling beer
6. Miss Murdstone: the elder sister of Mr. Murdstone
7. Mr. Murdstone: the stepfather of David Copperfield
8. lithe and limber: soft and easy to bend
9. flogged: being hit by a whip; here Mr. Murdstone is preparing the cane for David Copperfield, hoping David to be tamed under the whip.
10. this: what Miss Murdstone had said
11. returned: replied
12. apprehensive: worried
13. sought: tried to catch a glimpse of Mr. Murdstone
14. that: Mr. Murdstone's eye on me
15. freshener: something to refresh one's spirit
16. no checking: no time to check
17. distinguishing myself: to behave well
18. stoical: enduring suffering and hardship without complaining
19. formal parade of executing justice: to beat David under the name of justice
20. as in a vice: he nipped my head like a vice; vice: a metal tool used to turn screws
21. Peggotty: a loyal servant to David and his mother
22. puny: weak
23. stillness: silence
24. reign: to control or rule
25. smart: pain
26. wicked: bad; evil
27. stripes: wounds left by whipping

28. afresh: again

29. atrocious: bad; cruel

30. sill: windowsill

31. listlessly: depressed

32. retired: left

33. improbable: not likely to happen

34. weighed down: being worried or anxious

35. that permission: I was permitted to walk in the garden for half an hour.

36. gone down on my knees: knelt down

37. besought: the past tense of "beseech", equals "beg"

38. escorted: accompanied and protected; here David was closely monitored.

39. the devotional posture: the gesture of pray

40. linen wrapper: wrap something with a type of cloth

41. the fleeting intervals of something like cheerfulness: the feeling of happiness lasted too short

42. restraint: my imprisonment in this room

43. fit: faint; the state of unconsciousness

44. this: the cat

45. I was obliged to: I was forced to

46. shooting…of its own: what I heard from the keyhole was off and on

47. compassion: sympathy

48. no scholar: illiterate

49. soul: person

50. comical affection: an amusing feeling

51. grieved: sad

52. repent: to feel regret

Questions for Discussion

(1) Why does Mr. Murdstone mistreat David? Is David being rebellious?

(2) Why does David's mother fail to protect her son? Analyze this question from a female perspective at the time.

(3) Dickens' portrait of people living at the bottom of social strata is quite impressive. Take Peggotty as an example and try to interpret this character.

(4) Read this novel in its entirety and analyze David's epiphany after the shipwreck.

(5) David Copperfield is considered a semiautobiographical work. How do you understand the influence brought by his childhood experience?

(6) Compare *David Copperfield* with Dicken's novel *Oliver Twist* on their similarities and differences.

Suggested Reading

(1) Charles Dickens. *David Copperfield*. Beijing: China Translation and Publishing Corporation, 2011.

(2) Donald V. Bodeen. *A Critical Study of Charles Dickens: Humor, Satire and Pathos of Era*. New Delhi: Dominant Publishers and Distributors, 2009.

(3) Brown Ivor. *Dickens in His Time*. London: Thomas Nelson and Sons, 1963.

(4) 查尔斯·狄更斯：《大卫·科波菲尔》（上、下），宋兆霖译，南京：译林出版社，2017年。

(5) 罗经国编著：《狄更斯评论集》，上海：上海译文出版社，1981年。

(6) 赵炎秋：《狄更斯长篇小说研究》，北京：社会科学文献出版社，1996年。

24. William Makepeace Thackeray

William Makepeace Thackeray(1811–1863) is now recognized as the major author of the Victorian age and is famous for his masterpiece *Vanity Fair*. Thackeray was born in India, the son of an official of the East India Company. His father died when he was only 3 years old, but he inherited a large amount of money, which made it possible for him to receive a good education in public schools in London. In 1820, Thackeray entered Trinity College of Cambridge, but he didn't like life there and left Cambridge without taking a degree. He tried different kinds of jobs and developed his interest in drawing. In 1833, the failure of the Indian bank where he deposited his money made his life difficult. In 1836, he married Isabella Shawe and since then he turned seriously to literature. He wrote most of the time for some magazines and gradually his stories attracted people's attention. In 1847, his masterpiece *Vanity Fair* was published in serial form with his own illustrations. This novel established his fame, and later, he created some other novels like *Pendennis* (1849–1850) and *The Newcomes* (1853–1855). Besides novels, Thackeray also wrote short stories, sketches and poems, too. He died suddenly in London in 1863.

Vanity Fair is a social satire, in which Thackeray mainly described the lives of aristocrats and rich businessmen. Thackeray showed anger and indignation at their hypocrisy, vanity, snobbery and selfishness. From the name of this novel, we can also see this. Thackeray took the name of this novel from John Bunyan's *The Pilgrim's Progress*, in which vanity fair is the place where everything can be sold including husband, wife, children, name, body and soul. Thackeray wanted to present his characters as they are in real life and his cynical attitude toward life.

Vanity Fair

(Chapter I   Chiswick Mall)

While the present century was in its teens[1], and on one sunshiny morning in June, there drove up to the great iron gate of Miss Pinkerton's academy for young ladies, on Chiswick Mall[2], a large family coach, with two fat horses in blazing harness[3], driven by a fat coachman in a three-cornered hat and wig[4], at the rate of four miles an hour. A black servant, who reposed[5] on the box beside the fat coachman, uncurled[6] his bandy legs[7] as soon as the equipage[8] drew up opposite Miss Pinkerton's shining brass plate[9], and as he pulled the bell at least a score of young heads were seen peering out of the narrow windows of the stately[10] old brick house. Nay, the acute observer might have recognized the little red nose of good-natured Miss Jemima Pinkerton herself, rising over some geranium[11] pots in the window of that lady's own drawing-room.

"It is Mrs. Sedley's coach, sister," said Miss Jemima. Sambo, the black servant, has just rung the bell; and the coachman has a new red waistcoat.

"Have you completed all the necessary preparations incident to Miss Sedley's departure, Miss Jemima?" asked Miss Pinkerton herself, that majestic lady–the Semiramis of Hammersmith[12], the friend of Doctor Johnson[13], the correspondent of Mrs. Chapone[14] herself.

"The girls were up at four this morning, packing her trunks, sister," replied Miss Jemima; "we have made her a bow-pot[15]."

"Say a bouquet[16], sister Jemima, 'tis more genteel."

"Well, a booky as big almost as a hay-stack; I have put up two bottles of gillyflower-water for Mrs. Sedley, and the receipt for making it, in Amelia's box."

"And I trust, Miss Jemima, you have made a copy of Miss Sedley's account[17]. This is it, is it? Very good–ninety-three pounds four shillings. Be kind enough to address it to John Sedley, Esquire[18], and to seal this billet[19] which I have written to his lady."

In Miss Jemima's eyes an autograph letter[20] of her sister, Miss Pinkerton, was an object of as deep veneration[21] as would have been a letter from a sovereign[22]. Only when her pupils quitted the establishment[23], or when they were about to be married, and once, when poor Miss Birch died of the scarlet fever, was Miss Pinkerton known to write personally to the parents of her pupils; and it was Jemima's opinion that if anything could console Mrs. Birch for her daughter's loss, it would be that pious and eloquent composition in which Miss Pinkerton announced the event.

In the present instance Miss Pinkerton's "billet" was to the following effect:

THE MALL, CHISWICK, JUNE 15,18 —.

Madame–After her six years' residence at the Mall, I have the honor and happiness of presenting Miss Amelia Sedley to her parents, as a young lady not unworthy to occupy a fitting position in their polished and refined circle. Those virtues which characterize the young English gentlewoman, those accomplishments which become her birth and station[24], will not be found wanting in the amiable Miss Sedley, whose industry[25] and obedience have endeared her to her instructors, and whose delightful sweetness of temper has charmed her aged and her youthful companions.

In music, in dancing, in orthography[26], in every variety of embroidery[27] and needlework, she will be found to have realized her friends' fondest wishes. In geography there is still much to be desired[28]; and a careful and undeviating use of the backboard[29], for four hours daily during the next three years, is recommended as necessary to the acquirement of that dignified deportment and carriage so requisite for every young lady of fashion.

In the principles of religion and morality, Miss Sedley will be found worthy of an establishment which has been honored by the presence of The Great Lexicographer and the patronage of the admirable Mrs. Chapone. In leaving the Mall, Miss Amelia carries with her the hearts of her companions, and the affectionate regards of her mistress, who has the honor to subscribe herself,

Madame, Your most obliged humble servant,

BARBARA PINKERTON.

P. S, –Miss Sharp accompanies Miss Sedley. It is particularly requested that Miss Sharp's stay in Russell Square may not exceed ten days. The family of distinction with whom she is engaged desire to avail[30] themselves of her services as soon as possible.

This letter completed. Miss Pinkerton proceeded to write her own name and Miss Sedley's in the fly-leaf[31] of a Johnson's Dictionary–the interesting work which she invariably presented to her scholars, on their departure from the Mall. On the cover was inserted a copy of "Lines addressed to a young lady on quitting Miss Pinkerton's school, at the Mall; by the late revered Doctor Samuel Johnson." In fact, the lexicographer's name was always on the lips of this majestic woman[32], and a visit he had paid to her was the cause of her reputation and her fortune.

Being commanded by her elder sister to get "the Dictionary" from the cupboard, Miss Jemima had extracted two copies of the book from the receptacle in question[33]. When Miss Pinkerton had finished the inscription in the first, Jemima, with rather a dubious and timid air, handed her the second.

"For whom is this, Miss Jemima?" said Miss Pinkerton, with awful coldness.

"For Becky Sharp," answered Jemima, trembling very much, and blushing over her withered face and neck, as she turned her back on her sister. "For Becky Sharp; she's going, too."

"MISS JEMIMA!" exclaimed Miss Pinkerton, in the largest capitals. "Are you in your senses[34]?" Replace the Dixonary[35] in the closet, and never venture to take such a liberty in future.

"Well, sister, it's only two and ninepence[36], and poor Becky will be miserable if she don't get one."

"Send Miss Sedley instantly to me," said Miss Pinkerton. And so venturing not to say another word, poor Jemima trotted off[37], exceedingly flurried and nervous.

Miss Sedley's papa was a merchant in London, and a man of some wealth; whereas Miss Sharp was an articled[38] pupil, for whom Miss Pinkerton had done, as she thought, quite enough, without conferring upon her at parting the high honor of the Dixonary.

Although schoolmistresses' letters are to be trusted no more nor less than churchyard epitaphs[39]; yet, as it sometimes happens that a person departs this life who is really deserving of all the praises the stone-cutter carves over his bones; who *is* a good Christian, a good parent, child, wife or husband; who actually *does* leave a disconsolate family to mourn his loss–so in academies of the male and female sex it occurs every now and then that the pupil is fully worthy of the praises bestowed by the disinterested[40] instructor. Now, Miss Amelia Sedley was a young lady of this singular species[41], and deserved not only all that Miss Pinkerton said in her praise, but had many charming qualities which that pompous old Minerva[42] of a woman could not see, from the differences of rank and age between her pupil and herself.

For she could not only sing like a lark, or a Mrs. Billington[43], and dance like Hillisberg[44] or Parisot[45], and embroider beautifully, and spell as well as Dixonary itself, but she had such a kindly, smiling, tender, gentle, generous heart of her own as won the love of everybody who came near her, from Minerva herself down to the poor girl in the scullery[46] and the one-eyed tart-woman's daughter, who was permitted to vend her wares once a week to the young ladies in the Mall. She had twelve intimate and bosom friends out of the twenty-four young ladies. Even envious Miss Briggs never spoke ill of her: high and mighty Miss Saltire (Lord Dexter's granddaughter) allowed[47] that her figure was genteel; and as for Miss Swartz, the rich woolly haired mulatto[48] from St. Kitt's, on the day Amelia went away, she was in such a passion of tears that they were obliged to send for Dr. Floss, and half tipsify her with sal volatile[49]. Miss Pinkerton's attachment was, as may be supposed, from the high position and eminent virtues of that lady, calm and dignified; but Miss Jemima had already whimpered several times at the idea of Amelia's departure, and, but for[50] fear of her sister, would have gone off in downright hysterics, like the heiress (who paid double[51]) of St. Kitt's. Such luxury of grief[52], however, is only allowed to parlor-boarders[53]. Honest Jemima had all the bills, and the washing, and the mending and the puddings, and the plate and crockery, and the servants to superintend. But why speak about her? It is probable that we shall not hear of her again from this moment to the end of time, and that when the great filigree iron gates are once closed on her, she and her awful sister will never issue therefrom[54] into this little world of history.

But as we are to see a great deal of Amelia, there is no harm in saying, at the outset of[55] our acquaintance, that she was a dear little creature; and a great mercy it is, both in life and in novels, which (and the latter especially) abound in villains of the most sombre sort, that we are to have for a constant companion so guileless[56] and good-natured a person. As she is not a heroine, there is no need to describe her person; indeed I am afraid that her nose was rather short than otherwise, and her cheeks a great deal too round and red for a heroine; but her face blushed with rosy health, and her lips with the freshest of smiles, and she had a pair of eyes which sparkled with the brightest and honestest goodhumor, except indeed when they filled with tears, and that was a great deal too often: for the silly thing would cry over a dead canary-bird, or over a mouse that the cat haply[57] had seized upon; or over the end of a novel, were it ever so stupid; and as for saying an unkind word to her, were any persons hard-hearted enough to do so[58]–why, so much the worse for them.[59] Even Miss Pinkerton, that austere[60] and god-like woman, ceased scolding her after the first time, and though she no more comprehended sensibility than she did algebra[61], gave all masters and teachers particular orders to treat Miss Sedley with the utmost gentleness, as harsh treatment was injurious to her.

So that when the day of departure came, between her two customs of laughing and crying, Miss Sedley was greatly puzzled how to act. She was glad to go home, and yet most woefully sad at leaving school. For three days before, little Laura Martin, the orphan, followed her about, like a little dog. She had to make and receive at least fourteen presents–to make fourteen solemn promises of writing every week: "Send my letters under cover to my grandpapa, the Earl of Dexter," said Miss Saltire (who, by the way, was rather shabby); "Never mind the postage but write every day, you dear darling," said the impetuous and woolly-headed, but generous and affectionate,

Miss Swartz; and the orphan, little Laura Martin (who was just in round-hand), took her friend's hand and said, looking up in her face wistfully, "Amelia, when I write to you I shall call you mamma." All which details, I have no doubt, JONES[62], who reads this book at his club, will pronounce to be excessively foolish, trivial, twaddling[63], and ultra-sentimental. Yes; I can see Jones at this minute (rather flushed with his joint of mutton and half pint of wine), taking out bis pencil and scoring under the words "foolish, twaddling," etc., and adding to them his own remark of *"quite true."* Well, he is a lofty man of genius, and admires the great and heroic in life and novels; and so had better take warning and go elsewhere.[64]

Well, then. The flowers, and the presents, and the trunks, and bonnet-boxes of Miss Sedley having been arranged by Mr. Sambo in the carriage, together with a very small and weather-beaten old cow's skin trunk with Miss Sharp's card neatly nailed upon it, which was delivered by Sambo with a grin, and packed by the coachman with a corresponding sneer[65]—the hour for parting came; and the grief of that moment was considerably lessened by the admirable discourse which Miss Pinkerton addressed to her pupil. Not that the parting speech caused Amelia to philosophize[66], or that it armed her in any way with a calmness, the result of argument; but it was intolerably dull, pompous, and tedious; and having the fear of her schoolmistress greatly before her eyes, Miss Sedley did not venture, in her presence, to give way to any ebullitions[67] of private grief. A seed-cake and a bottle of wine were produced in the drawing-room, as on the solemn occasions of the visits of parents, and these refreshments being partaken of, Miss Sedley was at liberty to depart.

"You'll go in[68] and say good-by to Miss Pinkerton, Becky," said Miss Jemima to a young lady of whom nobody took any notice, and who was coming down-stairs with her own bandbox.

"I suppose I must," said Miss Sharp calmly, and much to the wonder of Miss Jemima; and the latter having knocked at the door, and received permission to come in, Miss Sharp advanced in a very unconcerned[69] manner, and said in French, and with a perfect accent, "Mademoiselle, je viens vous faire mes adieux[70]."

Miss Pinkerton did not understand French; she only directed those who did; but biting her lips and throwing up her venerable and Roman-nosed head (on the top of which figured a large and solemn turban), she said, "Miss Sharp, I wish you a good-morning." As the Hammersmith Semiramis spoke, she waved one hand, both by way of adieu and to give Miss Sharp an opportunity of shaking one of the fingers of the hand which was left out for that purpose.

Miss Sharp only folded her own hands with a very frigid smile and bow, and quite declined to accept the proffered[71] honor; on which Semiramis tossed up her turban more indignantly than ever. In fact, it was a little battle between the young lady and the old one, and the latter was worsted[72]. "Heaven bless you, my child," said she, embracing Amelia, and scowling the while over the girl's shoulder at Miss Sharp[73]. "Come away, Becky," said Miss Jemima, pulling the young woman away in great alarm, and the drawing-room door closed upon them forever.

Then came the struggle and parting below. Words refuse to tell it. All the servants were there in the hall–all the dear friends–all the young ladies–the dancing-master who had just arrived; and there was such a scuffling, and hugging, and kissing, and crying, with the hysterical *yoops*[74] of Miss Swartz, the parlor-boarder, from her room, as no pen can depict and the tender heart would fain pass over. The embracing was over; they parted–that is, Miss Sedley parted from her friends. Miss Sharp had demurely entered the carriage some minutes before. Nobody cried for leaving *her*.

Sambo of the bandy legs slammed the carriage-door on his young weeping mistress. He sprang up behind the carriage. "Stop!" cried Miss Jemima, rushing to the gate with a parcel.

"It's some sandwiches, my dear," said she to Amelia. "You may be hungry, you know; and Becky, Becky Sharp,[75] here's a book for you that my sister–that is, I–Johnson's Dixonary, you know; you mustn't leave us without that. Good-by. Drive on, coachman. God bless you!"

And the kind creature retreated into the garden, overcome with emotion.

But, lo! and just as the coach drove off, Miss Sharp put her pale face out of the window and actually flung[76] the book back into the garden.

This almost caused Jemima to faint with terror. "Well, I never[77]." said she. "What an audacious–" Emotion prevented her from completing either sentence. The carriage rolled away; the great gates were closed; the bell rang for the dancing lesson. The world is before two young ladies; and so, farewell to Chiswick Mall.

Notes

1. in its teens: This novel was published in 1847, so "in its teens" refers to the second decade in the 19th century.

2. Chiswick Mall: Chiswick street

3. harness: *n.* a set of leather bands used to control a horse

4. three-cornered hat and wig: Here the hat worn by the coachman and his wig (artificial hair) indicate that this coach is from a rich family.

5. repose: *v.* (literary) rest

6. uncurl: *v.* stretch out from a curled position

7. bandy legs: Legs are curved, so that the knees do not touch.

8. equipage: the large coach (large four-wheeled carriage pulled by horses)

9. shining brass plate: It refers to the plate with the name of this school.

10. stately: *adj.* imposing; grand

11. geranium: a plant with red, pink, or white flowers

12. Semiramis: *n.* a legendary queen in the ancient Babylonian country, who came to rule the country after her husband died; Hammersmith is where the school is located; here "the Semiramis of Hammersmith" refers to Miss Pinkerton and "Semiramis" also echoes with the word "majestic".

13. Doctor Johnson: Samuel Johnson, who was a well-known dictionary writer in Britain

14. Mrs. Chapone: a woman writer but not that famous; the author just wants to show the taste of Miss Pinkerton.

15. bow-pot: a bunch of flowers

16. bouquet: *n.* (French) bunch of flowers for carrying in the hand; Jemima used booky, which sounds like "bouquet" ; here the author just made mock of her that she doesn't know French, in fact, neither does her sister.

17. account: *n.* statement of money owed for services

18. John Sedley, Esquire: Miss Sedley's father; it is a polite way to address gentleman at that time.

19. billet: *n.* a brief of letter; note

20. autograph letter: letter signed by a person's signature

Part Six   The Victorian Literature   167

21. veneration: *n.* respect

22. sovereign: *n.* king or queen; here it shows Jemima's admiration for her sister.

23. establishment: *n.* organization; here it refers to this school.

24. become her birth and station: it means what Amelia learned from this school would match her status.

25. industry: *n.* quality of being hard-working

26. orthography: *n.* spelling

27. embroidery: *n.* the activity of decorating cloth with colored stitches

28. In geography there is still much to be desired: Amelia did not know much about geography.

29. backboard *n.* It is used for straightening the back of women.

30. avail: *v.* be of value or help

31. fly-leaf: *n.* a page at the beginning or end of a book, on which there is no printing

32. In fact, the lexicographer's name was always on the lips of this majestic woman: Miss Pinkerton always talked about Samuel John, the lexicographer to show off her acquaintance with famous people.

33. the receptacle in question: the cupboard mentioned before

34. Are you in your senses?: Are you mad?

35. Dixonary: This spelling of "dictionary" here is to make fun of Miss Pinkerton's pronunciation.

36. two and ninepence: two shillings and nine pence; shilling is an old British coin, used in Britain until 1971.

37. trot off: run with short steps

38. article: *v.* employ someone under contract as a trainee; here it means Miss Sharp was employed by Miss Pinkerton to accompany the girls to study.

39. churchyard epitaph: *n.* words inscribed on a tombstone; here it shows the author thinks the words on the tombstone are overstated, just like the letters written by the school masters.

40. disinterested: *n.* impartial

41. a young lady of this singular species: Miss Sedley does have some good qualities and deserves the praises for her.

42. Minerva: Roman goddess of wisdom; here the author just uses this to mock Miss Pinkerton.

43. Mrs. Billington: a singer at that time

44. Hillisberg: a dancer at that time

45. Parisot: a dancer at that time

46. scullery: *n*. A scullery is a small room next to a kitchen where washing and other household tasks are done.

47. allow: admit or agree

48. mulatto: people who have one black parent and one white

49. volatile: *n*. a smelling salt, used for stimulating people's senses

50. but for: if it had not been for

51. pay double: pay twice as much as the tuition fee

52. luxury of grief: to express one's grief only for the girls from rich families, not for the poor girls

53. parlor-boarder: *n*. privileged students who paid more in boarding school

54. therefrom: from that

55. at the outset of : at the beginning of

56. guileless: *adj*. behaving in an honest way

57. haply: *adv*. by chance

58. were any persons hard-hearted to do so: if any persons were hard-hearted enough to do so

59. so much the worse for them: that is even worse for them; here it means Amelia will cry even harder.

60. austere: *adj*. strict or serious

61. though she no more comprehended sensibility than she did algebra: though she knew nothing about deep feelings and algebra

62. JONES: "John" is a common name in Britain, by which the author referred to

63. twaddling: *adj*. silly or untrue

64. had better take warning and go elsewhere: The author says there are no heroes in this book, so he advises those who want to read stories with great people to choose some other ones to read.

65. with a grin/with a corresponding sneer: The author uses these actions to show

that the coach man and the black servant are very snobbish.

66. to philosophize: to look at something with a tolerant attitude; here the author means Amelia was calm when she listened to Miss Pinkerton's parting speech, not because there was something meaningful in it, but because her presence made her feel scared.

67. ebullition: display

68. You'll go in: This is in the imperative mood expressing an order.

69. unconcerned: uninterested

70. "Mademoiselle, je viens vous faire mes adieux": (French) I have come to say goodbye to you.

71. proffer: *v.* offer

72. worsted: defeated; here it means Miss Sharp refused to shake hands with Miss Pinkerton, which was a humiliation to her.

73. and scowling the while over the girl's shoulder at Miss Sharp: while embracing Amelia, Miss Pinkerton looked at Miss Sharp angrily.

74. yoops: *adj.* sound of weeping

75. Becky, Becky Sharp: Jemima was kind-hearted to call the name Miss Sharp, but she was afraid of her sister, so she added the family name "Sharp".

76. fling: *v.* throw violently

77. Well, I never: I have never seen this

Questions for Discussion

(1) What is the symbolic importance of Becky Sharp throwing the gift of Samuel Johnson's Dictionary out the window of her coach as she leaves Chiswick Mall?

(2) Thackeray's novels presented his characters as they are real in life and the failings of these characters are shown in a humorous and satirical way. Find some examples to show the author's use of humor and satire in this chapter.

(3) Throughout the novel, Thackeray frequently interjects his own commentary into the narrative. What is the effect of these interruptions and how do they contribute to the novel's narrative strategy?

(4) Thackeray and Dickens are both the most well-known novelists in the Victorian period in Britain, but the world described by Thackeray is a little different

from that in Dickens'. What are the differences between these two writers?

Suggested Reading

(1) Frances Theresa Russell. *Satire in the Victorian Novel*. New York: Macmillan, 1920.

(2) William Thackeray. *Vanity Fair*. New York: William Collins, 2011.

(3) William Thackeray. *Vanity Fair*. London: Penguin Classics, 2012.

(4) 范一亭：《维多利亚小说的资本、文化与性别研究》，北京：北京大学出版社，2014 年。

(5) 萨克雷：《名利场》(杨绛点烦本)，杨必译，北京：人民文学出版社，2016 年。

(6) 杨绛：《隐身的串门儿：读书随笔》，北京：生活·读书·新知三联书店，2015 年。

25. Matthew Arnold

Matthew Arnold (1822–1888) received an excellent education in his childhood at Rugby School, Winchester, a public school where his father Thomas Arnold had been the headmaster. At the age of 17, Arnold matriculated at Balliol College, Oxford, where he probed enthusiastically into classical studies and won a Newdigate prize with a poem on Oliver Cromwell. After graduation from college, he worked for a while as a fellow at Oriel College, another famous college in Oxford University. In 1847, Arnold became the secretary to Lord Lansdowne. Four years later, he became an inspector of schools, a post that occupied the rest of Arnold's 35 years of life. Probably under the influence of his father (though Thomas Arnold died in 1842), Arnold exerted much of his time, energy and enthusiasm on his career by traveling extensively across England inspecting schools. He made detailed observation records on what he saw, heard, read, and felt in these schools. These invaluable materials became the first-hand sources of his critical reflection. Arnold developed ideas to improve education in England, especially secondary education. Furthermore, from 1859 to 1865, he visited the European continental countries conducting investigations on their educational systems from which he formed his own insightful and thought-provoking reports, arguing heatedly that England could learn from the European continental education system. As a result, Arnold earned a reputation as a critic on social, cultural, and even economic issues. He also suffered several personal life tragedies, including the death of three of his six children and one of the sons living such a reckless life that Arnold had to undertake lectures in America.

Arnold's literary career can be clearly defined into two stages: the early stage when he devoted himself to poetry writing and the later stage when he was almost fully engaged in prose criticism. His renowned poems include "Dover Beach", "The Scholar Gipsy", "Tristram and Iseult", "Thyrsis", and his representative critical prose works consist of *Essays in Criticism, Culture and Anarchy, Friendship's Garland*. The historical changes and his continental trips influenced Arnold to a great extent. He sharply criticized Philistinism (barbarian state), utilitarianism and materialism of life and culture in England while resolutely supporting the introduction of Hellenic and Hebrew elements (as he called them "light and sweetness" in *Culture and Anarchy*), which originated and developed in Europe. Arnold was one of the few men of letters in his time who had paid special attention to Celtic literature. Arnold wrote *On the Study of Celtic Literature* in 1867, which directly or indirectly resonated with the Celtic Movement taking place in Ireland.

Dover Beach[1]

The sea is calm tonight.
The tide is full, the moon lies fair
Upon the straits[2]–on the French coast the light
Gleams and is gone; the cliffs of England[3] stand;
Glimmering[4] and vast, out in the tranquil[5] bay.
Come to the window, sweet is the night air!
Only, from the long line of spray[6]
Where the sea meets the moon-blanched land[7],

Listen! you hear the grating[8] roar

Of pebbles which the waves draw back, and fling[9],

At their return, up the high strand,

Begin, and cease[10], and then again begin,

With tremulous cadence slow[11], and bring

The eternal note of sadness in.

Sophocles[12] long ago

Heard it on the Aegean[13], and it brought

Into his mind the turbid[14] ebb and flow[15]

Of human misery[16]; we

Find also in the sound a thought,

Hearing it by this distant northern sea[17].

The Sea of Faith[18]

Was once, too, at the full, and round earth's shore

Lay like the folds[19] of a bright girdle[20] furled[21].

But now I only hear

Its melancholy, long, withdrawing roar,

Retreating, to the breath

Of the night wind, down the vast edges drear

And naked shingles[22] of the world.

Ah, love, let us be true

To one another! for the world, which seems

To lie before us like a land of dreams,

So various, so beautiful, so new,

Hath really neither joy, nor love, nor light,

Nor certitude[23], nor peace, nor help for pain[24];

And we are here as on a darkling[25] plain

Swept with confused alarms of struggle and flight,

Where ignorant[26] armies clash[27] by night.

Notes

1. Dover: a coast city in southeast England and across the strait the city on the French side is Calais; notice that in this poem the metrical and rhyming schemes are not strictly followed; this poem is a special kind of poem that is called Dramatic Monologue (戏剧独白诗).

2. fair: white and beautiful; straits: the straits of Dover; notice that the scene of these lines is like this: the poet is talking to someone (his lover) when he is looking at the views of the Dover straits by the window of a hotel.

3. cliff: high steep rock area at the edge of sea or ocean; cliffs of England: the white steep cliffs of Dover coast, which present a spectacular view

4. glimmer: shine with an unsteady light

5. tranquil: calm and steady

6. spray: wave

7. moon-blanched land: the sand land/beach that looks like pure white under the moonlight

8. grating: the action of rubbing two hard surfaces that makes loud or unpleasant sound

9. fling: throw; push away

10. cease: stop; halt

11. tremulous cadence slow: tremulous and slow cadence, turbulent and slow motion or rhythm; this is a typical case of Miltonic structure of modifying a noun, that is, *adj.* + *n.*+ another *adj*.

12. Sophocles: (c. 496 BC–406 BC), one of the great tragedy writers of ancient Greece with such prominent works as *Oedipus Tyrannus* and *Antigone*, expressing the theme of uncertain fate for humans

13. the Aegean: the Aegean Sea, the sea that symbolizes the ancient Greek civilization

14. turbid: mixed or muddy; rough and swift

15. ebb and flow: come and go; wax and wane; up and down

16. human misery: This may refer to the uncertain fate of Oedipus or Antigone who both went through great life tragedies and ended in pricking out their two eyes

and in taking their own life.

17. distant northern sea: Compared with the Aegean sea, Dover is a far-away northern cost city.

18. The Sea of Faith: the sea of religious belief (Christianity)

19. folds: parts of something that are curved, folded or laid in layers

20. girdle: belt

21. furled: folded, rolled or fastened up; the meaning of these lines is: The Sea of Faith once was full and it was around the world's shore, like a furled bright girdle with folds round the earth.

22. naked shingles: mass of small smooth stones on beach that were not covered by weeds or sea water

23. certitude: certainty

24. help for pain: cure or treatment for pain

25. darkling: total darkness

26. ignorant: without knowledge or information; notice here Arnold maybe is calling up the knowledge of Europe to cure the Philistinism in England.

27. The "clash" may refer to the turbulent and uncertain situations in England in Arnold's time and it may also refer to the ancient warfare recorded in Thucydides' *History of the Peloponnesian War*.

Questions for Discussion

(1) Why is Arnold using the irregular pattern of meter and rhyme in this poem? Is it to show his powerful and spontaneous feelings? Is he trying to develop or change traditional English poetry?

(2) Most scholars agreed "Dover Beach" was written during Arnold's honeymoon with his wife in Dover. Take out the lines that are indicative of the dramatic monologue technique in the poem and figure out how it is different from other lyrical or narrative poems.

(3) Compare "Dover Beach" and Robert Browning's "My Last Duchess" and distinguish the similarities (mainly in poetic technique) and more importantly the differences between the two.

(4) The "light and sweetness" are two key elements of cure to Philistinism and materialism in England, as far as Matthew Arnold is concerned. Can you distinguish these two elements in "Dover Beach"? Illustrate your argument with more reading of Arnold's works such as *Culture and Anarchy*.

(5) Why do you think Arnold attaches so much importance to Hellenic and Hebrew culture? What is the origin and development of European cultures and their influence on English literature and culture?

(6) Matthew Arnold and his works have been introduced and translated quite early in China by such scholars as Wu Mi (吴宓). Try your best to find Wu Mi's poetry and his discussion and comments on poetry(《吴宓诗集》,《吴宓诗话》) and read the parts that are related to Arnold. What are Wu Mi's reasons for the introduction of Arnold and his works?

Suggested Reading

(1) Collini Stefan. *Matthew Arnold: A Critical Portrait*. New York: Oxford University Press, 2008.

(2) Park Honan. *Matthew Arnold: A Life*. Cambridge: Harvard University Press, 1983.

(3) Matthew Arnold. *The Works of Matthew Arnold*. London: Wordsworth Editions Ltd. 1995.

(4) 马修·阿诺德：《文化与无政府状态：政治与社会批评》，韩敏中译，北京：生活·读书·新知三联书店，2002年。

(5) 刘锋：《〈圣经〉的文学性诠释与希伯来精神的探求》，北京：北京大学出版社，2007年。

(6) 李振中：《追求和谐的完美——评马修·阿诺德文学与文化批评理论》，上海：上海外语教育出版社，2009年。

26. Charlotte Brontë

Charlotte Brontë (1816–1855), the eldest of the famous Brontë sisters (Charlotte Brontë, Emily Brontë, and Anne Brontë), was born in a Catholic family in Thornton, Yorkshire. Their father, Patrick Brontë, was an Irishman who was born into a peasant family and later became a clergyman in a poor and isolated village on Yorkshire moors. The girls' mother died when they were very young, leaving six children to their domineering father. Life in the remote and lonely village of Haworth gave them little opportunity to contact with the outside world. In 1824, Charlotte and Emily were sent to the Clergy Daughters' School at Cowan Bridge, joining their two eldest sisters. The poor living condition and harsh discipline made a painful impression on young Charlotte's mind. In *Jane Eyre*, the description of protagonist Jane's horrible experience at Lowood School was based on Charlotte's life at Cowan Bridge. After the two eldest sisters died of tuberculosis, Charlotte and Emily were brought home, and taught by their father for the next five or six years. During this period, Charlotte cultivated a fondness for literature by reading and writing stories and plays. Later, she and her two sisters became teachers and governesses. In 1846 they published their poems together under male pseudonyms, and started novel writing. Charlotte's first novel *The Professor*, based on her own experience as a governess, was refused by a publisher, and not published until 1857, two years after her death. Her second novel *Jane Eyre* (1847) was a success, which established her as a promising novelist of the age. She also published two more novels *Shirley* (1849) and *Villette* (1853), both related to her life experience. With only her four semi-autobiographical novels, Charlotte Brontë occupied a very important place in English literature.

With the most successful novel, *Jane Eyre*, Charlotte Brontë created one of the most unforgettable heroines of all time. Jane is an orphan left in the care of her aunt and uncle where she suffers ten years of ill-treatment and abuse. Later she is sent to a charity school for clergyman's daughters. After enduring incredible hardships and cruel environment at Lowood School, she finds a post as a governess to the ward of Mr. Rochester in Thornfield. She falls in love with her employer Mr. Rochester and accepts his proposal for marriage. But on their wedding day, she learns that Mr.

Rochester has a mad wife locked in the attic of Thornfield. She leaves him at once and almost dies from illness on her escape. She is rescued by a kind-hearted clergyman who later asks Jane to marry him and go to India as a missionary. Jane refuses him and finds out Rochester is ruined and blinded by the fire set off by his mad wife. Having already inherited some money from her uncle, she goes back to Rochester and marries him. The central theme of a poor orphan girl's fight for independence and true love is the source of the novel's enduring popularity. Jane, plain in appearance but strong in mind, demonstrates a new type of heroine who is courageous, passionate, and independent. The realistic description of Jane's painful and abusive orphan childhood, her horrible experience in Lowood school, and class and gender inequality expose the cruel reality of Victorian social values and problems.

Jane Eyre

(Chapter XXIII)

A splendid Midsummer shone over England: skies so pure, suns so radiant as were then seen in long succession, seldom favour even singly, our wave-girt land. It was as if a band of Italian days had come from the South, like a flock of glorious passenger birds, and lighted to rest them on the cliffs of Albion[1]. The hay was all got in; the fields round Thornfield were green and shorn; the roads white and baked; the trees were in their dark prime; hedge and wood, full-leaved and deeply tinted, contrasted well with the sunny hue of the cleared meadows between.

On Midsummer-eve[2], Adele, weary with gathering wild strawberries in Hay Lane half the day, had gone to bed with the sun. I watched her drop asleep, and when I left her, I sought the garden.

…

"I grieve to leave Thornfield: I love Thornfield: —I love it, because I have lived in it a full and delightful life, —momentarily at least. I have not been trampled on. I have not been petrified. I have not been buried with inferior minds, and excluded from every glimpse of communion with what is bright and energetic and high. I have talked, face to face, with what I reverence[3], with what I delight in, —with an original, a vigorous, an expanded mind. I have known you, Mr. Rochester; and it strikes me with terror and anguish to feel I absolutely must be torn from you for ever. I see the necessity of departure; and it is like looking on the necessity of death."

"Where do you see the necessity?" he asked suddenly.

"Where? You, sir, have placed it before me."

"In what shape?"

"In the shape of Miss Ingram; a noble and beautiful woman, –your bride."

"My bride! What bride? I have no bride!"

"But you will have."

"Yes; –I will! –I will!" He set his teeth.

"Then I must go: –you have said it yourself."

"No: you must stay! I swear it–and the oath shall be kept."

"I tell you I must go!" I retorted[4], roused to something like passion. "Do you think I can stay to become nothing to you? Do you think I am an automaton[5]? –a machine without feelings? and can bear to have my morsel[6] of bread snatched from my lips, and my drop of living water dashed from my cup? Do you think, because I am poor, obscure, plain, and little, I am soulless and heartless? You think wrong! –I have as much soul as you, –and full as much heart! And if God had gifted me with some beauty and much wealth, I should have made it as hard for you to leave me, as it is now for me to leave you. I am not talking to you now through the medium of custom, conventionalities, nor even of mortal flesh; –it is my spirit that addresses your spirit; just as if both had passed through the grave, and we stood at God's feet, equal, –as we are!"

"As we are!" repeated Mr. Rochester–"so," he added, enclosing me in his arms. Gathering me to his breast, pressing his lips on my lips: "so, Jane!"

"Yes, so, sir," I rejoined: "and yet not so; for you are a married man–or as good as a married man, and wed to one inferior to you–to one with whom you have no sympathy–whom I do not believe you truly love; for I have seen and heard you sneer at her. I would scorn such a union[7]: therefore I am better than you–let me go!"

"Where, Jane? To Ireland?"

"Yes–to Ireland. I have spoken my mind, and can go anywhere now."

"Jane, be still; don't struggle so, like a wild frantic bird that is rending its own plumage[8] in its desperation."

"I am no bird; and no net ensnares me; I am a free human being with an independent will, which I now exert to leave you."

Another effort set me at liberty, and I stood erect before him.

"And your will shall decide your destiny," he said: "I offer you my hand, my heart, and a share of all my possessions."

"You play a farce, which I merely laugh at."

"I ask you to pass through life at my side–to be my second self, and best earthly companion."

"For that fate you have already made your choice, and must abide by it."

"Jane, be still a few moments: you are over-excited: I will be still too."

A waft of wind came sweeping down the laurel-walk, and trembled through the boughs[9] of the chestnut: it wandered away–away–to an indefinite distance–it died. The nightingale's[10] song was then the only voice of the hour: in listening to it, I again wept. Mr. Rochester sat quiet, looking at me gently and seriously. Some time passed before he spoke; he at last said–

"Come to my side, Jane, and let us explain and understand one another."

"I will never again come to your side: I am torn away now, and cannot return."

"But, Jane, I summon you as my wife: it is you only I intend to marry."

I was silent: I thought he mocked me.

"Come, Jane–come hither[11]."

"Your bride stands between us."

He rose, and with a stride reached me.

"My bride is here," he said, again drawing me to him, "because my equal is here, and my likeness. Jane, will you marry me?"

Still I did not answer, and still I writhed myself from his grasp: for I was still incredulous.

"Do you doubt me, Jane?"

"Entirely."

"You have no faith in me?"

"Not a whit.[12]"

"Am I a liar in your eyes?" he asked passionately. "Little sceptic, you SHALL be convinced. What love have I for Miss Ingram? None: and that you know. What love has she for me? None: as I have taken pains to prove: I caused a rumour to reach her that my fortune was not a third of what was supposed, and after that I presented myself to see the result; it was coldness both from her and her mother. I would not–I could not–marry Miss Ingram. You–you strange, you almost unearthly[13] thing!–I love as my own flesh. You–poor and obscure, and small and plain as you are–I entreat to accept me as a husband."

"What, me!" I ejaculated[14], beginning in his earnestness–and especially in his incivility–to credit his sincerity: "me who have not a friend in the world but you–if you are my friend: not a shilling[15] but what you have given me?"

"You, Jane, I must have you for my own–entirely my own. Will you be mine? Say yes, quickly."

"Mr. Rochester, let me look at your face: turn to the moonlight."

"Why?"

"Because I want to read your countenance–turn!"

"There! you will find it scarcely more legible than a crumpled, scratched page. Read on: only make haste, for I suffer."

His face was very much agitated and very much flushed, and there were strong workings in the features, and strange gleams in the eyes.

"Oh, Jane, you torture me!" he exclaimed. "With that searching and yet faithful and generous look, you torture me!"

"How can I do that? If you are true, and your offer real, my only feelings to you must be gratitude and devotion–they cannot torture."

"Gratitude!" he ejaculated; and added wildly–"Jane accept me quickly. Say, Edward–give me my name–Edward–I will marry you."

"Are you in earnest? Do you truly love me? Do you sincerely wish me to be your wife?"

"I do; and if an oath is necessary to satisfy you, I swear it."

"Then, sir, I will marry you."

"Edward–my little wife!"

"Dear Edward!"

"Come to me–come to me entirely now," said he; and added, in his deepest tone, speaking in my ear as his cheek was laid on mine, "Make my happiness–I will make yours."

"God pardon me!" he subjoined ere[16] long; "and man meddle not with me: I have her, and will hold her."

"There is no one to meddle, sir. I have no kindred to interfere."

"No–that is the best of it," he said. And if I had loved him less I should have thought his accent and look of exultation savage; but, sitting by him, roused from the nightmare of parting–called to the paradise of union–I thought only of the bliss given me to drink in so abundant a flow. Again and again he said, "Are you happy, Jane?" And again and again I answered, "Yes." After which he murmured, "It will atone– it will atone. Have I not found her friendless, and cold, and comfortless? Will I not guard, and cherish, and solace her? Is there not love in my heart, and constancy in my resolves? It will expiate at God's tribunal[17]. I know my Maker[18] sanctions what I do. For the world's judgment–I wash my hands thereof. For man's opinion–I defy it."

But what had befallen the night? The moon was not yet set, and we were all in shadow: I could scarcely see my master's face, near as I was. And what ailed the chestnut tree? it writhed and groaned; while wind roared in the laurel walk, and came sweeping over us.

"We must go in," said Mr. Rochester: "the weather changes. I could have sat with thee[19] till morning, Jane."

"And so," thought I, "could I with you." I should have said so, perhaps, but a livid, vivid spark leapt out of a cloud at which I was looking, and there was a crack, a crash, and a close rattling peal; and I thought only of hiding my dazzled eyes against Mr. Rochester's shoulder.

The rain rushed down. He hurried me up the walk, through the grounds, and into the house; but we were quite wet before we could pass the threshold. He was taking off my shawl in the hall, and shaking the water out of my loosened hair, when Mrs. Fairfax emerged from her room. I did not observe her at first, nor did Mr. Rochester. The lamp was lit. The clock was on the stroke of twelve.

"Hasten to take off your wet things," said he; "and before you go, good-night– good-night, my darling!"

He kissed me repeatedly. When I looked up, on leaving his arms, there stood the widow, pale, grave, and amazed. I only smiled at her, and ran upstairs. "Explanation will do for another time," thought I. Still, when I reached my chamber[20], I felt a pang at the idea she should even temporarily misconstrue what she had seen. But joy soon effaced[21] every other feeling; and loud as the wind blew, near and deep as the thunder crashed, fierce and frequent as the lightning gleamed, cataract-like as the rain fell during a storm of two hours' duration, I experienced no fear and little awe. Mr. Rochester came thrice[22] to my door in the course of it, to ask if I was safe and tranquil: and that was comfort, that was strength for anything.

Before I left my bed in the morning, little Adele came running in to tell me that the great horse-chestnut at the bottom of the orchard had been struck by lightning in the night, and half of it split away.

Notes

1. Albion: a poetic or literary term for Britain or England (often used when referring to ancient or historical times)

2. Midsummer-eve: the night before Midsummer's Day (June 24)

3. reverence: *v.* regard or treat with deep respect

4. retort: *v.* to reply quickly to a comment, in an angry, offended or humorous way

5. automaton: *n.* a moving mechanical device made in imitation of a human being, used in similes and comparisons to refer to a person who seems to act in a mechanical or unemotional way

6. morsel: *n.* a small piece or amount of food; a mouthful

7. union: *n.* a marriage

8. plumage: *n.* feather

9. bough: *n.* a main branch of a tree

10. nightingale: *n.* a small European thrush with drab brownish plumage, noted for the rich melodious song of the male, heard especially at night in the breeding season

11. hither: *adv.* to or toward this place

12. not a whit: not a bit

13. unearthly: *adj.* unnatural or mysterious

14. ejaculate: *v.* to say something quickly and suddenly

15. shilling: *n.* a former British coin and monetary unit, equals one twentieth of a pound or twelve pence

16. ere: *prep.* before

17. tribunal: *n.* a court of justice

18. Maker: *n.* God; the Creator

19. thee: *pron.* archaic or dialect form of "you", as the singular object of a verb or preposition

20. chamber: *n.* a private room, typically a bedroom

21. efface: *v.* destroy or remove

22. thrice: *adv.* three times

Questions for Discussion

(1) Jane may be plain looking, but she has a strong sense of charm and beauty. In what way does she attract Mr. Rochester? Compared with Jane, Mr. Rochester has a large fortune and social status. Do you think their marriage would be an equal match? In your opinion, what is important in a marriage? Money, social status or love?

(2) Many critics believed that the heroine Jane in *Jane Eyre* was the voice of Charlotte Brontë to express her rather radical opinions on social class and gender equality. Based on your knowledge of Victorian values and social conventions in 19th century England, explain the role and status of women both in society and family at that time.

(3) *Jane Eyre* is considered one of the earliest feminist novels by many feminist critics, for Jane's self-respect and pursuit of equality and independence. Try to find scenes or dialogues that reflect Jane's feminist ideas in the text.

Suggested Reading

(1) Charlotte Brontë. *Jane Eyre*. New York: Signet Classics, 2008.

(2) Elizabeth Gaskell. *The Life of Charlotte Brontë*. London: Penguin Classics, 1998.

(3) Diane Long Hoeveler & Deborah Denenholz Morse, ed. *Time, Space, and Place in Charlotte Brontë*. New York: Routledge Publishing, 2016.

(4) 夏洛蒂·勃朗特：《简·爱》，吴钧燮译，北京：人民文学出版社，1990年。

(5) 盖斯凯尔夫人：《夏洛蒂·勃朗特传》，张淑荣等译，北京：团结出版社，2000年。

(6) 中国社会科学院外国文学研究资料丛刊编辑委员会编，杨静远编选：《勃朗特姐妹研究》，北京：中国社会科学出版社，1983年。

27. Emily Brontë

Emily Brontë (1818–1848) was the sister of Charlotte and Anne Brontë. They are called the "Brontë Sisters" in English history. Emily Brontë was born in a village in Yorkshire, the fifth child in this family. Their father was a clergyman, who had published his own literary works and taught his children a lot in reading and thinking. Emily was fond of nature and the wild, which later became the salient feature in her novel. When their mother died, four girls were sent to the Clergy Daughters' School to receive education in 1824. But with the severe spread of tuberculosis, only Charlotte and Emily came back safely. Emily was greatly inspired by her father and siblings. She and her sisters broke the shackles of women in many ways. They were once governesses and then published a collection *Poems by Currer, Ellis, and Acton Bell* together in 1846. At the time, most male novelists could not bear the idea that females produced literary works. In this way, the Brontë sisters wrote under their male pseudonyms. One year later, still under the male name Emily Brontë created *Wuthering Heights* (1847). Although this novel did not receive an active response at the time, the value of it finally underwent the trial of time. It became a priceless classic in English literature. At the age of thirty, Emily Brontë also died of tuberculosis. Her bold breakthrough in female writing was profound for the following generations.

Wuthering Heights belongs to the literary genre–gothic novel. With an isolated setting, gothic novels always generate an aura of horror and mystery. For example, the setting of *Jane Eyre* is a typical demonstration of gothic novels. The story in

Wuthering Heights happens on the remote moors. Opening with the visit of a tenant named Lockwood, this story is told by the housekeeper, Nelly Dean, in flashbacks. With the span of forty years, this whole story appears before Lockwood. Mr. Earnshaw, the father of Catherine and Hindley, brings a gypsy boy home. His name is Heathcliff. Catherine likes Heathcliff's company and soon they fall in love with each other. But Hindley despises Heathcliff and always treats him like a slave. Heathcliff's situation becomes worse after the death of Mr. Earnshaw. He has to bear the insult of Hindley in order to stay with Catherine, the love of his life. Then everything changes when Catherine marries Edgar Linton, the young master of Thrushcross Grange, the neighbor of Wuthering Heights. Catherine's betrayal is a heavy blow to Heathcliff. He leaves Wuthering Heights for three years. When he comes back, he becomes a total villain and takes revenge on all of them. The only thing that remains unchangeable is his crazy obsession with Catherine, which later destroys the lives of the next generation. This novel seems to be framed in a simple structure of cause and effect. In fact, it is contrived in an intricate network by which various themes await further interpretations. For example, how to define the character Heathcliff? A protagonist or an antagonist?

Wuthering Heights

(Chapter XV)

Another week over–and I[1] am so many days nearer health, and spring! I have now heard all my neighbour's history, at different sittings, as the housekeeper could spare time from more important occupations. I'll continue it in her own words, only a little condensed. She[2] is, on the whole, a very fair narrator, and I don't think I could improve her style.

In the evening, she said, the evening of my visit to the Heights, I knew, as well as if I saw him, that Mr. Heathcliff was about the place; and I shunned going out, because I still carried his letter[3] in my pocket, and didn't want to be threatened or teased any more. I had made up my mind not to give it till my master went somewhere, as I could not guess how its receipt would affect Catherine. The consequence was, that it did not reach her before the lapse of three days. The fourth was Sunday, and I brought it into her room after the family were gone to church. There was a manservant left to keep the house with me, and we generally made a practice of locking the doors during the hours of service; but on that occasion the weather was so warm and pleasant that I set them wide open, and, to fulfil my engagement, as I knew who would be coming[4], I told my companion that the mistress wished very much for some oranges, and he must run over to the village and get a few, to be paid for on the morrow. He departed, and I went upstairs.

Mrs. Linton sat in a loose, white dress, with a light shawl[5] over her shoulders, in the recess of the open window, as usual. Her thick, long hair had been partly removed at the beginning of her illness, and now she wore it simply combed in its natural tresses over her temples and neck. Her appearance was altered, as I had told Heathcliff; but when she was calm, there seemed unearthly[6] beauty in the change. The flash of her eyes had been succeeded by a dreamy and melancholy softness; they no longer gave the impression of looking at the objects around her: they appeared always to gaze beyond, and far beyond–you would have said out of this world. Then the paleness of her face–its haggard[7] aspect having vanished as she recovered flesh–and the peculiar expression arising from her mental state, though painfully suggestive of their causes, added to the touching interest which she awakened; and–invariably to me, I know, and to any person who saw her, I should think–refuted more tangible proofs of convalescence, and stamped[8] her as one doomed to decay.

A book lay spread on the sill before her, and the scarcely perceptible wind fluttered its leaves at intervals. I believe Linton had laid it there: for she never endeavoured to divert herself with reading, or occupation of any kind, and he would spend many an hour in trying to entice her attention to some subject which had formerly been her amusement. She was conscious of his aim, and in her better moods endured his efforts placidly, only showing their uselessness by now and then suppressing a wearied sigh, and checking him at last with the saddest of smiles and kisses. At other times, she would turn petulantly away, and hide her face in her hands, or even push him off angrily; and then he took care to let her alone, for he was certain of doing no good.

Gimmerton chapel bells were still ringing; and the full, mellow flow of the beck in the valley came soothingly on the ear. It was a sweet substitute for the yet absent murmur of the summer foliage, which drowned that music about the Grange[9] when the trees were in leaf. At Wuthering Heights it always sounded on quiet days following a great thaw or a season of steady rain. And of Wuthering Heights Catherine was thinking as she listened: that is, if she thought or listened at all; but she had the vague, distant look I mentioned before, which expressed no recognition of material things either by ear or eye.

'There's a letter for you, Mrs Linton,' I said, gently inserting it in one hand that rested on her knee. 'You must read it immediately, because it wants an answer. Shall I break the seal?'

'Yes,' she answered, without altering the direction of her eyes. I opened it–it was very short. 'Now', I continued, 'read it.' She drew away her hand, and let it fall. I replaced it in her lap, and stood waiting till it should please her to glance down; but that movement was so long delayed that at last I resumed:

'Must I read it, ma'am? It is from Mr Heathcliff.'

There was a start and a troubled gleam[10] of recollection, and a struggle to arrange her ideas. She lifted the letter, and seemed to peruse it; and when she came to the signature she sighed: yet still I found she had not gathered its import, for, upon my desiring to hear her reply, she merely pointed to the name, and gazed at me with mournful and questioning eagerness.

'Well, he wishes to see you,' said I, guessing her need of an interpreter. 'He's in the garden by this time, and impatient to know what answer I shall bring.'

As I spoke, I observed a large dog lying on the sunny grass beneath raise its ears as if about to bark, and then smoothing them back, announce, by a wag of the tail, that someone approached whom it did not consider a stranger. Mrs Linton bent forward, and listened breathlessly. The minute after a step traversed the hall; the open house was too tempting for Heathcliff to resist walking in: most likely he supposed that I was inclined to shirk my promise[11], and so resolved to trust to his own audacity. With straining eagerness Catherine gazed towards the entrance of her chamber. He did not hit the right room directly, she motioned me to admit[12] him, but he found it out ere I could reach the door, and in a stride or two was at her side, and had her grasped in his arms.

He neither spoke nor loosed his hold for some five minutes, during which period he bestowed[13] more kisses than ever he gave in his life before, I dare say: but then my mistress had kissed him first, and I plainly saw that he could hardly bear, for downright agony, to look into her face! The same conviction had stricken him as me, from the instant he beheld her, that there was no prospect of ultimate recovery there—she was fated, sure to die.

'Oh, Cathy! Oh, my life! how can I bear it?' was the first sentence he uttered, in a tone that did not seek to disguise his despair. And now he stared at her so earnestly that I thought the very intensity of his gaze would bring tears into his eyes; but they burned with anguish: they did not melt.

'What now?' said Catherine, leaning back, and returning his look with a suddenly clouded[14] brow: her humour[15] was a mere vane for constantly varying caprices[16]. 'You and Edgar have broken my heart, Heathcliff! And you both came to bewail[17] the deed to me, as if you were the people to be pitied! I shall not pity you, not I. You have killed me—and thriven on[18] it, I think. How strong you are! How many years do you mean to live after I am gone?'

Heathcliff had knelt on one knee to embrace her; he attempted to rise, but she seized his hair, and kept him down.

'I wish I could hold you,' she continued bitterly, 'till we were both dead! I shouldn't care what you suffered. I care nothing for your sufferings. Why shouldn't you suffer? I do! Will you forget me? Will you be happy when I am in the earth? Will you say twenty years hence, "That's the grave of Catherine Earnshaw. I loved her long ago, and was wretched to lose her; but it is past. I've loved many others since: my children are dearer to me than she was; and at death, I shall not rejoice that I am going to her: I shall be sorry that I must leave them!" Will you say so, Heathcliff?'

'Don't torture me till I am as mad as yourself,' cried he, wrenching his head free, and grinding his teeth.

The two, to a cool spectator, made a strange and fearful picture. Well might Catherine deem that heaven would be a land of exile to her, unless with her mortal body she cast away her moral character also. Her present countenance had a wild vindictiveness[19] in its white cheek, and a bloodless lip and scintillating[20] eye; and she retained in her closed fingers a portion of the locks[21] she had been grasping. As to her companion, while raising himself with one hand, he had taken her arm with the other;

and so inadequate was his stock of gentleness to the requirements of her condition, that on his letting go I saw four distinct impressions left blue in the colourless skin.

'Are you possessed with a devil,' he pursued savagely, 'to talk in that manner to me when you are dying? Do you reflect that all those words will be branded[22] on my memory, and eating deeper eternally after you have left me? You know you lie to say I have killed you: and, Catherine, you know that I could as soon forget you as my existence[23]! Is it not sufficient for your infernal selfishness, that while you are at peace I shall writhe in the torments of hell?'

'I shall not be at peace,' moaned Catherine, recalled to a sense of physical weakness by the violent, unequal throbbing[24] of her heart, which beat visibly and audibly under this excess of agitation. She said nothing further till the paroxysm[25] was over; then she continued, more kindly—

'I'm not wishing you greater torment than I have, Heathcliff. I only wish us never to be parted: and should a word of mine distress you hereafter, think I feel the same distress underground, and for my own sake, forgive me! Come here and kneel down again! You never harmed me in your life. Nay, if you nurse anger[26], that will be worse to remember than my harsh words! Won't you come here again? Do!'

Heathcliff went to the back of her chair, and leant over, but not so far as to let her see his face, which was livid with emotion. She bent round to look at him; he would not permit it: turning abruptly, he walked to the fireplace, where he stood, silent, with his back towards us. Mrs Linton's glance followed him suspiciously: every movement woke a new sentiment in her. After a pause and a prolonged gaze, she resumed; addressing me in accents of indignant disappointment—

'Oh, you see, Nelly, he would not relent[27] a moment to keep me out of the grave. That is how I'm loved! Well, never mind. That is not my Heathcliff. I shall love mine yet; and take him with me: he's in my soul. And', added she, musingly, 'the thing that irks[28] me most in this shattered prison, after all. I'm tired, tired of being enclosed here. I'm wearying to escape into that glorious world, and to be always there: not seeing it dimly through tears, and yearning for it through the walls of an aching heart; but really with it, and in it. Nelly, you think you are better and more fortunate than I; in full health and strength: you are sorry for me—very soon that will be altered. I shall be sorry for you. I shall be incomparably beyond and above you all. I wonder he won't be near me!' She went on to herself. 'I thought he wished it. Heathcliff, dear! you should not be sullen[29] now. Do come to me, Heathcliff.'

In her eagerness she rose and supported herself on the arm of the chair. At that earnest appeal he turned to her, looking absolutely desperate. His eyes, wide and wet, at last flashed fiercely on her; his breast heaved convulsively. An instant they held asunder[30], and then how they met[31] I hardly saw, but Catherine made a spring[32], and he caught her, and they were locked in an embrace from which I thought my mistress would never be released alive: in fact, to my eyes, she seemed directly insensible. He flung himself into the nearest seat, and on my approaching hurriedly to ascertain if she had fainted, he gnashed at me, and foamed like a mad dog, and gathered her to him with greedy jealousy. I did not feel as if I were in the company of a creature of my own species: it appeared that he would not understand, though I spoke to him; so I stood off, and held my tongue, in great perplexity.

A movement of Catherine's relieved me a little presently: she put up her hand to clasp his neck, and bring her cheek to his as he held her; while he, in return, covering her with frantic caresses[33], said wildly–

'You teach me now how cruel you've been–cruel and false. Why did you despise me? Why did you betray your own heart, Cathy? I have not one word of comfort. You deserve this. You have killed yourself. Yes, you may kiss me, and cry; and ring out my kisses and tears: they'll blight[34] you–they'll damn[35] you. You loved me–then what right had you to leave me? What right–answer me–for the poor fancy you felt for Linton? Because misery and degradation, and death, and nothing that God or Satan could inflict would have parted us, you, of your own will, did it. I have not broken your heart–you have broken it; and in breaking it, you have broken mine. So much the worse for me, that I am strong. Do I want to live? What kind of living will it be when you–oh, God! would you like to live with your soul in the grave?'

'Let me alone. let me alone,' sobbed Catherine. 'If I have done wrong, I'm dying for it. It is enough! You left me too: but I won't upbraid[36] you! I forgive you. Forgive me!'

'It is hard to forgive, and to look at those eyes, and feel those wasted[37] hands,' he answered. 'Kiss me again; and don't let me see your eyes! I forgive what you have done to me. I love my murderer–but yours! How can I?'

They were silent–their faces hid against each other, and washed by each other's tears. At least, I suppose the weeping was on both sides; as it seemed Heathcliff could weep on a great occasion like this.

I grew very uncomfortable, meanwhile; for the afternoon wore fast away, the man whom I had sent off returned from his errand, and I could distinguish, by the shine of the westering sun[38] up the valley, a concourse[39] thickening outside Gimmerton chapel porch.

'Service is over.' I announced. 'My master[40] will be here in half an hour.'

Heathcliff groaned a curse, and strained Catherine closer: she never moved.

Ere long[41] I perceived a group of the servants passing up the road towards the kitchen wing. Mr Linton was not far behind; he opened the gate himself and sauntered[42] slowly up, probably enjoying the lovely afternoon that breathed as soft as summer.

'Now he is here,' I exclaimed. 'For Heaven's sake, hurry down! You'll not meet anyone on the front stairs. Do be quick; and stay among the trees till he is fairly in[43].'

'I must go, Cathy,' said Heathcliff, seeking to extricate[44] himself from his companion's arms. 'But if I live, I'll see you again before you are asleep. I won't stray five yards from your window.'

'You must not go!' she answered, holding him as firmly as her strength allowed. 'You shall not, I tell you.'

'For one hour,' he pleaded earnestly.

'Not for one minute,' she replied.

'I must–Linton will be up immediately,' persisted the alarmed intruder.

He would have risen, and unfixed her fingers by the act–she clung fast, gasping: there was mad resolution in her face.

'No!' she shrieked[45]. 'Oh, don't, don't go. It is the last time! Edgar will not hurt us. Heathcliff, I shall die! I shall die!'

'Damn the fool! There he is,' cried Heathcliff, sinking back into his seat. 'Hush, my darling! Hush, hush, Catherine! I'll stay. If he shot me so, I'd expire with a blessing on my lips.'

And there they were fast again. I heard my master mounting[46] the stairs–the cold sweat ran from my forehead: I was horrified.

'Are you going to listen to her ravings[47]?' I said passionately. 'She does not know what she says. Will you ruin her, because she has not wit[48] to help herself? Get up! You could be free instantly. That is the most diabolical[49] deed that ever you did. We are all done for—master, mistress, and servant.

I wrung my hands, and cried out; Mr Linton hastened his step at the noise. In the midst of my agitation, I was sincerely glad to observe that Catherine's arms had fallen relaxed, and her head hung down.

'She's fainted or dead,' I thought: 'so much the better. Far better that she should be dead, than lingering a burden and a misery-maker to all about her.'

Edgar sprang to his unbidden guest[50], blanched[51] with astonishment and rage. What he meant to do, I cannot tell; however, the other stopped all demonstrations, at once, by placing the lifeless looking form in his arms.

'Look there!' he said; 'unless you be a fiend, help her first—then you shall speak to me!'

He walked into the parlour, and sat down. Mr Linton summoned me, and with great difficulty, and after resorting to many means, we managed to restore her to sensation; but she was all bewildered; she sighed, and moaned, and knew nobody. Edgar, in his anxiety for her, forgot her hated friend. I did not. I went, at the earliest opportunity, and besought him to depart; affirming that Catherine was better, and he should hear from me in the morning how she passed the night.

'I shall not refuse to go out of doors,' he answered; 'but I shall stay in the garden: and, Nelly, mind you keep your word tomorrow. I shall be under those larch trees. Mind! or I pay another visit, whether Linton be in or not.'

He sent a rapid glance through the half-open door of the chamber, and, ascertaining that what I stated was apparently true, delivered the house of his luckless presence.

Notes

1. I: the narrator of this novel, also a tenant of Wuthering Heights

2. She: Ellen Dean, the other narrator, a loyal servant to the Earnshaws and later the Lintons

3. his letter: Mr. Heathcliff's letter to Catherine who is now Mrs. Linton

4. who would be coming: Ellen knew that Mr. Heathcliff was about to visit Catherine.

5. shawl: a large piece of woolen cloth worn by females

6. unearthly: extraordinary

7. haggard: being tired

8. stamp: mark, implying that Catherine's health is declining

9. Grange: the Thrushcross Grange where the Lintons live

10. gleam: light

11. shirk my promise: avoid keeping my promise

12. admit: guide Mr. Heathcliff toward the room

13. bestow: give

14. clouded: gloomy

15. humour: the state of mood

16. caprices: sudden changes

17. bewail: lament

18. thriven on: enjoyed doing something unpleasant

19. vindictiveness: hatred to revenge

20. scintillating: twinkling

21. the locks: a small bunch of hairs

22. brand: stamp; last forever

23. I could…my existence: I could not forget you until my death.

24. throbbing: beating

25. paroxysm: a sudden occurrence of emotion

26. nurse anger: harbor anger all the time

27. relent: permit

28. irk: annoy

29. sullen: unpleasant; depressed

30. asunder: apart

31. meet: hug

32. spring: a jump

33. caresses: gentle touches with love

34. blight: damage

35. damn: curse

36. upbraid: scold

37. wasted: thin

38. westering sun: sunset was nearing

39. concourse: a large crowd of people

40. My master: Edgar Linton, Catherine's husband

41. ere long: before long

42. saunter: walk casually

43. till he is fairly in: till he enters the room

44. extricate: free

45. shriek: scream

46. mounting: climbing up

47. ravings: crazy talking

48. has not wit: has no wit

49. diabolical: evil

50. unbidden guest: unexpected guest

51. blanched: pale

Questions for Discussion

(1) Can you understand Heathcliff's love for Catherine? What has caused their tragedy?

(2) What is Heathcliff's role in the story? Is he a protagonist or an antagonist?

(3) Try to finish reading this novel and analyze the influence of the setting on the characters' personalities.

(4) Can Heathcliff's revenge be justified? How do you understand his revenge from the perspective of human nature?

(5) *Wuthering Heights* is considered a Gothic novel. What are the characteristics of Gothic novels?

(6) Compare this novel with *The Count of Monte Cristo* by Alexandre Dumas. What is the difference between Heathcliff and Edmond Dantes in their ways of revenge?

Suggested Reading

(1) Emily Brontë. *Wuthering Heights*. New York: Oxford University Press, 1995.

(2) Edward Chitham. *The Birth of Wuthering Heights*. New York: Palgrave Macmillan, 2001.

(3) Janet Gezari. *Last Things: Emily Brontë's Poems*. New York: Oxford University Press, 2007.

(4) 艾米莉·勃朗特：《呼啸山庄》，杨苡译，南京：译林出版社，2010年。

(5)《论埃米莉·勃朗特的〈呼啸山庄〉》，北京：人民文学出版社，1958年。

(6) 王喆：《多维视野中的〈呼啸山庄〉》，成都：四川大学出版社，2014年。

28. Alfred Tennyson

Alfred Tennyson(1809–1892) was an eminent Victorian poet. He held the position of Poet Laureate that was the highest official position of a poet after William Wordsworth. Some historians even addressed the period from 1832 to the time of his death as "the Age of Tennyson".

Tennyson was often called by his title, Alfred, Lord Tennyson. He was born into a clergyman's family. His father was well-educated and encouraged his children to read books. The Tennyson children all showed their literary talent when they were young. Because of the family library, Tennyson became familiar with many famous works and began writing poems at an early age. In 1827, Tennyson entered Trinity College, Cambridge and there he met Arthur Henry Hallam, who became his best friend in his life. In 1831, Tennyson's father died and the family was in debt, so Tennyson left Cambridge without a degree. He began to publish his poetry while still in college, but this and another collection did not receive much public attention. In 1833, his best friend Hallam suddenly died, which affected him deeply. Because of these reasons, Tennyson published nothing for ten years. Then in 1842, he came forth with two volumes of poetry that earned him great acclaim. Two long poems came out in 1847 and 1850–*The Princess* and *In Memoriam* considered his best piece – written in memory of Arthur Henry Hallam. In 1855, he published *Maud and Other Poems* and in 1859, he published *Idylls of the King*, which was based on the legend of King Arthur. In 1884, he was knighted. In 1892, he died and was buried in the Poets' Corner of the Westminster Abbey.

Tennyson's poetry is remarkable for its metrical variety, rich descriptive imagery, exquisite verbal melodies and various themes. From his poems, one can see his great interest in Greek mythology and Medieval legends, like *Ulysses* and *Idylls of the King*. In some of his poems, he also touched on themes of loneliness and death, such as "Break, Break, Break" and "Crossing the Bar".

Break, Break, Break[1]

Break, break, break[2],
On thy cold gray stones, O Sea[3]!
And I would[4] that my tongue could utter
The thoughts that arise in me[5].

O well for[6] the fisherman's boy,
That he shouts with his sister at play!
O well for the sailor lad[7],
That he sings in his boat on the bay!

And the stately[8] ships go on
To their haven[9] under the hill;
But O for the touch of a vanish'd hand[10],
And the sound of a voice that is still[11]!

Break, break, break,
At the foot of thy crags[12], O Sea!
But the tender grace of a day[13] that is dead
Will never come back to me.

Notes

1. This short poem, like the long poem *In Memoriam,* was written by Tennyson to express his lament over the death of his friend Arthur Henry Hallam. Hallam was the poet's best friend in Cambridge, and did much to shape his mind. These two friends once traveled through the English Channel to Spain in 1929. But unfortunately, Hallam died four years later in Vienna, which was a heavy blow for the poet. Later, the poet wrote many poems for his friend. "Break, Break, Break" expresses the poet's loneliness at the loss of his dear friend.

2. break: *v.* (of the sea) curl and fall in waves; here the poet uses the repetition of the word to describe the rolling waves toward the shore.

3. O sea: Here the poet addresses the sea.

4. I would: I wish

5. The thoughts that arise in me: The poet wishes that he could have the ability to express troubling thoughts that won't go away.

6. O well for: O, it would be well for

7. lad: *n.* young man or boy; these sentences show two different experience: the fisherman's boys and girls play and the young sailor sing, while the poet is in great sadness.

8. stately: *adj.* impressive and graceful

9. haven: *n.* a place where people feel safe, secure and happy

10. a vanish'd hand: the hand of his friend who has vanished

11. a voice that is still: the voice of his friend can no longer be heard

12. crag: *n.* high, steep or rugged mass of rock

13. tender grace of a day: the loving kindness of the day when I was enjoying your company

Crossing the Bar[1]

Sunset and evening star[2],
And one clear call for me!
And may there be no moaning of the bar[3],

When I put out to sea.

But such a tide as moving seems asleep,
Too full for sound and foam[4],
When that which drew from out the boundless deep
Turns again home[5]!

Twilight and evening bell,
And after that the dark[6]!
And may there be no sadness of farewell,
When I embark;

For though from out our bourne[7] of Time and Place
The flood may bear[8] me far,
I hope to see my Pilot[9] face to face
When I have crossed the bar.

Notes

1. This poem was written in 1889 when Tennyson's illness caused him to compose it. Though this poem was not the last poem written by the poet, it appears as the final poem of all his collections of work due to the theme of this poem: death and the acceptance of it. bar: *n.* bank or ridge of sand, etc. across the mouth of a river or the entrance to a bay; here the bar symbolizes the boundary of one's life.

2. Sunset and evening star: These two images depict a picture of the closing day, symbolizing the late years of one's life.

3. moaning of the bar: the mournful sound of the ocean beating on the bar

4. Too full for sound and foam: The tide is overflowing with sound and foam, thus it is calm.

5. Turns again home: the waves return to the deep ocean; here it refers to the eternal home of the soul.

6. the dark: Here the darkness refers to death.

7. bourne: *n.* domain; bound

8. bear: *v.* (formal) carry

9. Pilot: Here it refers to God.

Questions for Discussion

Questions for "Break, Break, Break":

(1) What is the significance of the repeated words in the title of this poem?

(2) Why is the sea a useful symbol in bringing comfort to the speaker?

(3) How do the last two lines "But the tender grace of a day that is dead/ Will never come back to me" compare with some other lines in Chinese poems which express similar feelings?

Questions for "Crossing the Bar":

(1) What does the sea symbolize in this poem?

(2) What does the line "And may there be no sadness of farewell" mean?

(3) Note the use of alliteration in "clear call", the use of two successive /c/ sounds to reinforce its meaning. Identify more examples of alliteration in this poem.

(4) Who is the Pilot? Why does the poet want to "see my Pilot face to face"?

(5) Read other poems by Tennyson and discuss how "the passion of the past" is reflected in his poems.

Suggested Reading

(1) Alfred Tennyson. *The Works of Alfred Tennyson*. London: British Library Historical Print Editions, 2011.

(2) Alfred Tennyson. *The Poems of Tennyson*, Volume I. II, III. 2nd ed. London: Edited by Christopher Ricks. Longman Group UK Limited, 1987.

(3) Herbert Tucker. *Critical Essays on Alfred Lord Tennyson*. New York: G.K. Hall & Co., 1993.

(4) 丁尼生：《丁尼生诗选》（英汉对照），黄杲炘译，北京：外语教学与研究出版社，2014 年。

(5) 阿尔弗雷德·丁尼生：《亚瑟王传奇：丁尼生诗歌故事》，诺拉·切森改写，上海：上海科学技术文献出版社，2014 年。

29. Robert Browning

Robert Browning (1812–1889) was one of the notable Victorian poets. He was not as famous as his contemporaries at first, but later his unique style in poetry–the subtle psychological analysis and the form of dramatic monologue–won him high praise. He was raised in a well-off family. His mother was a gifted musician and his father, also named Robert Browning, was a collector of literary books, which gave Browning great access to literature. In 1824, Robert Browning, finished his first poetry work, which he destroyed after failed publishing. Besides being a poet, Browning was also a multilingual speaker, fluent in Latin, Italian and Greek. Browning's style and thought in poetry were greatly influenced by the poetry works of a Romantic poet, Percy Shelley. In 1833, Browning anonymously published his first long poem "Pauline", but it was not well-received. With spiritual confession, this poem was fragmented and obscure. But soon after that in 1835, his poem "Paracelsus" provided him with his first success, gaining him popularity of the time. Then Browning started to write drama during the heyday of dramatic monologue, a special poetic form used earlier by John Donne and other poets. It was Browning who enriched the width and breadth of dramatic monologue. Before 1845, Browning produced several volumes. When he met Elizabeth Barrett in 1845, he fell in love with her and eloped with her to Italy. Browning's life in Italy cast a touch of exoticism over his works. Most readers at the time found Browning a pretty odd poet mixing alien subjects and implicit meaning. His dramatic monologue like the collection *Men and Women* (1855) addresses an imaginary audience with the exploration of the soul, producing a powerful impact on readers. Browning spent the rest of his life in England but died in Venice. Later in 1889, he was buried in the Poets' Corner of Westminster Abbey.

"My Last Duchess" is Robert Browning's masterpiece in which he employed his exquisite skill of dramatic monologue. The speaker in this poem is the duke himself; he was the Duke of Ferrara but also the real murderer of his late wife. When his second marriage comes, his negotiation with the envoy over the bride's dowry unmasks his cruel characteristics. In his eloquent monologue to the envoy, the duke shows the envoy the portrait of his late wife to suggest his privilege over women.

The duke's control over his wife testifies to his absolute tyranny and greed, which killed his last wife. It is beyond doubt that the same story is awaiting his new duchess. Through portraying this vicious character, Browning presents us with his excellent psychological probing.

My Last Duchess

That's my last duchess painted on the wall,
Looking as if she were alive. I call
That piece a wonder, now; Fra Pandolf's[1] hands
Worked busily a day, and there she stands.
Will't please you sit and look at her? I said
"Fra Pandolf" by design[2], for never read
Strangers like you[3] that pictured countenance,
That depth and passion of its earnest glance,
But to myself they turned (since none puts by
The curtain drawn for you, but I[4])   [10]
And seemed as they would ask me, if they durst[5],
How such a glance came there; so not the first
Are you to turn and ask thus[6]. Sir, 't was not
Her husband's presence only, called that spot
Of joy into the Duchess' cheek: perhaps
Fra Pandolf chanced to say "Her mantle laps
Over my lady's wrist[7] too much" or "Paint
Must never hope to reproduce the faint
Half-flush that dies along her throat:" such stuff
Was courtesy, she thought, and cause enough   [20]
For calling up that spot of joy. She had
A heart—how shall I say?—too soon made glad,
Too easily impressed: she liked whate'er
She looked on, and her looks went everywhere.
Sir, 't was all one! My favour[8] at her breast,

The dropping of the daylight in the West,
The bough of cherries some officious fool
Broke in the orchard for her, the white mule[9]
She rode with round the terrace—all and each
Would draw from her alike the approving speech, [30]
Or blush, at least. She thanked men—good! but thanked
Somehow—I know not how—as if she ranked
My gift of a nine-hundred-years-old name
With anybody's gift. Who'd stoop[10] to blame
This sort of trifling? Even had you skill
In speech—(which I have not)—to make your will
Quite clear to such a one, and say, "Just this
Or that in you disgusts me; here you miss
Or there exceed the mark"[11]—and if she let
Herself be lessoned so, nor plainly set [40]
Her wits to yours, forsooth[12], and made excuse
— E'en then would be some stooping; and I choose
Never to stoop. Oh sir, she smiled, no doubt,
Whene'er I passed her; but who passed without
Much the same smile? This grew; I gave commands;
Then all smiles stopped together[13]. There she stands
As if alive. Will 't please you rise? We'll meet
The company below, then. I repeat,
The Count your master's known munificence[14]
Is ample warrant that no just pretence[15] [50]
Of mine for dowry[16] will be disallowed[17];
Though his fair daughter's self[18], as I avowed
At starting is my object. Nay, we'll go
Together down, sir. Notice Neptune[19], though,
Taming a sea-horse, thought a rarity[20],
Which Claus of Innsbruck[21] cast in bronze[22] for me.

Part Six　The Victorian Literature

Notes

1. Fra Pandolf: an imaginary painter

2. by design: on purpose

3. never read… like you: Strangers like you never read (a countenance like this).

4. since none… you, but I: no one but I am allowed to put down the curtain covering the painting

5. durst: the past tense of "dare"

6. not the first… and ask thus: you are not the first to turn to me and ask about her countenance

7. my lady's wrist: the last duchess's wrist

8. My favour: gifts like jewellery that the Duke gave her

9. mule: an animal like a donkey and horse

10. stoop: degrade oneself

11. here you miss/Or there exceed the mark: the last duchess often misses or exceeds the yardstick required by the Duke

12. forsooth: indeed

13. Then all smiles stopped together: the duchess stopped smiling; she died because of the narrator's commands.

14. munificence: generosity

15. pretence: requirement

16. dowry: money or property a wife brings to her husband when getting married

17. no just pretence/Of mine for dowry will be disallowed: My just requirement for the dowry will not be refused since the Count is so generous.

18. his fair daughter's self: the beautiful new duchess, the daughter of the Count

19. Neptune: the Roman God of sea

20. rarity: a rare existence

21. Claus of Innsbruck: an imaginary local sculptor

22. cast in bronze: mold in bronze

Questions for Discussion

(1) This poem is written in the dramatic monologue. What is the function of this

narrative device?

(2) What is the Duke's attitude towards his former wife as inferred in his introduction?

(3) What does the Duke imply by saying "I gave commands; Then all smiles stopped together"? What happened to his former wife?

(4) What is the Duke's intention in showing the guest his rare art collection?

(5) What does the poem reveal about the new wife and her dowry?

(6) Compare dramatic monologue with stream of consciousness.

Suggested Reading

(1) Robert Browning. *My Last Duchess and Other Poems*. New York: Dover Publications, 1993.

(2) S. S. Curry. *Browning and the Dramatic Monologue*. Boston: Expression Company, 1980.

(3) H. F. Tucker. *Browning's Beginning: The Art of Disclosure*. Minn.: University of Minnesota Press, 1980.

(4) 勃朗宁：《勃朗宁诗选》(英汉对照)，汪晴、飞白译，北京：外语教学与研究出版社，2013年。

(5) 申丹：《叙述学与小说文体学研究》，北京：北京大学出版社，1998年。

30. Oscar Wilde

Oscar Wilde (1854–1900) was one of the greatest English writers and artists of the 19th century, best known for his plays, fairy tales and unique aesthetic viewpoints. He was born and grew up in Dublin, Ireland. His father was a distinguished surgeon, who was fond of literature, and his mother was a poet and writer. After graduating from Trinity College, Dublin, Wilde won a full scholarship to Oxford, in 1874. At Oxford, he was influenced by the aesthetic theories of Walter Pater and John Ruskin, and later became one of the leading figures of the Aesthetic Movement. He advocated "Art for Art's Sake", emphasizing the artificiality of art. Wilde's most outstanding success was as a dramatist. During 1892–1895 he wrote many famous plays, including *Lady Windermere's Fan* (1892), *A Woman of No Importance* (1893), *An Ideal Husband* (1895) and *The Importance of Being Earnest* (1895). His plays are mainly about upper-class manners and morals with full of joy and witty humor. He used his light and witty language to reveal the decay and chaos of the upper classes. Many of the famous quotes even come from negative characters, which makes the dialogue more interesting and makes the characterization more realistic. As a prolific writer, he also wrote essays, including "The Decay of Lying" (1889); poems, such as "The Ballad of Reading Gaol" (1898), and a novel *The Picture of Dorian Gray* (1891). His collection of fairy tales *The Happy Prince and Other Tales* (1888) and *A House of Pomegranates* (1891) also received wide popularity among readers. However, from 1895 to 1897, Wilde was imprisoned for his homosexuality with hard labor. After his release, divorced and disgraced, he went to Paris, where he died from cerebral meningitis at the age of 46.

"The Happy Prince" is chosen from *The Happy Prince and Other Tales*, a collection of fairy tales, which has been enjoying wide-popularity among readers around the world. "The Happy Prince" tells the story of a metal statue of a happy prince, who does not know what sorrow is in his life but witnesses all the ugliness and misery in his city after he dies. He befriends a kind-hearted swallow, and together they sacrifice themselves to bring happiness to the poor. In the end, they both receive their rewards in paradise. The story reflects the true reality of Victorian British society. By putting real social evils into the story, Wilde mercilessly exposed the issues of social injustice and the indifference of the upper-class towards those at the bottom of society, and showed his deep sympathy for the poor, helpless lower-class people. At the same time, the characterization of a selfless, kind, and generous prince and swallow expressed his longing for an ideal social system, and questioned the moral principles of the society at that time.

The Happy Prince

High above the city, on a tall column, stood the statue of the Happy Prince. He was gilded all over with thin leaves of fine gold, for eyes he had two bright sapphires, and a large red ruby glowed on his sword-hilt.

He was very much admired indeed. "He is as beautiful as a weathercock[1]," remarked one of the Town Councillors who wished to gain a reputation for having artistic tastes; "only not quite so useful," he added, fearing lest people should think him unpractical, which he really was not.

"Why can't you be like the Happy Prince?" asked a sensible mother of her little boy who was crying for the moon[2]. "The Happy Prince never dreams of crying for anything."

"I am glad there is some one in the world who is quite happy," muttered a disappointed man as he gazed at the wonderful statue.

"He looks just like an angel," said the Charity Children[3] as they came out of the cathedral in their bright scarlet cloaks and their clean white pinafores[4].

"How do you know?" said the Mathematical Master, "you have never seen one."

"Ah! but we have, in our dreams," answered the children; and the Mathematical Master frowned and looked very severe, for he did not approve of children dreaming.

One night there flew over the city a little Swallow. His friends had gone away to Egypt six weeks before, but he had stayed behind, for he was in love with the most beautiful Reed. He had met her early in the spring as he was flying down the river after a big yellow moth, and had been so attracted by her slender waist that he had stopped to talk to her.

"Shall I love you?" said the Swallow, who liked to come to the point at once, and the Reed made him a low bow. So he flew round and round her, touching the water with his wings, and making silver ripples. This was his courtship[5], and it lasted all through the summer.

"It is a ridiculous attachment," twittered the other Swallows; "she has no money, and far too many relations"; and indeed the river was quite full of Reeds. Then, when the autumn came they all flew away.

After they had gone he felt lonely, and began to tire of his lady-love. "She has no conversation," he said, "and I am afraid that she is a coquette[6], for she is always flirting with the wind." And certainly, whenever the wind blew, the Reed made the most graceful curtsies[7]. "I admit that she is domestic," he continued, "but I love travelling, and my wife, consequently, should love travelling also."

"Will you come away with me?" he said finally to her; but the Reed shook her head, she was so attached to her home.

"You have been trifling with me," he cried. "I am off to the Pyramids[8]. Good-bye!" and he flew away.

All day long he flew, and at night-time he arrived at the city. "Where shall I put up?" he said; "I hope the town has made preparations."

Then he saw the statue on the tall column.

"I will put up there," he cried; "it is a fine position, with plenty of fresh air." So he alighted[9] just between the feet of the Happy Prince.

"I have a golden bedroom," he said softly to himself as he looked round, and he prepared to go to sleep; but just as he was putting his head under his wing a large drop of water fell on him. "What a curious thing!" he cried; "there is not a single cloud in the sky, the stars are quite clear and bright, and yet it is raining. The climate in the north of Europe is really dreadful. The Reed used to like the rain, but that was merely her selfishness."

Then another drop fell.

"What is the use of a statue if it cannot keep the rain off?" he said; "I must look for a good chimney-pot[10]," and he determined to fly away.

But before he had opened his wings, a third drop fell, and he looked up, and saw– Ah! what did he see?

The eyes of the Happy Prince were filled with tears, and tears were running down his golden cheeks. His face was so beautiful in the moonlight that the little Swallow was filled with pity.

"Who are you?" he said.

"I am the Happy Prince."

"Why are you weeping then?" asked the Swallow; "you have quite drenched[11] me."

"When I was alive and had a human heart," answered the statue, "I did not know what tears were, for I lived in the Palace of Sans-Souci[12], where sorrow is not allowed to enter. In the daytime I played with my companions in the garden, and in the evening I led the dance in the Great Hall. Round the garden ran a very lofty wall, but I never cared to ask what lay beyond it, everything about me was so beautiful. My courtiers[13] called me the Happy Prince, and happy indeed I was, if pleasure be happiness. So I lived, and so I died. And now that I am dead they have set me up here so high that I can see all the ugliness and all the misery of my city, and though my heart is made of lead yet I cannot chose but weep."

"What! is he not solid gold?" said the Swallow to himself. He was too polite to make any personal remarks out loud.

"Far away," continued the statue in a low musical voice, "far away in a little street there is a poor house. One of the windows is open, and through it I can see a woman seated at a table. Her face is thin and worn, and she has coarse, red hands, all pricked by the needle, for she is a seamstress. She is embroidering passion-flowers on a satin[14] gown for the loveliest of the Queen's maids-of-honour[15] to wear at the next Court-ball. In a bed in the corner of the room her little boy is lying ill. He has a fever, and is asking for oranges. His mother has nothing to give him but river water, so he is crying. Swallow, Swallow, little Swallow, will you not bring her the ruby out of my sword-hilt? My feet are fastened to this pedestal[16] and I cannot move."

"I am waited for in Egypt," said the Swallow. "My friends are flying up and down the Nile, and talking to the large lotus- flowers. Soon they will go to sleep in the tomb of the great King. The King is there himself in his painted coffin. He is wrapped in yellow linen, and embalmed[17] with spices. Round his neck is a chain of pale green jade, and his hands are like withered leaves."

"Swallow, Swallow, little Swallow," said the Prince, "will you not stay with me for one night, and be my messenger? The boy is so thirsty, and the mother so sad."

"I don't think I like boys," answered the Swallow. "Last summer, when I was staying on the river, there were two rude boys, the miller's sons, who were always throwing stones at me. They never hit me, of course; we swallows fly far too well for that, and besides, I come of a family famous for its agility; but still, it was a mark of disrespect."

But the Happy Prince looked so sad that the little Swallow was sorry. "It is very cold here," he said; "but I will stay with you for one night, and be your messenger."

"Thank you, little Swallow," said the Prince.

So the Swallow picked out the great ruby from the Prince's sword, and flew away with it in his beak over the roofs of the town.

He passed by the cathedral tower, where the white marble angels were sculptured. He passed by the palace and heard the sound of dancing. A beautiful girl came out on the balcony with her lover. "How wonderful the stars are," he said to her, "and how wonderful is the power of love!"

"I hope my dress will be ready in time for the State-ball," she answered; "I have ordered passion-flowers to be embroidered on it; but the seamstresses are so lazy."

He passed over the river, and saw the lanterns hanging to the masts of the ships. He passed over the Ghetto[18], and saw the old Jews bargaining with each other, and weighing out money in copper scales. At last he came to the poor house and looked in. The boy was tossing feverishly on his bed, and the mother had fallen asleep, she was so tired. In he hopped, and laid the great ruby on the table beside the woman's thimble. Then he flew gently round the bed, fanning the boy's forehead with his wings. "How cool I feel," said the boy, "I must be getting better"; and he sank into a delicious slumber[19].

Then the Swallow flew back to the Happy Prince, and told him what he had done. "It is curious," he remarked, "but I feel quite warm now, although it is so cold."

"That is because you have done a good action," said the Prince. And the little Swallow began to think, and then he fell asleep. Thinking always made him sleepy.

When day broke he flew down to the river and had a bath. "What a remarkable phenomenon," said the Professor of Ornithology[20] as he was passing over the bridge. "A swallow in winter!" And he wrote a long letter about it to the local newspaper. Every one quoted it, it was full of so many words that they could not understand.

"To-night I go to Egypt," said the Swallow, and he was in high spirits at the prospect. He visited all the public monuments, and sat a long time on top of the church steeple. Wherever he went the Sparrows chirruped, and said to each other, "What a distinguished stranger!" so he enjoyed himself very much.

When the moon rose he flew back to the Happy Prince. "Have you any commissions for Egypt?" he cried; "I am just starting."

"Swallow, Swallow, little Swallow," said the Prince, "will you not stay with me one night longer?"

"I am waited for in Egypt," answered the Swallow. "To-morrow my friends will fly up to the Second Cataract[21]. The river-horse couches there among the bulrushes, and on a great granite[22] throne sits the God Memnon[23]. All night long he watches the stars, and when the morning star shines he utters one cry of joy, and then he is silent. At noon the yellow lions come down to the water's edge to drink. They have eyes like green beryls, and their roar is louder than the roar of the cataract.

"Swallow, Swallow, little Swallow," said the Prince, "far away across the city I see a young man in a garret[24]. He is leaning over a desk covered with papers, and in a tumbler by his side there is a bunch of withered violets. His hair is brown and crisp, and his lips are red as a pomegranate, and he has large and dreamy eyes. He is trying to finish a play for the Director of the Theatre, but he is too cold to write any more. There is no fire in the grate, and hunger has made him faint."

"I will wait with you one night longer," said the Swallow, who really had a good heart. "Shall I take him another ruby?"

"Alas! I have no ruby now," said the Prince; "my eyes are all that I have left. They are made of rare sapphires, which were brought out of India a thousand years ago. Pluck out[25] one of them and take it to him. He will sell it to the jeweller, and buy food and firewood, and finish his play."

"Dear Prince," said the Swallow, "I cannot do that"; and he began to weep.

"Swallow, Swallow, little Swallow," said the Prince, "do as I command you."

So the Swallow plucked out the Prince's eye, and flew away to the student's garret. It was easy enough to get in, as there was a hole in the roof. Through this he darted, and came into the room. The young man had his head buried in his hands, so he did not hear the flutter of the bird's wings, and when he looked up he found the beautiful sapphire lying on the withered violets.

"I am beginning to be appreciated," he cried; "this is from some great admirer. Now I can finish my play," and he looked quite happy.

The next day the Swallow flew down to the harbour. He sat on the mast of a large vessel and watched the sailors hauling big chests out of the hold with ropes. "Heave a-hoy!" they shouted as each chest came up. "I am going to Egypt"! cried the Swallow, but nobody minded, and when the moon rose he flew back to the Happy Prince.

"I am come to bid you good-bye," he cried.

"Swallow, Swallow, little Swallow," said the Prince, "will you not stay with me one night longer?"

"It is winter," answered the Swallow, "and the chill snow will soon be here. In Egypt the sun is warm on the green palm-trees, and the crocodiles lie in the mud and look lazily about them. My companions are building a nest in the Temple of Baalbec, and the pink and white doves are watching them, and cooing to each other. Dear Prince, I must leave you, but I will never forget you, and next spring I will bring you back two beautiful jewels in place of those you have given away. The ruby shall be redder than a red rose, and the sapphire shall be as blue as the great sea."

"In the square below," said the Happy Prince, "there stands a little match-girl. She has let her matches fall in the gutter, and they are all spoiled. Her father will beat her if she does not bring home some money, and she is crying. She has no shoes or stockings, and her little head is bare. Pluck out my other eye, and give it to her, and her father will not beat her."

"I will stay with you one night longer," said the Swallow, "but I cannot pluck out your eye. You would be quite blind then."

"Swallow, Swallow, little Swallow," said the Prince, "do as I command you."

So he plucked out the Prince's other eye, and darted down with it. He swooped[26] past the match-girl, and slipped the jewel into the palm of her hand. "What a lovely bit of glass," cried the little girl; and she ran home, laughing.

Then the Swallow came back to the Prince. "You are blind now," he said, "so I will stay with you always."

"No, little Swallow," said the poor Prince, "you must go away to Egypt."

"I will stay with you always," said the Swallow, and he slept at the Prince's feet.

All the next day he sat on the Prince's shoulder, and told him stories of what he had seen in strange lands. He told him of the red ibises, who stand in long rows on the banks of the Nile, and catch gold-fish in their beaks; of the Sphinx[27], who is as old as the world itself, and lives in the desert, and knows everything; of the merchants, who walk slowly by the side of their camels, and carry amber beads in their hands; of the King of the Mountains of the Moon, who is as black as ebony, and worships a large crystal; of the great green snake that sleeps in a palm-tree, and has twenty priests to feed it with honey-cakes; and of the pygmies[28] who sail over a big lake on large flat leaves, and are always at war with the butterflies.

"Dear little Swallow," said the Prince, "you tell me of marvellous things, but more marvellous than anything is the suffering of men and of women. There is no Mystery so great as Misery. Fly over my city, little Swallow, and tell me what you see there."

So the Swallow flew over the great city, and saw the rich making merry in their beautiful houses, while the beggars were sitting at the gates. He flew into dark lanes, and saw the white faces of starving children looking out listlessly[29] at the black streets. Under the archway of a bridge two little boys were lying in one another's arms to try and keep themselves warm. "How hungry we are!" they said. "You must not lie here," shouted the Watchman, and they wandered out into the rain.

Then he flew back and told the Prince what he had seen.

"I am covered with fine gold," said the Prince, "you must take it off, leaf by leaf, and give it to my poor; the living always think that gold can make them happy."

Leaf after leaf of the fine gold the Swallow picked off, till the Happy Prince looked quite dull and grey. Leaf after leaf of the fine gold he brought to the poor, and the children's faces grew rosier, and they laughed and played games in the street. "We have bread now!" they cried.

Then the snow came, and after the snow came the frost. The streets looked as if they were made of silver, they were so bright and glistening; long icicles like crystal daggers hung down from the eaves of the houses, everybody went about in furs, and the little boys wore scarlet caps and skated on the ice.

The poor little Swallow grew colder and colder, but he would not leave the Prince, he loved him too well. He picked up crumbs outside the baker's door when the baker was not looking and tried to keep himself warm by flapping his wings.

But at last he knew that he was going to die. He had just strength to fly up to the Prince's shoulder once more. "Good-bye, dear Prince!" he murmured, "will you let me kiss your hand?"

"I am glad that you are going to Egypt at last, little Swallow," said the Prince, "you have stayed too long here; but you must kiss me on the lips, for I love you."

"It is not to Egypt that I am going," said the Swallow. "I am going to the House of Death. Death is the brother of Sleep, is he not?"

And he kissed the Happy Prince on the lips, and fell down dead at his feet.

At that moment a curious crack sounded inside the statue, as if something had broken. The fact is that the leaden heart had snapped right in two. It certainly was a dreadfully hard frost.

Early the next morning the Mayor was walking in the square below in company with the Town Councillors. As they passed the column he looked up at the statue: "Dear me! how shabby the Happy Prince looks!" he said.

"How shabby indeed!" cried the Town Councillors, who always agreed with the Mayor; and they went up to look at it.

"The ruby has fallen out of his sword, his eyes are gone, and he is golden no longer," said the Mayor in fact, "he is little better than a beggar!"

"Little better than a beggar," said the Town Councillors.

"And here is actually a dead bird at his feet!" continued the Mayor. "We must really issue a proclamation that birds are not to be allowed to die here." And the Town Clerk made a note of the suggestion.

So they pulled down the statue of the Happy Prince. "As he is no longer beautiful he is no longer useful," said the Art Professor at the University.

Then they melted the statue in a furnace, and the Mayor held a meeting of the Corporation to decide what was to be done with the metal. "We must have another statue, of course," he said, "and it shall be a statue of myself."

"Of myself," said each of the Town Councillors, and they quarrelled. When I last heard of them they were quarrelling still.

"What a strange thing!" said the overseer of the workmen at the foundry. "This broken lead heart will not melt in the furnace. We must throw it away." So they threw it on a dust-heap where the dead Swallow was also lying.

"Bring me the two most precious things in the city," said God to one of His Angels; and the Angel brought Him the leaden heart and the dead bird.

"You have rightly chosen," said God, "for in my garden of Paradise this little bird shall sing for evermore[30], and in my city of gold the Happy Prince shall praise me."

Notes

1. weathercock: *n.* a weathervane in the form of a rooster

2. cry for the moon: strive for the impossible [illusory]

3. Charity Children: children from the orphanage

4. pinafores: *n.* a sleeveless apronlike garment worn over a child's dress

5. courtship: *n.* (old-fashioned) a period during which a couple develops a romantic relationship, especially with a view to marriage

6. coquette: *n.* (literary, often disapproving) a woman who behaves in a way that is intended to attract men

7. curtsies: *n.* a woman's or girl's formal greeting made by bending the knees with one foot in front of the other

8. Pyramids: *n.* ancient stone buildings with four triangular sloping sides; the most famous pyramids are those built in ancient Egypt to contain the bodies of their kings and queens.

9. alight: *v.* (of a bird or an insect) to land in or on something after flying to it

10. chimney-pot: *n.* a short pipe on the top of a chimney, which increases the draught and directs the smoke upwards

11. drench: *v.* wet thoroughly; soak

12. the Palace of Sans-Souci: the Palace without sorrow

13. courtiers: *n.* noblemen and women who attend a royal court as companions or advisers to the king or queen

14. satin: *n.* a smooth, shiny kind of cloth, usually made from silk

15. maid-of-honour: an unmarried noblewoman attending a queen or princess

16. pedestal: *n.* the base that a column, statue, etc. rests on

17. embalm: *v.* preserve (a corpse) from decay, originally with spices and now usually by arterial injection of a preservative

18. Ghetto: *n.* a quarter of a city in which Jews were formerly required to live

19. slumber: *n.* sleep

20. Ornithology: *n.* the scientific study of birds

21. the Second Cataract: (literary) a large steep waterfall in Egypt

22. granite: *n.* a type of hard grey stone, often used in building

23. Memnon: *n.* a king of Ethiopia, son of Eos, slain by Achilles in the Trojan War

24. garret: *n.* a top-floor or attic room, especially a small dismal one (traditionally inhabited by an artist)

25. pluck out: pull out

26. swoop: *v.* (of a bird) move rapidly downward through the air

27. the Sphinx: an ancient Egyptian stone figure having a lion's body and a human or animal head, especially the huge statue near the Pyramids at Giza

28. pygmy: *n.* a member of a race of very short people living in parts of Africa and Southeast Asia

29. listlessly: *adv.* without energy or enthusiasm, coldly

30. for evermore: *adv.* forever

Questions for Discussion

(1) In "The Happy Prince," the prince was admired by all for his handsome and noble appearance. But what moved the readers and brought the prince real happiness was his "inner beauty" which was reflected by his sacrifice of "outer beauty." Based on the change of the outer and the inner image of the prince, analyze the author's aesthetic view and discuss why it is important to develop a healthy aesthetic view.

(2) What is the position or particularity of fairy tales in English literature?

(3) The symbolism of the story is presented with great skill. What are the symbolic meanings of the Happy Prince, the Swallow, and the beautiful Reed in the tale?

(4) The people that the Happy Prince helped (the seamstress who did needlework, the poor youth who wrote plays, the little match-girl, etc.) are all from the lower class. Considering the fact that Wilde himself was born an aristocrat, what does this reflect about Wilde's thoughts?

(5) Wilde's aestheticism has influenced many modern Chinese writers, such as Tian Han and Hong Shen, etc. Do you think this kind of influence is one-way? Will modern Chinese literature influence Western literature?

Suggested Reading

(1) Oscar Wilde. *The Happy Prince and Other Stories*. London: Penguin Popular Classics, 2008.

(2) Oscar Wilde. *The Collected Works of Oscar Wilde*. Ware: Wordsworth Editions Ltd, 2007.

(3) Richard Ellmann. *Oscar Wilde*. London: Vintage Classics, 1988.

(4) Kerry Powell & Peter Raby, ed. *Oscar Wilde in Context*. Cambridge: Cambridge University Press, 2017.

(5) 王尔德：《快乐王子》，巴金译，上海：上海译文出版社，2014年。

(6) 王尔德：《奥斯卡·王尔德自传》，孙宜学译，北京：团结出版社，2005年。

(7) 吴刚：《王尔德文艺理论研究》，上海：上海外语教育出版社，2009年。

31. Thomas Hardy

Thomas Hardy (1840–1928) was one of the most renowned novelists and poets of the Victorian period. He was born on 2 June 1840 in Higher Bockhampton (then Upper Bockhampton), a hamlet in the parish of Stinsford to the east of Dorchester in Dorset. England Hardy was educated at home by his mother until he went to his first school at Bockhampton at the age of eight. Growing up in a quiet and isolated country life shaped Hardy's personality that it became the major setting in his novels, casting his works with an impressive touch of local color. At the age of sixteen, Hardy was an apprentice architect and even was offered a vocation in London. Later, Hardy realized his zeal for literature was overwhelming. Influenced by the works of Robert Browning, Hardy commenced his literary journey. His first novel *The Poor Man and the Lady* failed to be published but soon his second novel *Desperate Remedies* (1871) was successfully published. His marriage to Emma Gifford in 1874 was beneficial for Hardy's literary career with Emma persuading him to put more efforts into writing. In 1874, his novel *Far from the Maddening Crowd* won Hardy lasting reputation.

The publications of *The Mayor of Casterbridge* (1886) rendered Hardy a formidable novelist in England. However, *Tess of the d'Urbervilles* (1891) and *Jude the Obscure* (1895) received mixed reviews, which symbolized the summit of his literary career. In his later life, Hardy became prolific in the creation of poetry, finishing almost nine hundred poems on different themes. In 1928, Hardy died and his body was buried in Poets' Corner, but his heart was buried near his first wife Emma Gifford in Stinson. The death of Hardy, a prominent novelist and poet, was an irreparable loss in the history of literature. His controversial perspectives were recognized later as acute timeless insights into reality.

"Afterwards", as the tile implies, is the last poem in Hardy's poetry collection *Moments of Vision*. This poem is interpreted as Hardy's reflections on his life and his outlook for the future. This poem includes five stanzas, following the rhyme of ABAB. Almost in each stanza, there is a natural image for the speaker to ponder about the world after his death, such as the dewfall-hawk, the hedgehog, and a crossing breeze. Though these natural images, the speaker initiates a dialogue to complete meditation on his former days and the afterlife.

Afterwards

When the Present[1] has latched its postern[2] behind my tremulous stay[3],
And the May month flaps its glad green leaves like wings,
Delicate-filmed[4] as new-spun silk, will the neighbours say,
"He was a man who used to notice such things"?
If it be in the dusk when, like an eyelid's soundless blink,
The dewfall-hawk comes crossing the shades to alight
Upon the wind-warped[5] upland thorn, a gazer may think,
"To him this must have been a familiar sight."

If I pass[6] during some nocturnal blackness, mothy and warm,
When the hedgehog travels furtively over the lawn,
One may say, "He strove[7] that such innocent creatures[8] should come to no harm,
But he could do little for them; and now he is gone."

If, when hearing that I have been stilled⁹ at last, they stand at the door,
Watching the full-starred heavens that winter sees,
Will this thought rise on those who will meet my face no more,
"He was one who had an eye for such mysteries"?

And will any say when my bell of quittance¹⁰ is heard in the gloom,
And a crossing breeze cuts a pause in its outrollings¹¹,
Till they rise again, as they were a new bell's boom,
"He hears it not now, but used to notice such things?"

Notes

1. Present: for the time being; this is an employment of personification.

2. latch its postern: lock the back door

3. tremulous stay: my trembling life on earth

4. delicate-filmed: the finest thread; film=thread

5. wind-warped: twisted or bent because of wind

6. pass: stop existing

7. strive: try hard

8. innocent creatures: Hardy was a defender of animals.

9. stilled: dead

10. my bell of quittance: it is my time to leave; "bell of quittance" refers to the toll of the church bell to recognize death; here it implies death is approaching.

11. in its outrollings: The breeze discontinues the tolling of bell.

Questions for Discussion

(1) What does this poem written as an epitaph show of his personality?

(2) Analyze images such as "dewfall-hawk", "hedgehog" and "full-starred heavens" as revealing Hardy's contemplation from different perspectives.

(3) What do the "my bell of quittance" and the "a new bell's boom" represent respectively?

(4) How do you interpret Hardy's passion for nature in terms of ecology?

(5) Compare this poem with John Keats' "When I have Fears that I may Cease to Be" on their attitudes towards death.

Suggested Reading

(1) James Gibson. *The Complete Poems of Thomas Hardy*. London and Basingstoke: Macmillan, 1976.

(2) Tom Paulin. *Thomas Hardy: The Poetry of Perception*. London and Basingstoke: Macmillan, 1975.

(3) Dale Kramer. *The Cambridge Companion to Thomas Hardy*. Cambridge: Cambridge University Press, 1999.

(4) 托马斯·哈代：《哈代诗选》，刘新民译，成都：四川文艺出版社，2018 年.

(5) 颜学军：《哈代诗歌研究》，北京：人民文学出版社，2006 年.

Jude the Obscure is Hardy's fourteenth novel. Published in 1895, it was criticized for its controversial elements such as the bold description of sex and the critique of Christianity. Jude is a schoolboy. After his teacher Mr. Richard Phillotson leaves for college, Jude longs to follow his footsteps to Christminster. However, Jude is always occupied with other external matters, like his failed marriage with Arabella and his complicated relationship with Sue. Jude's dream to become an academic never realizes. In this selected chapter, Jude is overlooking the distant Christminster which he desires to go in the future. His passion and yearning for the university are clearly revealed, while plenty of adversities await him ahead.

Jude the Obscure

(Part I Chapter 3)

NOT a soul[1] was visible on the hedgeless highway, or on either side of it, and the white road seemed to ascend and diminish till it joined the sky. At the very top it was crossed at right angles by a green "ridgeway"–the Ickneild Street and original Roman road through the district. This ancient track ran east and west for many miles, and down almost to within living memory had been used for driving flocks and herds[2] to fairs and markets. But it was now neglected and overgrown.

The boy had never before strayed so far north as this from the nestling hamlet[3] in which he had been deposited[4] by the carrier from a railway station southward, one dark evening some few months earlier, and till now he had had no suspicion that such a wide, flat, low-lying country lay so near at hand, under the very verge of his upland world. The whole northern semicircle between east and west, to a distance of forty or fifty miles, spread itself before him; a bluer, moister atmosphere, evidently, than that he breathed up here.

Not far from the road stood a weather-beaten old barn of reddish-grey brick and tile. It was known as the Brown House by the people of the locality. He was about to pass it when he perceived a ladder against the eaves; and the reflection[5] that the higher he got, the further he could see, led Jude to stand and regard it. On the slope of the roof two men were repairing the tiling. He turned into the ridgeway and drew towards the barn.

When he had wistfully watched[6] the workmen for some time he took courage, and ascended the ladder till he stood beside them.

"Well, my lad, and what may you want up here?"

"I wanted to know where the city of Christminster[7] is, if you please."

"Christminster is out across there, by that clump[8]. You can see it–at least you can on a clear day. Ah, no, you can't now."

The other tiler, glad of any kind of diversion from the monotony of his labour, had also turned to look towards the quarter[9] designated. "You can't often see it in weather like this," he said. "The time I've noticed it is when the sun is going down in a blaze of flame, and it looks like–I don't know what."

"The heavenly Jerusalem[10]," suggested the serious urchin[11].

"Ay–though I should never ha' thought of it myself.... But I can't see no Christminster to-day."

The boy strained his eyes also; yet neither could he see the far-off city. He descended from the barn, and abandoning Christminster with the versatility of his age[12] he walked along the ridge-track, looking for any natural objects of interest that might lie in the banks thereabout. When he repassed the barn to go back to Marygreen he observed that the ladder was still in its place, but that the men had finished their day's work and gone away.

It was waning[13] towards evening; there was still a faint mist, but it had cleared a little except in the damper tracts[14] of subjacent country and along the river-courses. He thought again of Christminster, and wished, since he had come two or three miles from his aunt's house on purpose, that he could have seen for once this attractive city of which he had been told. But even if he waited here it was hardly likely that the air would clear before night. Yet he was loth[15] to leave the spot, for the northern expanse became lost to view on retreating towards the village only a few hundred yards.

He ascended the ladder to have one more look at the point the men had designated, and perched himself on the highest rung, overlying the tiles. He might not be able to come so far as this for many days. Perhaps if he prayed, the wish to see Christminster might be forwarded. People said that, if you prayed, things sometimes came to you, even though they sometimes did not. He had read in a tract[16] that a man who had begun to build a church, and had no money to finish it, knelt down and prayed, and the money came in by the next post. Another man tried the same experiment, and the money did not come; but he found afterwards that the breeches[17] he knelt in were made by a wicked Jew. This was not discouraging, and turning on the ladder Jude knelt on the third rung, where, resting against those above it, he prayed that the mist might rise.

He then seated himself again, and waited. In the course of ten or fifteen minutes the thinning mist dissolved altogether from the northern horizon, as it had already done elsewhere, and about a quarter of an hour before the time of sunset the westward clouds parted, the sun's position being partially uncovered, and the beams streaming out in visible lines between two bars of slaty cloud[18]. The boy immediately looked back in the old direction.

Some way within the limits of the stretch of landscape, points of light like the topaz[19] gleamed. The air increased in transparency with the lapse[20] of minutes, till the topaz points showed themselves to be the vanes[21], windows, wet roof slates, and other shining spots upon the spires[22], domes, freestone-work, and varied[23] outlines that were faintly revealed. It was Christminster, unquestionably; either directly seen, or miraged[24] in the peculiar atmosphere.

The spectator gazed on and on till the windows and vanes lost their shine, going out almost suddenly like extinguished candles. The vague city became veiled in mist. Turning to the west, he saw that the sun had disappeared. The foreground of the scene had grown funereally[25] dark, and near objects put on the hues and shapes of chimaeras[26].

He anxiously descended the ladder, and started homewards at a run, trying not to think of giants, Herne the Hunter[27], Apollyon[28] lying in wait for Christian, or of the captain with the bleeding hole in his forehead and the corpses round him that remutinied[29] every night on board the bewitched ship[30]. He knew that he had grown out of belief in these horrors, yet he was glad when he saw the church tower and the lights in the cottage windows, even though this was not the home of his birth, and his great-aunt did not care much about him.

Inside and round about that old woman's "shop" window, with its twenty-four little panes set in lead-work[31], the glass of some of them oxidized with age, so that you could hardly see the poor penny articles exhibited within, and forming part of a stock which a strong man could have carried, Jude had his outer being for some long tideless time. But his dreams were as gigantic as his surroundings were small.

Through the solid barrier of cold cretaceous upland to the northward he was always beholding[32] a gorgeous city—the fancied place he had likened to the new Jerusalem, though there was perhaps more of the painter's imagination and less of the diamond merchant's in his dreams thereof than in those of the Apocalyptic writer[33]. And the city acquired a tangibility, a permanence, a hold on his life, mainly from the one nucleus of fact that the man for whose knowledge and purposes he had so much reverence was actually living there; not only so, but living among the more thoughtful and mentally shining ones therein.

In sad wet seasons, though he knew it must rain at Christminster too, he could hardly believe that it rained so drearily[34] there. Whenever he could get away from the confines of the hamlet for an hour or two, which was not often, he would steal off to the Brown House on the hill and strain his eyes persistently; sometimes to be rewarded by the sight of a dome or spire, at other times by a little smoke, which in his estimate had some of the mysticism of incense.

Then the day came when it suddenly occurred to him that if he ascended to the point of view after dark, or possibly went a mile or two further, he would see the night lights of the city. It would be necessary to come back alone, but even that consideration did not deter[35] him, for he could throw a little manliness[36] into his mood, no doubt.

The project was duly executed. It was not late when he arrived at the place of outlook, only just after dusk, but a black north-east sky, accompanied by a wind from the same quarter, made the occasion dark enough. He was rewarded; but what he saw was not the lamps in rows, as he had half expected. No individual light was visible, only a halo or glow-fog over-arching the place against the black heavens behind it, making the light and the city seem distant but a mile or so.

He set himself to wonder on the exact point in the glow where the schoolmaster might be–he who never communicated with anybody at Marygreen now; who was as if dead to them here. In the glow he seemed to see Phillotson[37] promenading[38] at ease, like one of the forms in Nebuchadnezzar's furnace[39].

He had heard that breezes travelled at the rate of ten miles an hour, and the fact now came into his mind. He parted his lips as he faced the north-east, and drew in the wind as if it were a sweet liquor.

"You," he said, addressing the breeze caressingly[40] "were in Christminster city between one and two hours ago, floating along the streets, pulling round the weather-cocks, touching Mr. Phillotson's face, being breathed by him; and now you are here, breathed by me–you, the very same."

Suddenly there came along this wind something towards him–a message from the place–from some soul residing there, it seemed. Surely it was the sound of bells, the voice of the city, faint and musical, calling to him, "We are happy here!"

He had become entirely lost to his bodily situation during this mental leap, and only got back to it by a rough recalling[41]. A few yards below the brow of the hill on which he paused a team of horses made its appearance, having reached the place by dint of [42] half an hour's serpentine[43] progress from the bottom of the immense declivity[44]. They had a load of coals behind them–a fuel that could only be got into the upland by this particular route. They were accompanied by a carter, a second man, and a boy, who now kicked a large stone behind one of the wheels, and allowed the panting animals to have a long rest, while those in charge took a flagon[45] off the load and indulged in a drink round.

They were elderly men, and had genial[46] voices. Jude addressed them, inquiring if they had come from Christminster.

"Heaven forbid, with this load!" said they.

"The place I mean is that one yonder[47]." He was getting so romantically attached to Christminster that, like a young lover alluding to his mistress, he felt bashful at mentioning its name again. He pointed to the light in the sky–hardly perceptible to their older eyes.

"Yes. There do seem a spot a bit brighter in the nor'east than elsewhere, though I shouldn't ha' noticed it myself, and no doubt it med be Christminster."

Here a little book of tales which Jude had tucked up under his arm, having brought them to read on his way hither before it grew dark, slipped and fell into the road. The carter eyed him while he picked it up and straightened the leaves[48].

"Ah, young man," he observed, "you'd have to get your head screwed on t'other way before you could read what they read there."

"Why?" asked the boy.

"Oh, they never look at anything that folks like we can understand," the carter continued, by way of passing the time. "On'y foreign tongues used in the days of the Tower of Babel[49], when no two families spoke alike. They read that sort of thing as fast as a night-hawk will whir. 'Tis all learning there–nothing but learning, except religion. And that's learning too, for I never could understand it. Yes, 'tis a serious-minded place[50]. Not but there's wenches[51] in the streets o' nights.... You know, I suppose, that they raise pa'sons there like radishes in a bed? And though it do take–how many years, Bob?–five years to turn a lirruping hobble-de-hoy chap into a solemn preaching man with no corrupt passions, they'll do it, if it can be done, and polish un off like the workmen they be, and turn un out wi' a long face, and a long black coat and waistcoat, and a religious collar and hat, same as they used to wear in the Scriptures, so that his own mother wouldn't know un sometimes.... There, 'tis their business, like anybody else's."

"But how should you know–"

"Now don't you interrupt, my boy. Never interrupt your senyers. Move the fore hoss aside, Bobby; here's som'at coming.... You must mind that I be a-talking of the college life. 'Em lives on a lofty level; there's no gainsaying[52] it, though I myself med not think much of 'em. As we be here in our bodies on this high ground, so be they in their minds–noble-minded men enough, no doubt–some on 'em–able to earn hundreds by thinking out loud. And some on 'em be strong young fellows that can earn a'most as much in silver cups. As for music, there's beautiful music everywhere in Christminster. You med be religious, or you med not, but you can't help striking in your homely note with the rest. And there's a street in the place–the main street–that ha'n't another like it in the world. I should think I did know a little about Christminster!"

By this time the horses had recovered breath and bent to their collars again. Jude, throwing a last adoring look at the distant halo, turned and walked beside his remarkably well-informed friend, who had no objection to telling him as they moved on more yet of the city–its towers and halls and churches. The waggon turned into a cross-road, whereupon Jude thanked the carter warmly for his information, and said he only wished he could talk half as well about Christminster as he.

"Well, 'tis oonly what has come in my way," said the carter unboastfully. "I've never been there, no more than you; but I've picked up the knowledge here and there, and you be welcome to it. A-getting about the world as I do, and mixing with all classes of society, one can't help hearing of things. A friend o' mine, that used to clane the boots at the Crozier Hotel in Christminster when he was in his prime, why, I knowed un as well as my own brother in his later years."

Jude continued his walk homeward alone, pondering so deeply that he forgot to feel timid. He suddenly grew older. It had been the yearning of his heart to find something to anchor on, to cling to–for some place which he could call admirable. Should he find that place in this city if he could get there? Would it be a spot in which, without fear of farmers, or hindrance, or ridicule, he could watch and wait, and set himself to some mighty undertaking like the men of old of whom he had heard? As the halo had been to his eyes when gazing at it a quarter of an hour earlier, so was the spot mentally to him as he pursued his dark way.

"It is a city of light," he said to himself.

"The tree of knowledge[53] grows there," he added a few steps further on.

"It is a place that teachers of men spring from and go to."

"It is what you may call a castle, manned by scholarship and religion."

After this figure he was silent a long while, till he added:

"It would just suit me."

Notes

1. soul: person
2. flocks and herds: groups of cows and sheep
3. the nestling hamlet: the remote village
4. deposit: leave the boy there
5. the reflection: the thought
6. wistfully watch: watch with longing
7. Christminster: the name of a place; here it refers to Oxford University.
8. clump: a group of trees, bushes or other plants
9. the quarter: district
10. The heavenly Jerusalem: the new Jerusalem, God's city in New Testament
11. urchin: referring to a young, dirty and poor boy
12. the versatility of his age: the caprices of his age; doing something on a whim
13. waning: becoming dark
14. tracts: large areas of land
15. was loth to: was unwilling to; loth: loath
16. a tract: a pamphlet
17. breeches: short trousers
18. slaty cloud: dark cloud
19. topaz: referring to the color of topaz; topaz: a precious stone
20. lapse: the passing of time
21. vane: a flat blade moved by the wind
22. spires: the pointed tops of buildings
23. varied: vague
24. miraged: reflected; mirage: an illusory image caused by hot air
25. funereally: dimly
26. chimaera: a hybrid monster in Greek mythology

27. Herne the Hunter: a ghost in English folklore
28. Apollyon: the Destroyer in New Testament
29. remutiny: rebel against
30. bewitched ship: haunted ship
31. panes set in lead-work: panes of glass in the lead-made frame
32. beholding: watching
33. the Apocalyptic writer: the writer who wrote the Apocalypse of John
34. drearily: dull and depressing
35. deter: prevent; stop
36. manliness: the typical qualities of a man
37. Phillotson: the schoolmaster
38. promenading: walking
39. Nebuchadnezzar's furnace: Nebuchadnezzar, the king of Babylon, threw three persons Shadrach, Meshach, and Abednego into the blazing fiery furnace but found there were four men walking around in the fire.
40. caressingly: gently
41. a rough recalling: a sudden loud sound
42. by dint of: by means of
43. serpentine: twisting
44. declivity: a downward slope
45. flagon: a container of wine
46. genial: friendly
47. yonder: over there
48. leaves: pages
49. the Tower of Babel: Tower of Babel, in biblical literature, is a structure built in the land of Shinar (Babylonia) after the Deluge. The story of its construction is an attempt to explain the existence of diverse human languages.
50. a serious-minded place: Christminster, referring to the Oxford of University
51. wench: prostitute
52. there's no gainsaying…: there's no denying…
53. the tree of knowledge: It grows in the Garden of Eden, is a symbol of the absolute knowledge of good and bad.

Questions for Discussion

(1) Why is Jude so focused on where Christminster is? What does Christminster mean to him?

(2) Analyze the description of the environment. What is the implication for Jude's destiny?

(3) There are a lot of Biblical elements in this chapter, such as "heavenly Jerusalem", "Apollyon". Is Jude a devout Christian?

(4) Read the novel in its entirety. Does Jude achieve his educational aspiration? Why or why not?

(5) Compare Jude with Fang Hongjian in *Fortress Besieged* by Qian Zhongshu over their pursuit of education.

Suggested Reading

(1) Thomas Hardy. *Jude the Obscure*. London: Cambridge University Press, 2013.

(2) D. H. Lawrence. *Study of Thomas Hardy and Other Essays*. London: Cambridge University Press, 1985.

(3) Scott Rode. *Reading and Mapping Hardy's Roads*. New York: Routledge, 2006.

(4) 哈代：《无名的裘德》，张谷若译，北京：人民文学出版社，1958 年。

(5) 李田意：《哈代评传》，上海：商务印书馆，1938 年。

(6) 聂珍钊：《悲戚而刚毅的艺术家——托玛斯·哈代小说研究》，武汉：华中师范大学出版社，1992 年。

Part Seven

The Twentieth Century

32. William Butler Yeats

    William Butler Yeats (1865–1939) was born in a landed gentry's home in Dublin, Ireland. He spent his childhood and youth in various places such as Dublin, London and County Sligo, the western coast town where his maternal grandparents' big family was living. He also received his education in these places and formed a passionate enthusiasm for literary writing while studying arts in Dublin. Since his family lost its power and land because of the tumultuous land movement since the middle of the 19th century, Yeats had to spend long stays and visits in Sligo where he enjoyed the wealthy atmosphere with his maternal grandparents. He was obsessed with the local folklore, myths and fairy tales. Yeats devoted himself to his literary career and was deeply involved with the Irish Renaissance Movement that aimed to realize national independence and revival through literary movement. He wrote poems, plays and prose to participate in the movement, while holding his idea of artistic creation at the same time. After meeting Maud Gonne when he was 26, Yeats spent the next 26 years seeking the hand of Gonne, only to be refused once and again, until he married Georgie Hyde-Lees in 1917. This, however, did not influence his creativity and Yeats continued to write his personal and characteristic works. He was awarded the Nobel Prize for Literature in 1923 and after participating in public affairs management for a period of time he retired himself to more philosophical and mysterious reflection for the rest of his life. He died in Italy and was brought back with a national navy ship to be buried in Sligo with words from his poetry on the tombstone–Cast a cold eye/ On life, on death/ Horseman, pass by!

Yeats' early career in poetry writing is mostly related to love and national literary revival with such works as "The Lake Isle of Innisfree", "The Wind Among the Reeds", and "When You are Old". His middle-stage poetry is more inclined to touch upon religious and political topics with such works as "Sailing to Byzantium", "The Second Coming" and so forth. His late-stage poetry is more reflective of his philosophical concepts that sometimes are full of occultism. In contrast with his poetry, Yeats' early plays such as The *Countess Cathleen* and *Cathleen Ni Houlihan* are more directly related to the Irish Renaissance Movement. His middle and late stage plays are full of his own interpretation of eastern and western philosophical and Japanese artistic principles such as Noh (能剧). Throughout his life Yeats had the habit of rewriting and reediting his earlier works, the majority of which can be considered symbolic in one way or another. However, to consider Yeats as a pure writer of Symbolism is to neglect his inheriting tradition of English literature, his obsession with mysterious and spiritual power that is characteristic of Celtic culture, and his profound, sometimes bizarre, reflection on the destiny of human history.

The Lake Isle of Innisfree[1]

I will arise and go now, and go to Innisfree,[2]
And a small cabin build there, of clay and wattles[3] made:
Nine bean-rows will I have there, a hive for the honey-bee;
And live alone in the bee-loud glade[4].

And I shall have some peace there, for peace comes dropping slow[5],
Dropping from the veils of the morning to where the cricket sings;[6]
There midnight's all a glimmer, and noon a purple glow[7],
And evening full of the linnet's[8] wings.

I will arise and go now, for always night and day
I hear lake water lapping[9] with low sounds by the shore;
While I stand on the roadway, or on the pavements grey,

I hear it in the deep heart's core.[10]

Notes

1. Innisfree: the name of an isle in Lough Gill (Gill Lake), Sligo; this poem of Yeats was written under the influence of reading *Walden*, the Transcendentalist masterpiece by David Thoreau; notice in this poem that Yeats still used traditional technique as iambic pentameter and so on, but not so strictly; however, Yeats paid special attention to rhyming, for instance, in this poem the rhyming pattern for each stanza is abab.

2. This line is an imitation of biblical sentences–I will arise and go to my father; Yeats held a skeptical view towards religion but he was still profoundly affected by reading biblical texts.

3. wattles: sticks twisted together to make fences or walls

4. the bee-loud glade: a small piece of empty land in a forest that is full of the buzzing sound of bees

5. dropping slow: coming slowly

6. The meaning for these two lines is: Peace comes slowly as it comes in gradual dropping motion; it comes from the twilight fog in the morning (largely stillness) and it also comes from the singing of the cricket (motion); compare this poem with John Keats' sonnet "On the Grasshopper and the Cricket".

7. purple glow: a light with purple color

8. linnet: a brownish twittering bird; notice the atmosphere Yeats created in this stanza–a cozy, harmonious, slowly-paced, mysterious land that resonated the fairy land in Celtic mythology.

9. lapping: moving from side to side

10. roadway/grey pavements: streets in cities and towns; according to Yeats' own description, he once stood at a square in London and suddenly there arose a great emotion in him and the image of Isle Innisfree came out immediately; these lines show that no matter where the poet is, he would miss the quiet, peaceful and fairy surroundings in Sligo.

When You are Old[1]

When you are old and gray and full of sleep
And nodding by the fire[2], take down this book[3],
And slowly read, and dream of the soft look
Your eyes had once, and of their shadows deep[4];

How many loved your moments of glad grace[5],
And loved your beauty with love false or true,
But one man loved the pilgrim soul in you[6],
And loved the sorrows of your changing face[7];

And bending down beside the glowing bars[8],
Murmur, a little sadly, how Love[9] fled
And paced upon the mountains overhead,
And hid his[10] face amid a crowd of stars.[11]

Notes

1. Notice that Yeats' spelling in certain works is not standardized English; so "are" is not capitalized here; this poem is an imitation of a sonnet by French poet Pierre Ronsard (1524–1585) with Yeats' own adaptations both in form and in meaning; the metrical scheme is iambic pentameter and the rhyming scheme is abba cddc effe.

2. fire: fire in an oven

3. this book: the book of poems that Yeats wrote to Maud Gonne

4. shadows deep: deep shadows of eyes that show the clearness and profoundness of the eyes

5. moments of glad grace: pleasure in glad moments; pleasure on the surface level

6. the pilgrim soul in you: the spirit of a pilgrim in you (Maud Gonne); Maud Gonne is an active nationalist and Yeats praises her national spirit as the spirit of a pilgrim in religious faith.

7. sorrows of your changing face: changes happening in growing old and sometimes some people may consider them as sorrows or pains; see Shakespeare's

"Sonnet 18".

    8. bars: long and straight pieces of metal used in a fireplace

    9. Love: God of Love; Cupid

    10. his: Cupid's

    11. The last three lines are Yeats' imagination and a further confirmation of his loving of the soul of the other party.

The Second Coming[1]

Turning and turning in the widening gyre[2]
The falcon[3] cannot hear the falconer[4];
Things fall apart; the centre cannot hold;
Mere anarchy[5] is loosed upon[6] the world,
The blood-dimmed tide[7] is loosed, and everywhere
The ceremony of innocence[8] is drowned;
The best lack all conviction[9], while the worst
Are full of passionate intensity[10].

Surely some revelation[11] is at hand[12];
Surely the Second Coming is at hand.
The Second Coming! Hardly are those words out
When a vast image out of *Spiritus Mundi*[13]
Troubles my sight: somewhere in sands of the desert
A shape with lion body and the head of a man,
A gaze blank[14] and pitiless as the sun,
Is moving its slow thighs[15], while all about[16] it
Reel[17] shadows of the indignant[18] desert birds.[19]
The darkness drops again; but now I know
That twenty centuries of stony sleep[20]
Were vexed[21] to nightmare by a rocking cradle[22],
And what rough beast[23], its hour come round at last,
Slouches[24] towards Bethlehem[25] to be born?[26]

Notes

1. According to Christian tradition, after the crucifixion of Jesus, he will come to the world for a second time, bringing peace and order in reign. At the same time, "anti-Christ" will also come along the way, bringing chaos, disorder and messing up; the poem describes the scene of this second coming with the poet's imagination.

2. gyre: This is an image that Yeats brought from ancient Celtic culture; it starts from a point and turns in a wider and wider spiral until it falls apart.

3. falcon: a bird of prey with long pointed wings 鹰隼

4. falconer: the person who trains and keeps a falcon usually for hunting; here it means something/the world is out of control.

5. anarchy: state of being in great disorder; the situation of a country or region that is without government, order or control

6. loose upon: spread across; run unchecked

7. the blood-dimmed tide: the tide that is full of blood; brutal fighting or battle scene; studies point out that here Yeats may hint at the happening of WWI (1914–1918) or the turbulent situation in Ireland, or the revolution in contemporary Russia.

8. ceremony of innocence: proper rituals, behavioral principles and conducts that are necessary for a civilized world; notice that "loose" is used three times to show the seriousness of disorder and fighting in the world while the ceremony is drowned.

9. conviction: pious faith (for religion or creed)

10. passionate intensity: the extremest state or situation of passion

11. revelation: (religion) something that is considered to be the sign or message from God

12. at hand: going to happen soon

13. *Spiritus Mundi*: (Latin) the Spirit of the Universe; Yeats once explained it as "a general storehouse of images which have ceased to be the property of any personality or spirit"; to some extent, it equals the idea of Great Memory, mainly supported by Plato, the source of all lives; it is also similar to Jung's concept of "collective unconsciousness".

14. blank: empty and emotionless

15. slow thighs: (transferred epithet 移就) the thighs that are moving slowly

16. about: around

17. reel: fly in circles; hover

18. indignant: fierce

19. These lines are scenes that come to Yeats' mind in a vision that may relate to Egyptian deserts, sphinx, and vultures.

20. stony sleep: (transferred epithet) extremely profound sleep

21. vexed: stimulated; provoked

22. rocking cradle: Here hints the birth of Jesus Christ.

23. rough beast: the sphinx

24. slouch: move slowly with shoulders and head bent forward

25. Bethlehem: a small town in Israel and the birth place of Jesus Christ

26. According to Yeats, history moves in two thousand years' gyre (2000 years as a gyre); for Europe, the first gyre starts with Zeus and Leda and then turns and turns until it falls apart, and here it begins with another gyre; this time it starts with the birth of Jesus Christ and when Yeats wrote the poem (1919) he thinks that the Christian civilization turns for almost 2000 years and it falls apart; but what will come for the next 2000 years Yeats himself does not know either.

Questions for Discussion

(1) Studies have shown that "The Lake Isle of Innisfree" is not only Yeats' reminiscence of the beautiful and peaceful scene in Sligo, also shows Yeats' land consciousness of Ireland. Look at a world map, locate the island of Ireland and try to figure out the land consciousness in some of Yeats' poetry.

(2) "The Lake Isle of Innisfree" and "When You are Old" are Yeats' early or middle stages' poetry that use traditional metrical and rhyming schemes, though not strictly. What do you think is Yeats' reason for doing that?

(3) Scholars point out that Yeats' poetry is also under enormous influence from English and Irish ballad traditions. What are some Irish ballads or folk tales features in Yeats' poetry?

(4) Yeats was not only fascinated by folk tales and fairy talks of countryside Ireland, but also interested in mysterious thoughts as in New Platonism and Jewish

Kabbalah mysticism. How do these influence his "The Second Coming"?

(5) Yeats spent some time in his youth collecting Irish folklore and stories with the help of Lady Gregory. However, Yeats did not understand Irish. In Irish Renaissance Movement, Yeats encouraged writers such as J. M. Synge to write Irish sources, but Yeats always wrote in English. What is his consideration when on the one hand he upheld the idea of reviving Celtic culture (language included) and on the other hand he wrote with no other language than English?

(6) Yeats was not only a prominent poet, but also a significant play writer. Read some of his plays and figure out the similarities and differences between these two genres of his works.

Suggested Reading

(1) William Butler Yeats. *The Collected Poems of W. B. Yeats*. Edited by Richard J. Finneran, New York: Simon & Schuster Inc., 1996.

(2) William Butler Yeats. *The Collected Works of W. B. Yeats Volume II: The Plays*. Edited by David R. Clark and Rosalind E. Clark, New York: Scribner, 2001.

(3) William Butler Yeats. *The Collected Works of W. B. Yeats Volume III: Autobiographies*. Edited by William H. O'Donnell and Douglas N. Archibald, New York: Scribner, 2001.

(4) 叶芝：《叶芝诗集》(上、中、下)，傅浩译，石家庄：河北教育出版社，2002年。

(5) 傅浩：《叶芝评传》，杭州：浙江文艺出版社，1999年。

(6) 欧光安：《借鉴与融合：叶芝诗学思想研究》，天津：南开大学出版社，2017年。

33. John Galsworthy

John Galsworthy(1867–1933), English novelist and playwright, winner of the Nobel Prize for Literature in 1932. He is most well-known for his Forsyte novels.

Galsworthy was born into a rich family. His father was a solicitor. He majored in law when he studied at Oxford University. Because of his interest in marine law, he took a voyage around the world, during which he encountered Joseph Conrad, then the mate of a merchant ship. They became lifelong friends. Influenced by Conrad, Galsworthy found law not to his taste and took to writing. From 1897 to 1901, Galsworthy published four works under the pseudonym John Sinjohn at his own expense. In 1904, Galsworthy published his first novel under his own name: *The Island Pharisees*, which was considered to be one of his most important works. In 1906, *The Man of Property* was included in his famous trilogy "The Forsyte Saga". The other two novels of the saga are *In Chancery* (1920) and *To Let* (1921). The story of the Forsyte family after World War I was continued in *The White Monkey* (1924), *The Silver Spoon* (1926), and *Swan Song* (1928), collected in *A Modern Comedy* (1929). Through this work, Galsworthy launched a severe attack on upper middle class families, to which he himself belonged. He then continued writing a number of novels, short stories and plays. *Strife*, written in 1907, is one of his most successful plays. In 1932, John Galsworthy was awarded the Nobel Prize in Literature. However, at that time he was too ill to receive the award in person and died within six weeks of it.

Galsworthy's works presented the life of the British middle-class in the late 19th and early 20th century. He used very simple language, but the characters were fresh before the readers. Irony is one of the chief methods used by Galsworthy. In the story *Told by the Schoolmaster*, Galsworthy began with "the beauty of the summer when the war broke out" to show the conflict between the peaceful countryside and the cruel war.

Told by the Schoolmaster[1]

We all remember still, I suppose, the beauty of the summer when the war broke out. I was then a schoolmaster in a village on the Thames. Nearly fifty, with a broken shoulder and very deficient sight, there was no question of my fitness for military service. The perfect weather, that beautiful countryside, with the corn harvest just beginning, and the apples already ripening, the quiet nights with their moonlight and shadow, and in it all, this great horror, the death-warrant of millions of young men signed[2]. Such summer loveliness walking hand in hand with murder was too ironical! One of those evenings towards the end of August, I left my house at the end of the village street, and walked up towards the Downs. I have never known anything more entrancing[3] than the beauty of that night. All was still, and coloured like the bloom of dark grapes, so warm, so pleasant. It was perhaps half-past nine when I passed two of my former scholars[4], a boy and a girl, standing silently at the edge of an old pit, opposite a beech tree. They looked up and greeted me. The moon itself was almost golden, as if it were warm to the touch, and from it came the light over sky and fields, woods, farmhouses, and the river down below. I remember thinking that Joe Beckett and Betty Roofe were too young to be sweethearting[5], if indeed they were, for they hadn't looked like it. They could hardly be sixteen yet, for they had only left school last year. Betty Roofe had been an interesting child, alert, self-contained[6], with a well shaped, dark-eyed little face, and a head set on very straight. She was the daughter of the village laundress, and I used to think that she was too good for washing clothes, but she was already doing it and as things went in that village, would probably go on doing it till she married. Joe Beckett was working on Carver's farm down there below me, and the pit was about half way between their homes. A good boy, Joe, freckled[7], reddish in the hair and rather too small in the head; with blue eyes that looked at you very straight and a short nose; a well-grown boy and very big for his age–altogether an interesting boy. I was still standing there when up he came on his way to Carver's and I look back to that next moment with as much regret as to any moment in my life. He held out his hand.

"Good-bye, sir, in case I don't see you again."

"Why, where are you off, Joe?"

"Joining up[8]..."

"Joining up? But, my dear boy, you're two years under age, at least."

He grinned. "I'm sixteen this month, but I bet I can make out to be eighteen. They aren't very particular, I'm told."

I looked him up and down. It was true, he could pass for eighteen well enough, with military needs as they were. And possessed, as every one was just then, by patriotism and anxiety at the news, all I said was:

"I don't think you ought to, Joe; but I admire your spirit."

He stood there silent, then said, "Well, good-bye, sir, I'm going to-morrow."

I gave his hand a good hard squeeze. He grinned again, and without looking back, ran off down the hill towards Carver's farm, leaving me alone once more that night. God! What a crime was war! From this peaceful place boys were hurrying off to that business of man-made death.

And we, –we could only admire them for it! Well! I could never forgive myself that I did not inform the recruiting authorities of that boy's real age.

Crossing back over the hill towards home, I came on[9] the child Betty, at the pit where I had left her.

"Well, Betty, was Joe telling you?"

"Yes, sir, he's going to join up."

"What did you say to him?"

"I said he was a fool, but he is so headstrong!"

Her voice was calm enough, but she was quivering all over.

"It's very plucky[10] of him, Betty."

"You know, Joe gets things into his head. I don't see why he has to go–and leave me."

I couldn't help a smile. She saw it, and said:

"Yes, I'm young, and so is Joe; but he is my boy!"

And then, ashamed at saying it, she ran off among the trees. I stood a few minutes, listening to the owls, then went home and read myself into forgetfulness on one of Scott's first books.

So Joe went, and we knew him no more for a whole year. And Betty continued with her mother washing for the village. In September 1915, just after term had begun, I was standing one afternoon in the village schoolroom pinning up on the wall a picture for my scholars and thinking, as usual, of the war and its deadlock[11]. On the far side of the street I could see a soldier standing with a girl. Suddenly he crossed over to the school, and there in the doorway was young Joe Beckett, in his khaki[12] jacket, square and tanned to the color of his freckles, looking indeed quite a man.

"How d'you do, sir?"

"And you, Joe?"

"Oh! I'm fine. I thought I'd like to see you. I've just got my marching orders. I'm off to France to-morrow. I've been having my leave."

I felt the catch at my throat that we all felt when youngsters whom we know were going out for the first time.

"Was that Betty with you out there?"

"Yes, –the fact is, I've got something to tell you, sir! She and I were married last week at M. We have been staying there since, and I brought her home to-day, as I must go to-night. She just went off there, and I joined her for my leave. We didn't want any fuss, you see, because of our being too young."

"Young!"

"Well, I was seventeen a week ago, and she'll be seventeen next month."

He went to the door, and whistled. Betty came in, dressed in dark blue, very neat and self-contained; only the flush on her round young face marked some disturbance.

"Show him your marriage certificate, and your ring."

The girl held out the official paper, and from it I read that a registrar had married them at M., under right names and wrong ages. Then she slipped a glove off, and held up her left hand, –there was the magic ring!

"Very good of you to tell me, Joe," I said at last. "Am I the first to know?"

"Yes, sir. You see, I've got to go at once. Betty's mother wouldn't like our marriage, because she was too young. I thought I'd like to tell you, in case people said it wasn't all straight and proper."

"Nothing I say will alter the fact that you've falsified your ages."

Joe grinned again.

"That's all right," he said. "I got it from a lawyer's clerk in my platoon. It's a marriage all the same."

"Yes, I believe that's so."

"Well, sir, there she is till! Come back."

Suddenly his face changed, he looked as if he were going to cry; and they stood gazing at each other as if they were alone.

"What time is it, sir?" Joe asked me suddenly.

"Five o'clock."

"Lord! I must run to the station. Could I leave her here, sir?"

I nodded, and walked into the little room beyond. When I came back she was sitting where she used to sit in school, bowed over her arms spread out on the inky desk. Her dark hair was all I could see, and the quivering movement of her young shoulders. Joe had gone. Well! That was the normal state of Europe, then! I went back into the little room to give her time, but when I returned once more, she, too, had gone.

The second winter passed, more muddy, more bloody even than the first, and with no hope of an ending. Betty showed me three or four of Joe's letters where he signed "Your loving Joe."

Her marriage was accepted in the village. Child-marriage was quite common then. In April it began to be obvious that their union was to be "blessed" as they call it. One day early in May I was passing Mrs. Roofe's when I saw that lady in her garden, and stopped to ask after Betty.

"She is nearing her time. I've written to Joe Beckett. Maybe he'll get leave."

"I think that was a mistake, Mrs. Roofe, I would have waited till it was over."

"Maybe you're right, sir, but Betty is so very young, you know, to have a child. I didn't have my first till I was twenty one."

"Everything goes fast these days, Mrs. Roofe."

"Not my washing. I can't get the help with Betty like this. It's a sad business about the baby coming, If he gets killed, I suppose she'll get a pension, sir?"

Pension? Married in the wrong age, with the boy still under service age, if they come to look into it, I really don't know.

"Oh! Surely, Mrs. Roofe, but we won't think about his being killed. Joe's a fine boy."

Mrs. Roofe's worn face darkened.

"He was a fool to join up before his time; plenty of chance after, and then to marry my girl, like this! Well, young folks are fools!"

I was sitting over my pensions work one evening a month later, for I had now decided to keep things listed in the village, when someone knocked at my door, and who should be standing there but Joe Beckett!

"Why, Joe! Got leave?"

"Ah! I had to come and see her. I haven't been there yet, didn't dare. How is she, sir?" Pale and dusty, as if from a hard journey, his uniform all muddy, and unbrushed, and his reddish hair standing up anyhow, –he looked wretched, poor boy! "She's all right, Joe. But it must be very near, from what her mother says."

"I haven't had any sleep for nights, thinking of her, –such a kid, she is!"

"Does she know you're coming?"

"No, I haven't written anything about it.";

"Better be careful. I wouldn't risk a shock. Have you anywhere to sleep?"

"No, sir."

"Well, you can stay here, if you like. They won't have room for you there."

"Thank you, sir. I wouldn't like to put you out[13]."

"Not a bit, Joe. Delighted to have you, and hear your adventures."

He shook his head. "I don't want to talk of them!" he said. "Don't you think I could see her to-night, sir? I've come a long way for it, my God! I have!"

"We'll try! But see her mother first."

"Yes, sir." And he touched his forehead. His face, so young a face, already had that look in the eyes of men who stare death in the face. He went away, and I didn't see him again that night. They had managed apparently to screw him into their tiny cottage. He was only just in time, for two days later Betty had a boy-child. He came to me the same evening, after dark, very excited.

"She's a wonder," he said. "But if I'd known, I'd never have done it, sir. I never would. You can't tell what you're doing till it's too late, it seems." Strange saying from that young father, till afterwards it was made too clear!

Betty recovered quickly and was out within three weeks.

Joe seemed to have long leave, for he was still in the village, but I had little talk with him, for, though always friendly, he seemed shy of me, and as to talking of the war, –not a word!

One evening I passed him and Betty leaning on a gate, close to the river, –a warm evening of early July. I saw those two young things, with their arms round each other, and their heads close together–her dark hair, and Joe's reddish hair, getting quite long! I took good care not to disturb them. His last night, perhaps, before he went back into the furnace! It was no business of mine to have my doubts, but I had been having them long before that very dreadful night when, just as I was going to bed, somebody knocked at my door, and going down, I found Betty outside, excited[14].

"Oh, sir, come quick! They've arrested Joe."

On our way, she told me: "Oh, sir, I was afraid there was some mistake about his leave, –it was so long. I thought he'd get into trouble over it, so I asked Bill Pateman (the village constable[15]) and now they've come and arrested him for deserting[16]. Oh! What have I done? What have I done? Outside the Roofe's cottage, Joe was standing between a corporal's[17] guard, and Betty threw herself into his arms. Inside I could hear Mrs. Roofe speaking with the corporal, and the baby crying."

I spoke to Joe. He answered quietly, in her arms:

"I asked for leave, but they wouldn't give it. I had to come. I couldn't stay there, knowing how it was with her."

"Where was your regiment[18]?"

"In the line."

"Good God!"

Just then the corporal came out. I took him apart.

"I was his schoolmaster, corporal," I said. "The poor chap joined up when he was just sixteen–he's still under age, you see, –and now he's got this child wife and a new born baby!"

The corporal nodded. His face was twitching, a decent face with a moustache.

"I know, sir," he muttered, "I know. Cruel work, but I've got to take him. He'll have to go back to France."

"What does it mean?"

He lifted his arms from his sides and let them drop, and that gesture was somehow the most expressive and dreadful I ever saw.

"Deserting in the face of the enemy," he whispered. "Bad business! Can you get that girl away, sir?"

But Joe freed himself from her arms, he kissed her hair and face; then with a groan, he pushed her into my arms and marched straight off between the guard.

And I was left in the dark street with that excited child struggling in my arms.

"Oh! My God! My God!"

And what could one say or do?

All the rest of that night, after Mrs. Roofe had got Betty back into the cottage, I sat up writing in duplicate[19] the facts about Joe Beckett.

I sent one copy to his regimental headquarters, the other to the chaplain[20] of his regiment in France. I sent fresh copies two days later with duplicates of his birth certificate. It was all 1 could do. Then came a fortnight of waiting for news. Betty was still excited. The thought that, through her anxiety, she herself had delivered him into their hands, nearly sent her off her mind. Probably her baby alone kept her from insanity or suicide. And all that time the battle raged, and hundreds of thousands of women in England and France and Germany were in daily terror for their menfolk. Yet none, I think, could have had quite the feelings of that child. Her mother, poor woman, would come over to me at the schoolhouse, and ask if I had heard anything.

"Better for the poor girl to know the worst," she said, "if it is the worst. The anxiety is killing her." But I had no news and could not get any at headquarters. The thing was being dealt with in France. Never was the world's horror more clear to me. This deadly little tragedy was as nothing, –just a fragment of straw whirling round in that terrible wind.

And then one day I got news, at last–a letter from the chaplain, and seeing what it was I put it into my pocket and hurried down to the river, –afraid to open it till I was alone. Crouched up there, with my back to a haystack, I took it out with trembling fingers.

"Dear Sir,

The boy Joe Beckett was shot this morning. I am distressed at having to tell you and the poor child, his wife. War is a cruel thing, indeed!"

I had known it. Poor Joe! Poor Betty! Poor, poor Betty! I read on:

"I did all I could; the facts you sent were put before the Court Martial[21] and the point of his age considered. But all leave had been stopped; his request had been definitely refused; the regiment was actually in the line, with fighting going on, –and the situation extremely critical in that sector. Private considerations count for nothing in such circumstances. 1 have been greatly distressed by the whole thing, and the court itself was much moved. The poor boy seemed dazed[22]; he wouldn't talk, didn't seem to take in anything; indeed they tell me that all he said after the verdict[23], certainly all I heard him say was: 'My poor wife!' over and over again. He stood up well at the end."

So that boy, like a million others, dripped to dust. A little ironical though that his own side should shoot him who went to fight for them two years before he needed, to shoot him who wouldn't be legal food for powder for another month.

Notes

1. In this novel, Galsworthy expressed his attitude toward war through the fate of an innocent country boy who joined the army under his age and was shot by his own people for he left the army without permission. Galsworthy didn't depict any scenes of the war, but the anxiety and grief brought by war can be felt deeply after reading the novel.

2. the death-warrant of millions of young men signed: If you say that someone is signing their own death warrant, you mean that they are behaving in a way which will cause their ruin or death.

3. entrancing: attractive

4. scholar: pupil

5. sweethearting: *adj.* (old) to be each other's girl friend and boy friend

6. self-contained: *adj.* not needing the company of others; reserved

7. freckled: *adj.* having freckles (small light brown spots on sb's skin)

8. joining up: to join the army

9. come on: go with sb

10. plucky: *adj.* brave and determined, usually refers to someone who is weak but faces difficulties with courage

11. deadlock: *n.* a situation in which a disagreement cannot be settled

12. khaki: *n.* a strong material of a greenish brown colour, used especially to make uniforms for soldiers

13. put... out: cause trouble to someone

14. excited: *adj.* worried or angry about something

15. constable: *n.* policeman of the lowest rank

16. desert: *v.* leave the job in the armed forces without permission

17. corporal: *n.* a low rank in the army

18. regiment: *n.* a British infantry unit

19. in duplicate: as two identical copies

20. chaplain: clergyman serving in the armed forces

21. Court Martial: *n.* a trial in a military court of a member of the armed forces who is charged with breaking a military law

22. dazed: *adj.* feeling confused and not able to think clearly

23. verdict: *n.* the decision that is given by the jury or judge at the end of a trial

Questions for Discussion

(1) This is a short story set in World War I. Compared with other novels which described the cruel scenes in the wars, how did Galsworthy deal with this topic?

(2) In this short story, the author deliberately created several ironies. Can you find them?

(3) Read more short stories by Galsworthy and discuss the characteristics of the use of language in his stories.

Suggested Reading

(1) 方岩、欧光安主编：《英语短篇小说选读》第二版，北京：北京大学出版社，2018 年。

(2) 陈焘宇编选：《高尔斯华绥中短篇小说集》，上海：上海译文出版社，1997 年。

(3) 高尔斯华绥：《诺贝尔文学奖作家短篇小说精选——高尔斯华绥》（英汉对照），青闰、刘建东、丹冰译注，北京：外文出版社，2013 年。

(4) 高尔斯华绥：《高尔斯华绥短篇小说精选——苹果树》，王勋等编译，北京：清华大学出版社，2015 年。

34. D. H. Lawrence

D. H. Lawrence (David Herbert Lawrence) (1885–1930), one of the most famous representative writers of British modernism, was born in a small village of

Eastwood, Nottinghamshire. His father was a miner and his mother was a teacher before she was married. Lawrence's early experience was very similar to that of Paul's in his most famous novel *Sons and Lovers* (1913). Disgusted by his father's vulgar and coarse behaviour, he was very much attached to his mother who was determined to change her son's social status by encouraging him to pursue higher education. But his feelings toward his parents were reversed when he grew up. After the death of his elder brother, Lawrence became the center of his mother's life. He was gradually overwhelmed by his mother's interference in his relationship with girls and felt imprisoned by her possessive love. After graduating from Nottingham University, he became a teacher. Later he met his future wife and went to Germany. Since then, he began his unsettled life. During the war, because of his wife's German origins and his strong objection to the war, he was constantly oppressed by the authorities. In order to search for an ideal and tolerable community, he and his wife moved from England to Australia, America, Mexico and settled in Italy. In 1930, he died of tuberculosis in France. During his lifetime, Lawrence's works were harshly criticized and often associated with pornography, because of his frank and direct description of sexual passion. *The Rainbow* (1915) and *Lady Chatterley's Lover* (1928) were both banned in the UK, while *Women in Love* (1921) could not find a publisher until four years after it was finished. Through his works, Lawrence expressed his deep moral concern for Western civilization. He despised ethical conventions and distrusted modern science. In his view, industrialization led to dehumanization; money and machines were the primary reason for the corruption of human nature. He believed that people should not oppress their sexual passion, for it is a part of human nature.

"The Rocking Horse Winner" is a short story published in 1926. The story takes place in England during the post-industrial revolution period. The young hero Paul, hearing his mother's complaint about having no enough money in their family, determines to get money through luck. Later he finds out that if he rides his rocking horse fast enough, he can somehow "hear" the name of the winning horse in the race. Together with his uncle and gardener, he wins a lot of money by gambling and secretly gives his money to his mother. However, the increasing desire for more money leads him to ride more furiously, and in the end, Paul falls into illness and dies. By describing a well-to-do family that still hungers for money, Lawrence criticized the insatiable pursuit of money and pleasure in modern society. Paul's efforts to make money to please his mother in order to gain luck and parental love expose the cruel reality of the importance of wealth and material possessions in a capitalist society. Like Lawrence's other controversial works, "The Rocking Horse Winner" received a large amount of scholarly debate. Some critics see the story as a reflection of money and relationships in industrial society, while others explore it from a psychoanalytic perspective. Paul's eagerness to provide his family can be interpreted as an unconscious fantasy to replace his father, a concept that psychologist Sigmund Freud termed the "Oedipus complex."

The Rocking Horse Winner

There was a woman who was beautiful, who started with all the advantages, yet she had no luck. She married for love, and the love turned to dust. She had bonny[1] children, yet she felt they had been thrust upon her, and she could not love them. They looked at her coldly, as if they were finding fault with her. And hurriedly she felt she must cover up some fault in herself. Yet what it was that she must cover up she never knew. Nevertheless, when her children were present, she always felt the center of her heart go hard. This troubled her, and in her manner she was all the more gentle and anxious for her children, as if she loved them very much. Only she herself knew that at the center of her heart was a hard little place that could not feel love, no, not for anybody. Everybody else said of her: "She is such a good mother. She adores her children." Only she herself, and her children themselves, knew it was not so. They read it in each other's eyes.

There were a boy and two little girls. They lived in a pleasant house, with a garden, and they had discreet servants, and felt themselves superior to anyone in the neighborhood.

Although they lived in style[2], they felt always an anxiety in the house. There was never enough money. The mother had a small income, and the father had a small income, but not nearly enough for the social position which they had to keep up. The father went in to town to some office. But though he had good prospects, these prospects never materialized[3]. There was always the grinding[4] sense of the shortage of money, though the style was always kept up.

At last the mother said: "I will see if I can't make something." But she did not know where to begin. She racked her brains, and tried this thing and the other, but could not find anything successful. The failure made deep lines come into her face. Her children were growing up; they would have to go to school. There must be more money, there must be more money. The father, who was always very handsome and expensive in his tastes, seemed as if he never *would* be able to do anything worth doing. And the mother, who had a great belief in herself, did not succeed any better, and her tastes were just as expensive.

And so the house came to be haunted by the unspoken phrase: *There must be more money! There must be more money!* The children could hear it all the time, though nobody said it aloud. They heard it at Christmas, when the expensive and splendid toys filled the nursery. Behind the shining modern rocking-horse, behind the smart doll's house, a voice would start whispering: "There *must* be more money! There *must* be more money!" And the children would stop playing, to listen for a moment. They would look into each other's eyes, to see if they had all heard. And each one saw in the eyes of the other two that they too had heard. "There *must* be more money! There *must* be more money!"

It came whispering from the springs of the still-swaying rocking-horse, and even the horse, bending his wooden, champing head, heard it. The big doll, sitting so pink and smirking in her new pram, could hear it quite plainly, and seemed to be smirking all the more self-consciously because of it. The foolish puppy, too, that took the place of the teddy-bear, he was looking so extraordinarily foolish for no other reason but that he heard the secret whisper all over the house: "There *must* be more money!"

Yet nobody ever said it aloud. The whisper was everywhere, and therefore no one spoke it. Just as no one ever says: "We are breathing!" in spite of the fact that breath is coming and going all the time.

"Mother," said the boy Paul one day, "why don't we keep a car of our own? Why do we always use uncle's, or else a taxi?"

"Because we're the poor members of the family," said the mother.

"But why *are* we, mother?"

"Well—I suppose," she said slowly and bitterly, "it's because your father has no luck."

The boy was silent for some time.

"Is luck money, mother?" he asked rather timidly.

"No, Paul. Not quite. It's what causes you to have money."

"Oh!" said Paul vaguely. "I thought when Uncle Oscar said *filthy lucker*, it meant money."

"*Filthy lucre*[5] does mean money," said the mother. "But it's lucre, not luck."

"Oh!" said Paul vaguely. "Then what *is* luck, mother?"

"It's what causes you to have money. If you're lucky you have money. That's why it's better to be born lucky than rich. If you're rich, you may lose your money. But if you're lucky, you will always get more money."

"Oh! Will you? And is father not lucky?"

"Very unlucky, I should say," she said bitterly. The boy watched her with unsure eyes.

"Why?" he asked.

"I don't know. Nobody ever know why one person is lucky and another unlucky."

"Don't they? Nobody at all? Does *nobody* know?"

"Perhaps God. But He never tells."

"He ought to, then. And aren't you lucky either, mother?"

"I can't be, if I married an unlucky husband."

"But by yourself, aren't you?"

"I used to think I was, before I married. Now I think I am very unlucky indeed."

"Why?"

"Well–never mind! Perhaps I'm not really," she said.

The child looked at her, to see if she meant it. But he saw, by the lines of her mouth, that she was only trying to hide something from him.

"Well, anyhow," he said stoutly[6], "I'm a lucky person."

"Why?" said his mother, with a sudden laugh.

He stared at her. He didn't even know why he had said it.

"God told me," he asserted, brazening it out[7].

"I hope He did, dear!" she said, again with a laugh, but rather bitter.

"He did, mother!"

"Excellent!" said the mother, using one of her husband's exclamations.

The boy saw she did not believe him; or, rather, that she paid no attention to his assertion. This angered him somewhat, and made him want to compel her attention[8].

He went off by himself, vaguely, in a childish way, seeking for the clue to "luck." Absorbed, taking no heed of other people, he went about with a sort of stealth[9], seeking inwardly for luck. He wanted luck, he wanted it, he wanted it. When the two girls were playing dolls in the nursery, he would sit on his big rocking-horse, charging madly into space, with a frenzy that made the little girls peer at him uneasily. Wildly the horse careered[10], the waving dark hair of the boy tossed, his eyes had a strange glare in them. The little girls dared not speak to him.

When he had ridden to the end of his made little journey, he climbed down and stood in front of his rocking-horse, staring fixedly into its lowered face. Its red mouth was slightly open, its big eye was wide and glassy-bright.

"Now!" he would silently command the snorting steed. "Now, take me to where there is luck! Now take me!"

And he would slash the horse on the neck with the little whip he had asked Uncle Oscar for. He *knew* the horse could take him to where there was luck, if only he forced it. So he would mount again, and start on his furious ride, hoping at last to get there. He knew he could get there.

"You'll break your horse, Paul!" said the nurse.

"He's always riding like that! I wish he'd leave off!" said his elder sister Joan.

But he only glared down on them in silence. Nurse gave him up. She could make nothing of him. Anyhow he was growing beyond her.

One day his mother and his Uncle Oscar came in when he was on one of his furious rides. He did not speak to them.

"Hallo, you young jockey[11]! Riding a winner?" said his uncle.

"Aren't you growing too big for a rocking-horse? You're not a very little boy any longer, you know," said his mother.

But Paul only gave a blue glare from his big, rather close-set eyes. He would speak to nobody when he was in full tilt. His mother watched him with an anxious expression on her face.

At last he suddenly stopped forcing his horse into the mechanical gallop, and slid down.

"Well, I got there!" he announced fiercely, his blue eyes still flaring, and his sturdy long legs straddling apart.

"Where did you get to?" asked his mother.

"Where I wanted to go," he flared back at her.

"That's right, son!" said Uncle Oscar. "Don't you stop till you get there. What's the horse's name?"

"He doesn't have a name," said the boy.

"Gets on without all right?" asked the uncle.

"Well, he has different names. He was called Sansovino last week."

"Sansovino, eh? Won the Ascot[12]. How did you know his name?"

"He always talks about horse-races with Bassett," said Joan.

The uncle was delighted to find that his small nephew was posted with all the racing news. Bassett, the young gardener, who had been wounded in the left foot in the war and had got his present job through Oscar Cresswell whose batman[13] he had been, was a perfect blade of the "turf." He lived in the racing events, and the small boy lived with him.

Oscar Cresswell got it all from Bassett.

"Master Paul comes and asks me, so I can't do more than tell him, sir," said Bassett, his face terribly serious, as if he were speaking of religious matters.

"And does he ever put anything on a horse he fancies?"

"Well–I don't want to give him away–he's a young sport, a fine sport, sir. Would you mind asking him himself? He sort of takes a pleasure in it, and perhaps he'd feel I was giving him away, sir, if you don't mind."

Bassett was serious as a church.

The uncle went back to his nephew, and took him off for a ride in the car.

"Say, Paul, old man, do you ever put anything on a horse?" the uncle asked.

The boy watched the handsome man closely.

"Why, do you think I oughtn't to?" he parried[14].

"Not a bit of it. I thought perhaps you might give me a tip for the Lincoln."

The car sped on into the country, going down to Uncle Oscar's place in Hampshire.

"Honor bright[15]?" said the nephew.

"Honor bright, son!" said the uncle.

"Well, then, Daffodil."

"Daffodil! I doubt it, sonny. What about Mirza?"

"I only know the winner," said the boy. "That's Daffodil."

"Daffodil, eh?"

There was a pause. Daffodil was an obscure horse comparatively.

"Uncle!"

"Yes, son?"

"You won't let it go any further, will you? I promised Bassett."

"Bassett be damned, old man! What's he got to do with it?"

"We're partners. We've been partners from the first. Uncle, he lent me my first five shillings, which I lost, I promised him, honor bright , it was only between me and him; only you gave me that ten-shilling note I started winning with, so I thought you were lucky. You won't let it go any further, will you?"

The boy gazed at his uncle from those big, hot, blue eyes, set rather close together. The uncle stirred and laughed uneasily.

"Right you are, son! I'll keep your tip private. Daffodil, eh? How much are you putting on him?"

"All except twenty pounds," said the boy. "I keep that in reserve."

The uncle thought it a good joke.

"You keep twenty pounds in reserve, do you, you young romancer? What are you betting, then?"

"I'm betting three hundred," said the boy gravely. "But it's between you and me, Uncle Oscar! Honor bright?"

The uncle burst into a roar of laughter.

"It's between you and me all right, you young Nat Gould[16]," he said, laughing. "But where's your three hundred?"

"Bassett keeps it for me. We're partners."

"You are, are you! And what is Bassett putting on Daffodil?"

"He won't go quite as high as I do, I expect. Perhaps he'll go a hundred and fifty."

"What, pennies?" laughed the uncle.

"Pounds," said the child, with a surprised look at his uncle. "Bassett keeps a bigger reserve than I do."

Between wonder and amusement Uncle Oscar was silent. He pursued the matter no further, but he determined to take his nephew with him to the Lincoln races.

"Now, son," he said, "I'm putting twenty on Mirza, and I'll put five for you on any horse you fancy. What's your pick?"

"Daffodil, uncle."

"No, not the fiver[17] on Daffodil!"

"I should if it was my own fiver," said the child.

"Good! Good! Right you are! A fiver for me and a fiver for you on Daffodil."

The child had never been to a race-meeting before, and his eyes were blue fire. He pursed his mouth tight, and watched. A Frenchman just in front had put his money on Lancelot. Wild with excitement, he flayed his arms up and down, yelling, "*Lancelot! Lancelot!*" in his French accent.

Daffodil came in first, Lancelot second, Mirza third. The child flushed and with eyes blazing, was curiously serene. His uncle brought him four five-pound notes, four to one.

"What am I to do with these?" he cried, waving them before the boy's eyes.

"I suppose we'll talk to Bassett," said the boy. "I expect I have fifteen hundred now; and twenty in reserve; and this twenty."

His uncle studied him for some moments.

"Look here, son!" he said. "You're not serious about Bassett and that fifteen hundred, are you?"

"Yes, I am. But it's between you and me, uncle. Honor bright!"

"Honor bright all bright, son! But I must talk to Bassett."

"If you'd like to be a partner, uncle, with Bassett and me, we could all be partners. Only, you'd have to promise, honor bright, uncle, not to let it go beyond us three. Bassett and I are lucky, and you must be lucky, because it was your ten shillings I started winning with...."

Uncle Oscar took both Bassett and Paul into Richmond Park for an afternoon, and there they talked.

"It's like this, you see, sir," Bassett said. "Master Paul would get me talking about racing events, spinning yearns, you know, sir. And he was always keen on knowing if I'd made or if I'd lost. It's about a year since, now, that I put five shillings on Blush of Dawn for him—and we lost. Then the luck turned, with that ten shillings he had from you, that we put on Singhalese. And since that time, it's been pretty steady, all things considering. What do you say, Master Paul?"

"We're all right when we're sure," said Paul. "It's when we're not quite sure that we go down."

"Oh, but we're careful then," said Bassett.

"But when are you *sure*?" smiled Uncle Oscar.

"It's Master Paul, sir," said Bassett, in a secret, religious voice. "It's as if he had it from heaven. Like Daffodil, now, for the Lincoln. That was as sure as eggs."

"Did you put anything on Daffodil?" asked Oscar Cresswell.

"Yes, sir. I made my bid."

"And my nephew?"

Bassett was obstinately silent, looking at Paul.

"I made twelve hundred, didn't I, Bassett? I told uncle I was putting three hundred on Daffodil."

"That's right," said Bassett, nodding.

"But where's the money?" asked the uncle.

"I keep it safe locked up, sir. Master Paul he can have it any minute he likes to ask for it."

"What, fifteen hundred pounds?"

"And twenty! And *forty*, that is, with the twenty he made on the course."

"It's amazing!" said the uncle.

"If Master Paul offers you to be partners, sir, I would if I were you; if you'll excuse me," said Bassett.

Oscar cresswell thought about it.

"I'll see the money," he said.

They drove home again, and sure enough, Bassett came round to the garden-house with fifteen hundred pounds in notes. The twenty pounds reserve was left with Joe Glee in the Turf Commission[18] deposit.

"You see, it's all right, uncle, when I'm *sure*! Then we go strong, for all we're worth. Don't we, Bassett?"

"We do that, Master Paul."

"And when are you sure?" said the uncle, laughing.

"Oh, well, sometimes I'm *absolutely* sure, like about Daffodil," said the boy; "and sometimes I have an idea; and sometimes I haven't even an idea, have I, Bassett? Then we're careful, because we mostly go down."

"You do, do you! And when you're sure, like about Daffodil, what makes you sure, sonny?"

"Oh, well, I don't know," said the boy uneasily. "I'm sure, you know, uncle; that's all."

"It's as if he had it from heaven, sir," Bassett reiterated[19].

"I should say so!" said the uncle.

But he became a partner. And when he Leger was coming on, Paul was "sure" about Lively Spark, which was a quite inconsiderable horse. The boy insisted on putting a thousand on the horse, Bassett went for five hundred, and Oscar Cresswell two hundred. Lively Spark came in first, and the betting had been ten to one against him. Paul had made ten thousand.

"You see," he said, "I was absolutely sure of him."

Even Oscar Cresswell had cleared[20] two thousand.

"Look here, son," he said, "this sort of thing makes me nervous."

"It needn't, uncle! Perhaps I shan't be sure again for a long time."

"But what are you going to do with your money?" asked the uncle.

"Of course," said the boy, "I started it for mother. She said she had no luck, because father is unlucky, so I thought if I was lucky, it might stop whispering."

"What might stop whispering?"

"Our house. I *hate* our house for whispering."

"What does it whisper?"

"Why—why" —the boy fidgeted—"why, I don't know. But it's always short of money, you know, uncle."

"I know it, son, I know it."

"You know people send mother writs, don't you, uncle?"

"I'm afraid I do," said the uncle.

"And then the house whispers, like people laughing at you behind your back. It's awful, that is! I thought if I was lucky ..."

"You might stop it," added the uncle.

The boy watched him with big blue eyes, that had an uncanny[21] cold fire in them, and he said never a word.

"Well, then!" said the uncle. "What are we doing?"

"I shouldn't like mother to know I was lucky," said the boy.

"Why not, son?"

"She'd stop me."

"I don't think she would."

"Oh!" –and the boy writhed in and odd way–"I *don't* want her to know, uncle."

"All right, son! We'll manage it without her knowing."

They managed it very easily. Paul, at the other's suggestion, handed over five thousand pounds to his uncle, who deposited it with the family lawyer, who was then to inform Paul's mother that a relative had put five thousand pounds into his hands, which sum was to be paid out a thousand pounds at a time, on the mother's birthday, for the next five years.

"So she'll have a birthday present of a thousand pounds for five successive years," said Uncle Oscar. "I hope it won't make it all the harder for her later."

Paul's mother had her birthday in November. The house had been "whispering" worse than ever lately, and, even in spite of his luck, Paul could not bear up against it.

He was very anxious to see the effect of the birthday letter, telling his mother about the thousand pounds.

When there was no visitors, Paul now took his meals with his parents, as he was beyond the nursery control. His mother went into town nearly every day. She had discovered that she had an odd knack of sketching furs and dress materials, so she worked secretly in the studio of a friend who was the chief "artist" for the leading drapers. She drew the figures of ladies in furs and ladies in silk and sequins for the newspaper advertisements. This young woman artist earned several thousand pounds a year, but Paul's mother only made several hundreds, and she was again dissatisfied. She so wanted to be first in something, and she did not succeed, even in making sketches for drapery advertisements.

She was down to breakfast on the morning of her birthday. Paul watched her face as she read her letters. He knew the lawyer's letter. As his mother read it, her face hardened and became more expressionless. Then a cold, determined look came on her mouth. She hid the letter under the pile of others, and said not a word about it.

"Didn't you have anything nice in the post for your birthday, mother?" said Paul.

"Quite moderately nice," she said, her voice cold and absent.

She went away to town without saying more.

But in the afternoon Uncle Oscar appeared. He said Paul's mother had had a long interview with the lawyer, asking if the whole five thousand could not be advanced at once, as she was in debt.

"What do you think, uncle?" said the boy.

"I leave it to you, son."

"Oh, let her have it, then! We can get some more with the other," said the boy.

"A bird in the hand is worth two in the bush, laddie!" said Uncle Oscar.

"But I'm sure to *know* for the Grand National[22]; or the Lincolnshire[23]; or else the Derby[24]. I'm sure to know for *one* of them," said Paul.

So Uncle Oscar signed the agreement, and Paul's mother touched the whole five thousand. Then something very curious happened. The voices in the house suddenly went mad, like a chorus of frogs on a spring evening. There were certain new furnishings, and Paul had a tutor. He was *really* going to Eton, his father's school, in the following autumn. There were flowers in the winter, and a blossoming of the luxury Paul's mother had been used to. And yet the voices in the house, behind the sprays of mimosa and almond blossom, and from under the piles of iridescent cushions, simply trilled and screamed in a sort of ecstasy: "There *must* be more money! Oh-h-h; there *must* be more money. Oh, now, now-w! Now-w-w–there *must* be more money!—more than ever! More than ever!"

It frightened Paul terribly. He studied away at his Latin and Greek with his tutors. But his intense hours were spent with Bassett. The Grand National had gone by: he had not "known", and had lost a hundred pounds. Summer was at hand. He was in agony for the Lincoln. But even for the Lincoln he didn't "know", and he lost fifty pounds. He became wild-eyed and strange, as if something were going to explode in him.

"Let it alone, son! Don't you bother about it!" urged Uncle Oscar. But it was as if the boy couldn't really hear what his uncle was saying.

"I've got to know for the Derby! I've got to know for the Derby!" the child reiterated, his big blue eyes blazing with a sort of madness.

His mother noticed how overwrought[25] he was.

"You'd better go to the seaside. Wouldn't you like to go now to the seaside, instead of waiting? I think you'd better," she said, looking down at him anxiously, her heart curiously heavy about him.

But the child lifted his uncanny blue eyes.

"I couldn't possibly go before the Derby, mother!" he said. "I couldn't possibly!"

"Why not?" she said, her voice becoming heavy when she was opposed. "Why not? You can still go from the seaside to see the Derby with your Uncle Oscar, if that's what you wish. No need for you to wait here. Besides, I think you care too much about these races. It's a bad sign. My family has been a gambling family, and you won't know till you grow up how much damage it has done. But it has done damage. I shall have to send Bassett away, and ask Uncle Oscar not to talk racing to you, unless you promise to be reasonable about it; go away to the seaside and forget it. You're all nerves!"

"I'll do what you like, mother, so long as you don't send me away till after the Derby," the boy said.

"Send you away from where? Just from this house?"

"Yes," he said, gazing at her.

"Why, you curious child, what makes you care about this house so much, suddenly? I never knew you loved it."

He gazed at her without speaking. He had a secret within a secret, something he had not divulged[26], even to Bassett or to his Uncle Oscar.

But his mother, after standing undecided and a little bit sullen for some moments, said:

"Very well, then! Don't go to the seaside till after the Derby, if you don't wish it. But promise me you won't let your nerves to go pieces. Promise you won't think so much about horse-racing and *events*, as you call them!"

"Oh, no," said the boy casually. "I won't think much about them, mother. You needn't worry. I wouldn't worry, mother, if I were you."

"If you were me and I were you," said his mother, "I wonder what we *should do*!"

"But you know you needn't worry, mother, don't you?" the boy repeated.

"I should be awfully glad to know it," she said wearily.

"Oh, well, you can, you know. I mean, you *ought* to know you needn't worry," he insisted.

"Ought I? Then I'll see about it," she said.

Paul's secret of secrets was his wooden horse, that which had no name. Since he was emancipated from a nurse and a nursery-governess, he had had his rocking-horse removed to his own bedroom at the top of the house.

"Surely, you're too big for a rocking-horse!" his mother had remonstrated.

"Well, you see, mother, till I can have a *real* horse, I like to have *some* sort of animal about," had been his quaint answer.

"Do you feel he keeps you company?" she laughed.

"Oh, yes! He's very good, he always keeps me company, when I'm there," said Paul.

So the horse, rather shabby, stood in an arrested prance in the boy's bedroom.

The Derby was drawing near, and the boy grew more and more tense. He hardly heard what was spoken to him, he was very frail, and his eyes were really uncanny. His mother had sudden strange seizures of uneasiness about him. Sometimes, for half-an-hour, she would feel a sudden anxiety about him that was almost anguish. She wanted to rush to him at once, and know he was safe.

Two nights before the Derby, she was at a big party in town, when one of her rushes of anxiety about her boy, her first-born, gripped her heart till she could hardly speak. She fought with the feeling, might and main[27], for she believed in common sense. But it was too strong. She had to leave the dance and go downstairs to telephone to the country. The children's nursery-governess was terribly surprised and startled at being rung up in the night.

"Are all the children all right, Miss Wilmot?"

"Oh, yes, they are quite all right."

"Master Paul? Is he all right?"

"He went to bed as right as a trivet[28]. Shall I run up and look at him?"

"No," said Paul's mother reluctantly. "No! Don't trouble. It's all right. Don't sit up. We shall be home fairly soon." She did not want her son's privacy intruded upon.

"Very good," said the governess.

It was about one o'clock when Paul's mother and father drove up to their house. All was still. Paul's mother went to her room and slipped off her white fur cloak. She had told her maid not to wait up for her. she heard her husband downstairs, mixing a whisky-and-soda.

And then, because of the strange anxiety at her heart, she stole upstairs to her son's room. Noiselessly she went along the upper corridor. Was there a faint noise? What was it?

She stood, with arrested[29] muscles, outside his door, listening. There was a strange, heavy, and yet not loud noise. Her heart stood still. It was a soundless noise, yet rushing and powerful. Something huge, in violent, hushed motion. What was it? What in God's name was it? She ought to know. She felt that she knew the noise. She knew what it was.

Yet she could not place it. She couldn't say what it was. And on and on it went, like a madness.

Softly, frozen with anxiety and fear, she turned the door-handle.

The room was dark. Yet in the space near the window, she heard and saw something plunging to and fro. She gazed in fear and amazement.

Then suddenly she switched on the light, and saw her son, in his green pajamas, madly surging on the rocking-horse. The blaze of light suddenly lit him up, as he urged the wooden horse, and lit her up, as she stood, blonde, in her dress of pale green and crystal, in the doorway.

"Paul!" she cried. "Whatever are you doing?"

"It's Malabar!" he screamed, in a powerful, strange voice. "It's Malabar!"

His eyes blazed at her for one strange and senseless second, as he ceased urging his wooden horse. Then he fell with a crash to the ground, and she, all her tormented motherhood flooding upon her, rushed to gather him up.

But he was unconscious, and unconscious he remained, with some brain-fever.

He talked and tossed, and his mother sat stonily by his side.

"Malabar! It's Malabar! Bassett, Bassett, I *know*! It's Malabar!"

So the child cried, trying to get up and urge the rocking-horse that gave him his inspiration.

"What does he mean by Malabar?" asked the heart-frozen mother.

"I don't know," said the father stonily.

"What does he mean by Malabar?" she asked her brother Oscar.

"It's one of the horses running for the Derby," was the answer.

And, in spite of herself, Oscar Cresswell spoke to Bassett, and himself put a thousand on Malabar: at fourteen to one.

The third day of the illness was critical: they were waiting for a change. The boy, with his rather long, curly hair, was tossing ceaselessly on the pillow. He neither slept nor regained consciousness, and his eyes were like blue stones. His mother sat, feeling her heart had gone, turned actually into a stone.

In the evening, Oscar Cresswell did not come, but Bassett sent a message, saying could he come up for one moment, just one moment? Paul's mother was very angry at the intrusion, but on second thought she agreed. The boy was the same. Perhaps Bassett might bring him to consciousness.

The gardener, a shortish fellow with a little brown moustache, and sharp little brown eyes, tiptoed into the room touched his imaginary cap to Paul's mother, and stole to the bedside, staring with glittering, smallish eyes, at the tossing, dying child.

"Master Paul!" he whispered. "Master Paul! Malabar came in first all right, a clean win. I did as you told me. You've made over seventy thousand pounds, you have; you've got over eight thousand. Malabar came in all right, Master Paul."

"Malabar! Malabar! Did I say Malabar, mother? Did I say Malabar? Do you think I'm lucky, mother? I knew Malabar, didn't I? Over eighty thousand pounds! I call that lucky, don't you, mother? Over eighty thousand pounds! I knew, didn't I know I knew? Malabar came in all right. If I ride my horse till I'm sure, then I tell you, Bassett, you can go as high as you like. Did you go for all you were worth, Bassett?"

"I went a thousand on it, Master Paul."

"I never told you, mother, that if I can ride my horse, and *get there*, then I'm absolutely sure–oh, absolutely! Mother, did I ever tell you? I *am* lucky!"

"No, you never did," said the mother.

But the boy died in the night.

And even as he lay dead, his mother heard her brother's voice saying to her: "My God, Hester, you're eighty-odd thousand to the good, and a poor devil of a son to the bad. But, poor devil, poor devil, he's best gone out of a life where he rides his rocking-horse to find a winner."

Notes

1. bonny: *adj.* (dialect, especially *ScotE*) very pretty
2. live in style: live in luxury
3. these prospects never materialized: these expectations will never be fulfilled
4. grinding: *adj.* (of a difficult situation) that never ends or improves
5. *Filthy lucre*: *n.* shameful profit; easy money
6. stoutly: *adv.* firmly; resolutely
7. brazen it out: to face trouble or blame with unashamed confidence, as if you have done nothing wrong
8. compel her attention: attract/catch her attention
9. stealth: *n.* the fact of doing something in a quiet or secret way
10. career: *v.* (of a person or vehicle) to move forward very quickly, especially in an uncontrolled way
11. jockey: *n.* a person who rides horses in races, especially as a job
12. Ascot: *n.* the most famous horse race in the world, which is held annually in a town called Ascot in Southern England
13. batman: *n.* the personal servant of an officer in the armed forces
14. parry: *v.* to avoid having to answer a difficult question, criticism, etc., especially by replying in the same way
15. honor bright: swear on one's honor
16. Nat Gould: Nathaniel Gould (1857–1919) , a British writer and journalist who has written more than 100 popular novels about horse racing
17. fiver: *n.* £5 or a five-pound note

18. Turf Commission: racing commission

19. reiterate *v.* to repeat something that you have already said, especially to emphasize it

20. clear: *v.* to gain or earn a sum of money as profit

21. uncanny: *adj.* strange and difficult to explain; weird

22. Grand National: *n.* an annual steeplechase run at Aintree, Liverpool, since 1839

23. Lincolnshire: Lincolnshire horse racing

24. Derby: An annual race for three-year-old horses, founded in 1780 by the 12th Earl of Derby. The race is run on Epsom Downs in England in late May or early June.

25. overwrought: *adj.* extremely upset and emotional

26. divulge: *v.* reveal

27. might and main: does her best

28. as right as a trivet: safe and sound

29. arrested: *adj.* tightened

Questions for Discussion

(1) Who killed Paul? Analyze the factors that led to Paul's tragic death.

(2) In the story, the rocking horse appears three times. Note the author's use of symbols, and analyze the symbolic meanings of the rocking horse.

(3) Does the house really whisper? What effects does the repetition of "There must be more money!" have?

(4) Lawrence used fable-like narration both at the beginning and end of the story. What are the advantages of such narrative techniques?

(5) Some analysts view Paul's tragic ending as a reflection of his desire to win parental love from a hard-hearted mother. Compare the maternal image he created in *Sons and Lovers*, and analyze the relationship between mother and son from a psychoanalytic perspective.

Suggested Reading

(1) D. H. Lawrence. *The Rocking-Horse Winner*. Whitefish: Kessinger

Publishing, 2004.

(2) Jeffrey Meyers. *D. H. Lawrence: A Biography*. New York: Cooper Square Press, 2002.

(3) Zhu Tongbo, ed. *D. H. Lawrence Selected Literary Critiques*. Shanghai: Shanghai Foreign Language Education Press, 2003.

(4) 劳伦斯：《劳伦斯论文艺》，黑马译，北京：团结出版社，2006 年。

(5) 约翰·沃森：《劳伦斯：局外人的一生》，石磊译，上海：上海书店出版社，2012 年。

(6) 刘宪之、饭田武郎、德拉尼、冈田泰治主编：《劳伦斯研究》，济南：山东友谊书社，1991 年。

(7) 罗婷：《劳伦斯研究——劳伦斯的生平、著作和思想》，长沙：湖南文艺出版社，1996 年。

35. James Joyce

James Joyce (1882–1941) is one of the most venerable Irish novelists in the twentieth century. Born in 1882, Joyce was brought up in a big family in Dublin. Although his father was a talented singer, his years of neglect of his family led to a financial plight. Joyce by his own intelligence learned a new language Norwegian and further he read a lot of works by Henrik Ibsen, Dante and so on. Later, he received a bachelor's degree from University College Dublin. His gift in language rendered him a multilingual speaker, an expert in seventeen languages. After the start of his literary career, Joyce flew to Trieste, an Italian city, with Nora Barnacle in 1904. There Joyce worked as a teacher while keep writing. From 1914 to 1916, two significant novels came out–*Dubliners* (1914) and *A Portrait of the Artist as a Young Man* (1916), which were not well-received commercially. During this period, he was acquainted with Ezra Pound and William Butler Yeats. Pond hailed Joyce as an unconventional voice. The year 1922 witnessed Joyce's literary milestone. With the publication of *Ulysses*, Joyce presented readers with his finest employment of a special literary device—the stream of consciousness, which recorded the narrator's flow of thought through his own visual observations and psychological changes. *Ulysses*, however, was not a reader-friendly work. It was even banned for several years under the doubt of pornography. It was not an easy road for the public finally read this novel, which was indeed a classic in English literature. All these adversities could not deny the fact that James Joyce had established quite a reputation as a novelist. In his later years, Joyce published *Finnegans Wake* (1939), which was a huge success. Two years later, Joyce died in Zurich.

Ulysses is a modern imitation of Homer's epic poem *Odyssey*, which tells the hero, Odysseus, encounters countless adversities, temptations and trials on his way back home to Ithaca. It takes Odysseus almost ten years to end his wandering after the Trojan War. Joyce's *Ulysses* encompasses three main characters Leopold Bloom, Stephen Dedalus and Marion Bloom; they are modern substitute characters for Odysseus Telemachus, and Penelope in *Odyssey*. Different from Odysseus' decade of hardships, the story in *Ulysses* is set in twenty-four hours. In eighteen episodes, it relates a simple story with complex images. The portrayal of psychological struggle is inextricably interwoven among the three main characters. Leopold Bloom roams in the streets for being a coward to disclose his wife Molly's affair with another man. Each scene in his eyes triggers his contemplation over life. When he encounters a child's funeral, Bloom ponders over his son, the poor little Rudy, who dies in infancy. The second protagonist is a young artist who lives in the abyss of guilt for disobeying his mother's last will. The only female character Molly is also wandering in her own stream of consciousness. In general, *Ulysses* is a simple novel set in a short time schedule, it describes the most ordinary daily life. Nevertheless, with various themes, the contrived structure, and the complicated context, *Ulysses* deserves more profound interpretations from generations to come. Lestrogonians in Homer's *Odyssey* are a tribe of giant cannibals. The fragment described by Joyce is a description of people eating in the restaurant with the intention to compare people who eat in the restaurant to the giant Lestrogonians in a sarcastic way.

Ulysses

([b. Lestrogonians])

His heart astir[1] he pushed in the door of the Burton restaurant. Stink gripped his trembling breath: pungent meatjuice, slop of greens. See the animals[2] feed.

Men, men, men.

Perched on high stools by the bar, hats shoved back, at the tables calling for more bread no charge, swilling, wolfing gobfuls of sloppy food[3], their eyes bulging, wiping wetted moustaches. A pallid suetfaced young man[4] polished his tumbler knife fork and spoon with his napkin. New set of microbes. A man with an infant's saucestained napkin tucked round him shovelled gurgling soup down his gullet. A man spitting back on his plate: halfmasticated gristle[5]: no teeth to chewchewchew[6] it. Chump chop from the grill. Bolting to get it over. Sad booser's eyes. Bitten off more than he can chew. Am I like that? See ourselves as others see us. Hungry man is an angry man. Working tooth and jaw. Don't! O! A bone! That last pagan king of Ireland Cormac in the schoolpoem choked himself at Sletty southward of the Boyne. Wonder what he was eating. Something galoptious[7]. Saint Patrick converted him to Christianity. Couldn't swallow it all however.

– Roast beef and cabbage.

– One stew.

Smells of men. His gorge rose[8]. Spaton sawdust, sweetish warmish cigarette smoke, reek of plug, spilt beer, men's beery piss, the stale of ferment.

Couldn't eat a morsel here. Fellow sharpening knife and fork, to eat all before him, old chap picking his tootles. Slight spasm, full, chewing the cud. Before and after. Grace[9] after meals. Look on this picture then on that. Scoffing up stewgravy with sopping sippets of bread[10]. Lick it off the plate, man! Get out of this.

He gazed round the stooled and tabled eaters, tightening the wings of his nose.

– Two stouts here.

– One corned and cabbage.

That fellow ramming[11] a knifeful of cabbage down as if his life depended on it. Good stroke. Give me the fidgets to look.[12] Safer to eat from his three hands. Tear it limb from limb. Second nature to him. Born with a silver knife in his mouth. That's witty, I think. Or no. Silver means born rich. Born with a knife. But then the allusion is lost.

An illgirt server gathered sticky clattering plates. Rock, the bailiff, standing at the bar blew the foamy crown from his tankard. Well up: it splashed yellow near his boot. A diner, knife and fork upright, elbows on table, ready for a second helping stared towards the foodlift across his stained square of newspaper. Other chap telling him something with his mouth full. Sympathetic listener. Table talk. I munched hum un thu Unchster Bunk un Munchday[13]. Ha? Did you, faith?

Mr Bloom raised two fingers doubtfully to his lips. His eyes said.

– Not here. Don't see him.

Out. I hate dirty eaters.

He backed towards the door. Get a light snack in Davy Byrne's. Stopgap. Keep me going. Had a good breakfast.

– Roast and mashed here.

– Pint of stout.

Every fellow for his own, tooth and nail. Gulp. Grub. Gulp. Gobstuff.

He came out into clearer air and turned back towards Grafton street. Eat or be eaten. Kill! Kill!

Notes

1. astir: (his heart) beats quickly

2. animals: referring to men dining in the restaurant

3. swilling, wolfing gobfuls of sloppy food: eating and swallowing food containing liquid

4. a pallid suetfaced young man: a young man with a pale and oily face

5. halfmasticated gristle: half chewed inedible meat

6. chewchewchew: chew

7. something galoptious: something hard to swallow

8. His gorge rose.: He felt physically sick.

9. Grace: a short prayer before a meal to thank God

10. scoffing up stewgravy with sopping sippets of bread: sipping the bread with left soup of stewed meat

11. ramming: putting something into one's mouth rudely

12. Give me the fidgets to look.: Looking at this scene makes me restless.

13. Munchday: Monday; Joyce gave the wrong spellings here on purpose.

Questions for Discussion

(1) Is Bloom's observation of customers in the restaurant rational? Why does Bloom feel sick when he sees the scene of eating?

(2) In the end, Bloom decides to get a light snack at Davy Byrne's. Why does he make such a decision?

(3) How do you understand the relationship between Bloom and Stephen? Do they resemble the relationship between father and son?

(4) Read this novel in its entirety. Will Bloom reveal Molly's cheating on him in the end? Why or why not?

(5) Is Bloom's stream of consciousness a mental torture to him? How do you understand his mental activities?

(6) *Ulysses* in structure parallels Homer's *Odyssey*. Compare their structures in chronological order.

Suggested Reading

(1) James Joyce. *Ulysses*. Hertfordshire: Wordsworth Classics, 2010.

(2) Joseph Campell. *Mythic Worlds, Modern Words: On the Art of James Joyce*. Novato: New World Library, 2016.

(3) Richard Ellman. *Ulysses on the Liffey*. New York: Oxford University Press, 1972.

(4) 詹姆斯·乔伊斯：《尤利西斯》，萧乾、文洁若译，南京：江苏凤凰文艺出版社，2018 年。

(5) 特伦斯·霍克斯：《结构主义和符号学》，瞿铁鹏译，刘峰校，上海：上海译文出版社，1987 年。

(6) 施琪嘉主编：《创伤心理学》，北京：人民卫生出版社，2013 年。

36. William S. Maugham

William S. Maugham (1874–1965), was an English novelist, playwright, short-story writer and one of the most reputed and well-known writers of his era, whose work is characterized by the simple style of writing, as well as sharp and accurate understanding and judgment of human nature.

Maugham was born in 1874 in Paris, where his father handled legal affairs for the British embassy. Unfortunately, he lost both parents when he was only 10 years old, after which he was sent to the UK to be brought up by an uncle. However, his uncle was proved to be cold and unsympathetic to young William. He was sent to King's school in Canterbury. Because French was his first language, he had very bad English, for which he was often mocked. He also developed a stammer which stayed throughout his life. At the age of 16, he refused to continue his education at King's school. So his uncle sent him to study at Heidelberg University. There he wrote his first book. Later, Maugham tried different jobs, and he even practiced medicine as a doctor, but was not really interested in these jobs. In 1897, he wrote his first novel *Liza of Lambeth*, which became an immediate success. After that, Maugham gave up medicine to take up writing as his preferred career. By 1914, Maugham had produced ten plays and published ten novels. Maugham traveled a lot in British colonies and he recorded his experience into his novels.

His major works are: *Of Human Bondage* (1915), a semi-autobiographical account of a young medical student's painful progress toward maturity; *The Moon and Sixpence* (1919), an account of an unconventional artist, suggested by the life of Paul Gauguin; and *The Razor's Edge* (1944), the story of a young American war veteran's quest for a satisfying way of life. In 1928, the publication of his collection of short stories *Ashenden* won him popular recognition as a superb storyteller. Many of his short stories portray the conflict of Europeans in alien surroundings that provoke strong emotions, and Maugham's skill in handling the plot is distinguished as economy and suspense.

Home

The farm lay among the Somersetshire hills, an old-fashioned stone house that was surrounded by barns. Over the doorway the date when it was built had been carved, 1673, and the house looked like a part of the landscape. An avenue of splendid elms[1] led from the road to the trim garden. The people who lived here were as unpretentious[2] as the house: their only boast was that ever since it was built from father to son in one unbroken line they had been born and died in it. For three hundred years they had farmed the surrounding land. George Meadows was now a man of fifty and his wife was a year or two younger. They were both fine people in the prime of life; and their children, two sons and three girls, were handsome and strong. They had no notions about being gentlemen and ladies; they knew their place and were proud of it. I have never seen a more united household. They were merry, industrious and kindly. Their life was patriarchal[3].

They were happy and they deserved their happiness. But the master of the house was not GEORGE Meadows: it was his mother. She was twice the man her son was[4], they said in the village. She was a woman of seventy, tall, upright, and dignified, with gray hair, and though her face was much wrinkled, her eyes were bright and shrewd. Her word was law in the house and on the farm; but she had humour, and if her rule was despotic[5] it was also kindly. She was a good business woman and you had to get up very early in the morning to best[6] her in a bargain. She was a character.

One day Mrs. George stopped me on my way home. (Her mother-in-law was the only Mrs. Meadows we knew: George's wife was known only as Mrs. George.)

"Who do you think is coming here today?" she asked me. "Uncle George Meadows. You know, he was in China."

"Why, I thought he was dead."

"We all thought he was dead."

I had heard the story of Uncle George Meadows a dozen times and it had amused me because it was like an old ballad; it was touching to come across it in real life. For Uncle George Meadows and Tom, his younger brother, had both courted Mrs. Meadows when she was Emily Green, fifty years and more ago, and when she married Tom, George had gone away to sea.

They heard that he was on the China coast. For twenty years now and then he sent them presents; then there was no more news of him. When Tom Meadows died his widow wrote to George and told him, but received no answer; and at last they came to the conclusion that he must be dead. But two or three days ago to their astonishment they had received a letter from the matron[7] of the sailors' home at Portsmouth[8]. It appeared that for the last ten years George Meadows, crippled with rheumatism[9], had been an inmate[10] and now, feeling that he had not much longer to live, wanted to see once more the house in which he was born. Albert Meadows had gone to Portsmouth in a car to fetch him and he was to arrive that afternoon.

"Just fancy," said Mrs. George, "he has not been here for more than fifty years. He has never seen my George who's fifty-one next year."

"And what does Mrs. Meadows think of it?" I asked.

"Well, you know what she is. She sits there and smiles to herself. All she says is 'He was a good-looking young fellow when he left, but not so steady as his brother.' That's why she chose my George's father. But he's probably quietened down[11] by now, she says."

Mrs. George asked me to look in and see him. With the simplicity of a country-woman who had never been further from her home than London, she thought that because we had both been in China we must have something in common. Of course I accepted.

I found the whole family assembled when I arrived; they were sitting in the great old kitchen with its stone floor, Mrs. Meadows in her usual chair by the fire, very upright, and I was amused to see that she had put on her best silk dress, while her son and his wife sat at the table with their children. On the other side of the fireplace sat an old man, hunched up[12] in a chair. He was very thin and his skin hung on his bones like an old suit much too large for him; his face was wrinkled and yellow and he had lost nearly all his teeth.

I shook hands with him.

"Well, I'm glad to see you've got here safely, Mr. Meadows," I said.

"Captain," he corrected.

"He walked here," Albert told me. "When he got to the gate he made me stop the car and said he wanted to walk."

"And mind you, I've not been out of my bed for two years. They carried me down and put me in the car. I thought I'd never walk again, but when I saw the elm trees I felt I could walk. I walked down that drive fifty-two years ago when I went away and now I've walked back again."

"Silly, I call it," said Mrs. Meadows.

"It's done me good. I feel better and stronger than I have for ten years. I'll see you out yet,[13] Emily."

"Don't you be too sure," she answered.

I suppose no one had called Mrs. Meadows by her first name for a generation. It gave me a little shock, as though the old man were taking a liberty with her[14]. She looked at him with a shrewd smile in her eyes and he, talking to her, grinned with his toothless mouth. It was strange to look at them, these two old people who had not seen one another for half a century, and to think that all that long time ago he had loved her and she had loved another. I wondered if they remembered what they had felt then and what they had said to one another.

I wondered if it seemed to him strange now that for that old woman he had left the home of his fathers, his lawful inheritance, and lived an exile's life.

"Have you ever been married, Captain Meadows?" I asked.

"Not me," he said in his low voice. "I know too much about women for that."

"That's what you say," remarked Mrs. Meadows. "If the truth was known I shouldn't be surprised to hear you'd had half-a-dozen black wives in your day."

"They're not black in China, Emily, you ought to know better than that, they're yellow."

"Perhaps that's why you've got so yellow yourself. When I saw you, I said to myself, why, he's got jaundice[15]."

"I said I'd never marry anyone but you, Emily, and I never have."

He said this not with pathos[16] or resentment, but as a mere statement of fact, as a man might say, "I said I'd walk twenty miles and I've done it." There was some satisfaction in the speech.

"Well, you might have regretted it if you had," she answered.

I talked a little with the old man about China.

"There's not a port in China that I don't know better than you know your coat pocket. Where a ship can go I've been. I could keep you sitting here all day long for six months and not tell you half the things I've seen in my day."

"Well, one thing you've not done, George, as far as I can see," said Mrs. Meadows, the mocking but not unkindly smile still in her eyes, "and that is to make a fortune."

"I'm not one to save money. Make it and spend it: that's my motto. But one thing I can say for myself: if I had the chance of going through my life again I'd take it. And there are not many who'll say that."

"No, indeed," I said.

I looked at him with admiration and respect. He was a toothless, crippled, penniless old man, but he had made a success of life, for he had enjoyed it.

When I left him he asked me to come and see him again next day. If I was interested in China he would tell me all the stories I wanted to hear.

Next morning I thought I would go and ask if the old man would like to see me. I walked down the avenue of elm trees and when I came to the garden saw Mrs. Meadows picking flowers.

I bade her good morning[17] and she raised herself. She had a huge armful of white flowers. I glanced at the house and saw that the blinds[18] were drawn: I was surprised, for Mrs. Meadows liked the sunshine.

"Time enough to live in the dark when you're buried," she always said.

"How's Captain Meadows?" I asked her.

"He always was a harun-scarum[19] fellow," she answered. "When Lizzie brought him a cup of tea this morning she found he was dead."

"Dead?"

"Yes. Died in his sleep. I was just picking these flowers to put in the room. Well, I'm glad he died in that old house. It always means a lot to the Meadows to do that."

They had had a good deal of difficulty in persuading him to go to bed. He had talked to them of all the things that had happened to him in his long life. He was happy to be back in his old home. He was proud that he had walked up the drive without assistance, and he boasted that he would live for another twenty years. But death had put the full stop in the right place.

Mrs. Meadows smelt the white flowers that she held in her arms.

"Well, I'm glad he came back," she said. "After I married Tom Meadows and

George went away, the fact is I was never quite sure that I'd married the right one."

Notes

1. elms: *n.* trees that have broad leaves

2. unpretentious: *adj.* modest

3. patriarchal: *adj.* ruled or controlled by men

4. She was twice the man her son was: She was much better and stronger than her son; it means she was the real ruler of this family.

5. despotic: *adj.* using power in a cruel and unreasonable way

6. best: *v.* defeat

7. matron: *n.* woman in charge of the nurses in a hospital

8. Portsmouth: a town and port on the south coast of England

9. rheumatism: *n.* an illness that makes your joints or muscles stiff and painful

10. inmate: *n* patient in a hospital

11. quieten down: less noisy or less active

12. hunch up: bend forward into a rounded shape

13. I will see you out yet: I could still escort you to the door when you want to go somewhere

14. take a liberty with (sb): (old-fashioned) to treat someone without respect by being too friendly too quickly

15. jaundice: *n.* an illness that makes your skin and eyes yellow

16. pathos: *n.* something that causes a feeling of pity or sadness

17. bid her good morning: say good morning to her

18. blind: *n.* a window cover that one pulls down from the top to the bottom

19. harun-scarum: *adj.* reckless; rash; impulsive

Questions for Discussion

(1) When did George Meadows return from China? Why did he go to the matron of the sailors' home at Portsmouth instead of his own home?

(2) What do you think of George's decision to leave his hometown because of the rejection from his loved one?

(3) What did Mrs. Meadows mean when she said "After I married Tom Meadows and George went away, the fact is I was never quite sure that I'd married the right one"?

(4) Read more short fictions by Maugham and discuss how his sharp observation of human nature made his short stories so popular with readers.

Suggested Reading

(1) William S. Maugham. *Sixty-five Short Stories*. London: William Heinemann Limited and Octopus Books Limited, 1976.

(2) 威廉·萨默塞特·毛姆：《生活的真相：毛姆短篇小说选》，叶雷等译，南京：译林出版社，2017 年。

(3) 毛姆：《爱德华·巴纳德的堕落 毛姆短篇小说全集 I》，陈以侃译，桂林：广西师范大学出版社，2016 年。

(4) 毛姆：《人性的因素 毛姆短篇小说全集 II》，陈以侃译，桂林：广西师范大学出版社，2018 年。

(5) 毛姆：《英国特工阿申登 毛姆短篇小说全集 III》，陈以侃译，桂林：广西师范大学出版社，2019 年。

(6) 威廉·萨默塞特·毛姆：《绅士肖像 毛姆短篇小说全集 IV》，陈以侃译，桂林：广西师范大学出版社，2020 年。

(7) 威廉·萨默塞特·毛姆：《月亮与六便士》，李继宏译，天津：天津人民出版社，2016 年。

(8) 秦宏：《掀开彩色的面纱：毛姆创作研究》，北京：人民出版社，2016 年。